The State and Nation-Building Processes in Kenya since Independence:

Remembering the Marginalised and
Forgotten Issues and Actors

I0110293

Edited by

Susan Waiyego Mwangi
Elias Omondi Opongo
Ephraim Wachira Wahome

Langaa Research & Publishing CIG
Mankon, Bamenda

Publisher

Langaa RPCIG
Langaa Research & Publishing Common Initiative Group
P.O. Box 902 Mankon
Bamenda
North West Region
Cameroon
Langaagrp@gmail.com
www.langaa-rpcig.net

Distributed in and outside N. America by African Books Collective
orders@africanbookscollective.com
www.africanbookscollective.com

ISBN-10: 9956-550-34-5

ISBN-13: 978-9956-550-34-0

List of Contributors

Susan Waiyego Mwangi is a lecturer of Political History and International Relations at Kenyatta University. She holds a PhD in Political History from Pau University in France and MA degree in Gender and Politics from Kenyatta University. She works at the Department of History, International relations, Peace and Security and Political studies. She has vast research experience in security and political studies, gender and conflict, transitional justice, state fragility and proliferation of arms, and democratic transitions in Africa.

Elias Omondi Opongo is the Director of Hekima Institute of Peace Studies and International Relations(HIPSIR) and holds a PhD in Peace and Conflict studies from the University of Bradford, UK and an MA in International Peace studies from the University of Notre Dame, USA. His research focuses on transitional justice and post conflict reconstruction. He has published books, contributed book chapters and articles on conflict resolution, transitional justice, peace building and catholic social teaching. He is a Jesuit priest from Kenya.

Peter Wafula Wekesa is a Senior Lecturer in the Department of History, Archaeology and Political studies at Kenyatta University, Nairobi. He teaches and researches on African Political History with a special bias in border issues, identity politics and international relations

Bethwel Ogot was educated at Maseno High School and at Makerere University where he studied mathematics and history. After teaching briefly at Alliance High School in Kenya he enrolled at the University of St. Andrews where he studied history and philosophy. He returned to East Africa as a history tutor at Makerere, and then went to the U.K. to the School of Oriental and African Studies as a Ph.D. student. In the late 1960s and early 1970s he was instrumental as a faculty member and chair in making the history department of the new University of Nairobi. Ogot was also the long-term president of the Historical Association of Kenya where he did a great deal to stimulate the publication of new research in the Kenya Historical

Review, Hadithi, and the Trans African Journal of History. His edited collection, Zamani (1968) was a key text in the development of research and teaching on East Africa. Later he was instrumental in the creation and publication of the UNESCO General History of Africa. He was the dean at the University of Nairobi, Director of the Louis Leakey Memorial Institute for African Prehistory, and professor of History at Kenyatta University and Director of research at Maseno University College. In 2003 he was appointed Chancellor at Moi University. In his career he has served on a series of important official commissions and boards. In addition he has been an influential and often controversial contributor to national debates about the role of Kenya's past in its present and future. A Fellow of the Kenya National Academy of Sciences, in 2008 Ogot received the African Studies Association, Distinguished Africanist Award.

Ephraim Wachira Wahome is an Associate Professor in the Department of History and Archaeology at the University of Nairobi. His area of research interest is cultural heritage conservation. He has also published in the areas of culture and human rights, among other areas. His current research covers diverse areas include cultural tourism, prehistory, culture and human rights, and architectural heritage. He is also Associate Dean of the Faculty of Arts. He is also a former Chairman of Department of History at the same university.

Christian Thibon is Professor of contemporary history, University of Pau and Pays de l'Adour, former Director of the IFRA 2010-14, specialist of the Great Lakes Region, political history and demographical history.

Felix Kiruthu is Senior Lecturer and head of Public Policy and Administration Department at Kenyatta University in Nairobi, Kenya. He is a historian specializing in economic and political History of Africa. Since 1997, Felix has taught in the Department of History, Archaeology, and Political Studies at Kenyatta University. His main research focus is in the history of political economy, and has researched on the urban history of Africa with special focus on labour relations, as well as on the history informal enterprises. His other research interests include: Biographies of prominent individuals; pedagogical methods in the study of history; as well as Peace and Conflict studies.

Francis M. Muchoki holds a bachelor's degree in education from the University of Nairobi. He also has a masters and a PhD in history from Kenyatta University. He is currently a Senior Lecturer at The Catholic University. Muchoki was first appointed as an Assistant Lecturer at Egerton University in 1989 where he rose to the level of lecturer and Associate Chairman of the History Department. He joined Catholic University in 1995 as a lecturer. At The Catholic University, he has served as a head of history Department, a Dean of Faculty and as a Deputy Vice-Chancellor. He has conducted research and published articles and book chapters in areas of his interest.

Albert Okinda is a Doctor of Philosophy candidate in the Department of Diplomacy and International Relations at Kenyatta University. Albert is a budding writer with interest in topical issues touching on International Relations, National security, Governance, Political Economy and Comparative Politics.

Zarina Patel is a writer, artist, human rights and race relations activist, environmentalist and campaigner for social justice. She played a major role in saving the Jeevanjee Gardens in Nairobi. She has also authored a number of books including: Challenge to Colonialism, AlibhaiMullaJevanjee and Manilal Ambalal Desai: The Stormy Petrel among others.

Gordon Omenya obtained his PhD in History from Université de Pau in France. He is currently a lecturer in the Department of History, Archaeology and Political Studies- Kenyatta University. His areas of interest include race relations, gender history, global history, popular culture and history of international relations. Dr Omenya is also a member of the French Institute of Research in Africa (IFRA), the British Institute of Research in East Africa (BIEA) and the Council for the Development of Social Science Research in Africa (CODESRIA).

Dorothy A. Nyakwaka, B.Ed. (University), M.Phil. (Moi University), Ph.D. (Egerton University). She is a senior lecturer at Egerton University in the Department of History. She is a Fulbright fellow and a member of CODESRIA and OSSREA. Most of her publications are on gender and governance, regionalism and conflict, including: 'The Challenges of Piracy in African Maritime Zones' in *Africa Insights* Vol. 39 (3) November 2009.

Mildred A.J. Ndeda, B.Ed., M.A. (University of Nairobi), PhD. (Kenyatta University). She is an associate professor of history at the Jaramogi Oginga Odinga University of Science and Technology. She taught at Kenyatta University for 28 years and also became chairperson of the Department of History, archaeology and Political Studies. She is a specialist in labour, gender and women's histories and studies and has published extensively. Amongst her publications is: 'The struggle for Sexual Rights among the Kikuyu Women of Central Kenya, 1918-2002,' in Toyin Falola and Nana A. Amponsah (Eds.), *Women, Gender and Sexuality in Africa*, CAP Africa World Series (Durham: Carolina Academic Press, 2013).

Washington Ndiiri is at present a senior lecturer in the Department of History, Archaeology and Political Studies at Kenyatta University. He served as the chairperson of the Department between 2012 and 2016. He has published widely in other related areas of History and Archaeology in a number of many professional bodies within and beyond the country.

Babere Kerata Chacha is Senior Lecturer in the Department of Public Affairs and Environmental Studies at Laikipia University. He has a PhD in History from Egerton University. He is currently a Global Visiting Fellow, School of Social Sciences, University of New South Wales, Australia. He is Co-ordinator Directorate of External Linkages and Human Rights at Laikipia University. In the past he has been a fellow of St. Antony's College Oxford, and Wolfson College Cambridge. In the past he has taught as an Adjunct Lecturer in history and development Studies at the University of Eastern Africa, Baraton and Kamagambo Adventist College. His research interest includes social history, environmental history, sexuality and rural studies. Chacha has also been engaged in teaching Military History and Military Thought at the Kenya Military Academy in Lanet.

Godfrey Muriuki is a distinguished professor, in the Department of History and Archaeology, University of Nairobi. His areas of interest include human migration and settlement, economic development and political organisation. He is keen on colonial and postcolonial history, and his work, *The History of the Kikuyu, 1550 – 1900,* represents his interest in political, oral, social, and economic aspects of African history.

Table of Contents

Acknowledgements

This book is a culmination of efforts and interactions by several individuals and institutions extending over a period of four years. It draws heavily from two conferences held in 2013 at IFRA, themed "Nationalism and Nationalists in Kenya." Participants of the two conferences were drawn from different universities and civil society institutions, with a major goal to revisit the debate on nationalism and the process of nation building in Kenya. In particular, the organisers of the first conference carefully and purposively selected the first generation of scholars of Kenya's history (the luminaries) with an aim of establishing whether their views regarding the topic had changed since 1977 when participants in the Historical Association of Kenya conference disagreed on the actors and the issues which should form the discourse on the topic. While one group of scholars from one region felt that the sacrifice of many of the freedom fighters had been swept under the carpet by the then President Jomo Kenyatta; yet another group felt that only those that were at the forefront of deliberations with the colonial government were true heroes of nation-building. The debate at the time had attracted the first and the second generations of scholars in history. Their main argument was on the question on the politics of knowledge production and consumption. After this conference, debates on the topic of nationalism continued with each group firmly holding their views. It is with this in mind that the organisers of the 2013 conference from Kenyatta University and IFRA, under the directorship of Professor Christian Thibon, invited the five main participants in the 1977 conference. These were Professor Bethwell Ogot, Professor Godfrey Muriuki, Professor William Ochieng, Prof Henry Mwanzi and Professor Henry Stanley Mwaniki. Each of them was invited to participate in the two conferences. Some were available for the first while the rest attended the second conference. We sincerely thank IFRA for bringing these professors together as well as a second and third generation of scholars of history together to deliberate on such an important topic. Interestingly, the views of each of the scholars have changed, albeit slightly, and they are all in agreement that the topic has not received as much attention as it should since the 1970s.

Amongst the papers presented in both conferences, twelve were selected for inclusion in this book. All the ideas of the participants were, however, in one way or the other taken into account when editing this book. Dr. Pius Kakai and , Dr. Julius Nabende from Kenyatta University; Prof. Peter Ndege from Moi University and Dr. Isaya Onjala of Jaramogi Oginga Odinga University, Dr. Benjamin Kipkorir and Dr. Marie-Aude Foure, Deputy Director, IFRA deserve special mention. Their participation as discussants and facilitators during the conferences enriched this volume. Dr. Marie-Aude Foure in particular was very helpful in mobilising researchers and ensuring that every participant was comfortable. Her ideas on the nuanced understanding of nation building in Tanzania and how this compares to Kenya indeed stimulated our debates.

This book would not have been written without the contribution by several universities in Kenya and France, which we acknowledge with gratitude. These are University of Nairobi, Kenyatta University, Moi University, Laikipia University, Jaramogi Oginga Odinga University, Catholic University, Hekima University College, all in Kenya, and the University of Pau et les Pays des L'adour in France. Each of the universities is well represented in this volume. Financial support was received from IFRA under the current Director, Dr. Marie-Emmanuelle and L'Afrique dans le Monde (LAM) Pau under Prof. Christian Thibon. The good and warm welcome that the editors received from the British Institute of East Africa and IFRA cannot go unmentioned.

Proof-reading, typesetting and formatting were done by Dr. Godwin Siundu of the University of Nairobi, Department of Literature. He is an editor of the journal *Eastern African Literary and Cultural Studies*

Foreword

Nationalism is not an easy term to grasp and play with. It is both a political slogan and a scientific concept, with multiple definitions and uses in each case. It had its finest hour in the postcolonial era, which faded away with the realisation that national states and identities could cohabit with more local and global political formations and belongings. Yet, nationalism has far from disappeared and its endurance deserves the attention that the authors of this book and the Institut français de recherches en Afrique (IFRA) gave it during two conferences held in Nairobi in 2013[1]. As part of the commemoration exercise, IFRA proposed to reflect more particularly on nationalism in Kenya. Here political debates and institutional experiments have constantly played around the idea of a disputed Kenyan nation. From *Majimbo* – a form of federalism – to the current devolution, from the Shifta War to the current idea of 'secession', the idea of who belongs to which country is a permanent feature of the conversation. The authors of the book – from a variety of generations – discuss a wealth of topics related to the formation of the Kenyan state and nation. They draw the institutional trajectory of the contemporary devolved state; they analyse the role of marginalised communities and individuals in the making of the nation; they explain the parallel rise of the nationalist idea and ethnicity; they do not shy away from some dark moments of the nation building process; they reflect on the role of history and social sciences in the nationalist narratives. Above all, they show how the idea of a Kenyan nation thrives in the citizens' imaginations and their daily practices

Marie-Emmanuelle Pommerolle
Director, IFRA

---

1 "The 50th Anniversary of African Independence: marginalized, forgotten and revived political actors", IFRA, 23-24 September 2013 and "Fifty years after Independence: the Nations in East Africa, revisiting nation building between particularism and universalism", IFRA, 12 13 June 2014.

Chapter 1

General Introduction

Susan Waiyego Mwangi and Elias Omondi Opongo

Kenya's nationalism during the late colonial period was marked by two main characteristics that feature in this book. First, the struggle for independence was mainly characterized by the claim for land that had been taken away by the colonizers. Second was the struggle for autonomy and self-determination, mainly through political resistance. Land is the definitional element of communal identity and cultural values, as well as the source of economic wealth for most African societies. Hence, the fact that a number of African communities had been robbed of their land meant that the nationalist sentiments were not only based on self-determination, but were also the basis of integrity for the affected families. The *Mau Mau* resistance and its subsequent memorialisation, demonstrates the significance of a nationalist resistance that the armed group put forward. The *Mau Mau* war, led by Dedan Kimathi Waciuri, was at its peak between 1952 and 1956. The group began its operations on September 26, 1952 (University of Arkansas, n.d.), but by 1956 it had been weakened by the much stronger colonial army. The armed *Mau Mau* group launched attacks and ambushes on British forces and civilians. But the *Mau Mau* also committed human rights abuses such as torture and murder against the local populations, particularly those deemed to be collaborators or sympathisers with the colonial government (Blacker, 2007). There are various accounts on the number of *Mau Mau* that were killed in the course of the armed struggle. It is, however, estimated that close to 12,000 were killed by the colonial government (Blacker, 2007) between 1952 and 1963.

The second characteristic of Kenya's nationalism was the struggle for autonomy and self-determination, which was mainly carried out through political resistance. The colonialists put into place a new system of governance that reduced the powers of local leadership (chiefs, kings, and clan leaders) and weakened the ethnic nations. In order to ensure that there was less resistance from organized groups across ethnic identities, the British colonial administration designed a strategy of governance that was based on a divide and rule policy. They confined different ethnic groups to specified boundaries and used the local leaders, through an indirect rule system, to govern the people. The indirect rule transferred some powers to the local ethnic leaders who later became known as 'chiefs'. To a great extent, this undermined the existing structures of local governance, subjected the community leaders to the authority of the colonialists and diminished the agency of the affected communities. The decentralization of power to ethnic jurisdictions meant that the central power of the colonial government was stable and undisturbed. The colonial government used this decentralized power structures as a means of achieving peace between the central and local government, and maintaining stability between different ethnic groups (Hornsby, 2012). Agitations for independence were both through political narratives and armed struggle, largely defined by calls for nationalism.

The struggle for independence in Africa was generally marked by diverse forms of nationalism embedded in political and military campaigns. To a great extent, the success or failure of attempts at nationalism depended on local leadership, the level of communal grievances against colonialists, and the capacity to mobilize and organize resistance, whether politically or militarily. Nationalism can be positively defined as a political ideology aimed at advocating for a people's territorial and communal autonomy or sovereignty over a dominant political, ideological, economic, or military dominance. A negative definition of nationalism would mainly refer to cultivation of differentiation elements against a particular group through the enhancement of superiority or marginalizing policies and ideologies. Generally, the first definition is what is commonly used in this book, although the two perspectives are not seamlessly different when it comes to the actual application of the phenomenon into political systems.

Political resistance in Kenya was born in June 1921 with the formation of the *Young Kikuyu Association* (later renamed the *East African Association* – EAA). Political activists like Harry Thuku, Waiganjo Ndotono, and George Mugekenyi put up political resistance against the British and were later arrested (University of

Arkansas, n.d.). The Young Kikuyu Association (KCA) introduced a sense of nationalism to the Kikuyu ethnic community and drew attention to the need to unite against colonialists. The KCA was later banned by the British colonial government. Later, in 1924, the KCA was replaced by the Kikuyu Central Association. In 1944, Harry Thuku became the first chairman and founder of the multi-ethnic Kenya African Study Union (KASU), which in 1946 became the Kenya African Union (KAU). Other parties emerged between 1954 and 1958 and, given the restrictions on movements by the colonial government, the parties were to a great extent regional or ethnic: Nairobi Peoples Convention Party (NPCP), Mombasa African Democratic Union (MADU), African District Association (Central Nyanza) (ADA), Abagusii Association (South Nyanza District) (AA), South Nyanza District African Political Association (SNDAPA), Taita African Democratic Union (TADU), Nakuru District Congress (NDC), Abaluhya People's Association (APA), Nakuru African Progressive Party (NAPP), Mwambao United Front (MUF), Nyanza North African Congress (NNAC), Kalenjin Political Alliance (KPA), Maasai United Front, Coast African People's Union (CAPU), and Somali National Association (SNA). These parties fronted a type of nationalism grounded on the need for ethnic representation. The immediate preoccupation was not a nationalist ideology based on aspirations for a single nation bringing together different ethnic communities, but one that ensured the protection of the needs of the respective immediate ethnic group. Hence the dominant ethnic groups or regions had their own ethnic kingpins (Ogot, 1995): Jomo Kenyatta and Harry Thuku (Kikuyuland), Oginga Odinga (Luoland), Paul Ngei (Kambaland), Ronald Ngala (Coastal region), amongst others.

The African nationalists demanded representation in the governing Legislative Council (LEGCO) were suspected *Mau Mau* fighters (Kyle, 1999; Maina, 2004). Following Waruhiu's death, the colonial government declared a state of emergency and suspended political activities. The state of emergency lasted between 1952 and 1960. Yet, the *Mau Mau* phenomenon, even at this point, led to certain important changes in the political organisation of Kenya. For instance, the British colonial government, in 1952, broadened the membership of the Legco to include: fourteen Europeans, one Arab,

3

and six elected Asians. There were also six Africans and one Arab nominated by the governor. However, multi-racial participation in the electoral process was only allowed in 1954, under the new constitutional framework known as the Lyttleton Constitution. By the same year (1954) the supreme instrument of governance was the council of ministers (United Kingdom, 1954).

In a bid for more representation of Africans and eventual independence, African leaders went to London to negotiate with the British government in 1960. An agreement was reached between the African delegates and the English settlers, under the New Kenya Group, which was led by Michael Blundell. The agreement recognized the need for independence of the Africans. Known as the first Lancaster House constitutional conference, the process gave birth to a new constitution. There were more Africans in the legislative council and council of ministers. For the first time, Africans were allowed to form parties with a national outlook. This paved way for the formation of the Kenya African National Union (KANU) under the leadership of James Gichuru, Oginga Odinga, and Tom Mboya – who was the Secretary General of the Kenya Federation of Labour. KANU was dominated mainly by the Kikuyus and Luos. The numerically smaller ethnic groups amalgamated their parties and formed the Kenya African Democratic Union (KADU) led by Ronald Ngala, Paul Ngei, Masinde Muliro, and Daniel Arap Moi. The nationalist aspirations were driven mainly by the decolonization agenda. In the 1961 elections, "KANU obtained 63% of the votes (16 seats) and KADU got 16% of the votes (11 seats)" (Adar, 1998). Nearing independence, KANU-KADU had a Constitutional Conference that struck a compromise to review the bicameral legislature in the constitution, allowing for "the *Lower House (House of Representatives) and the Upper House (Senate)* in which the interests of the smaller ethnic groups were largely reflected. KADU insisted on a regional (federal) form of the legislature, which was in the end provided for in the Kenyan Constitution" (Adar, 1998). This therefore meant that the 1963 general elections based on regionalism (also known in Kiswahili as *majimboism*) were favoured by KADU as a way of neutralizing the dominance of the larger tribes (Kikuyu and Luo) in KANU.

This historical analysis demonstrates that Kenya's struggle for independence had various undertones of varying nationalist perspectives. With the confining of political activities to ethnic-regions and restrictions on movements by the colonial government, it was difficult for nationalist leaders with a national outlook to emerge. The representation was first and foremost ethnic, then regional. There was an interesting spill-over into independence: while the nationalism agenda for the African leaders was grounded on ending the dominance of the colonialists and instituting the self-governance of the Africans, the divide and rule strategy of the colonial government soon became the defining factor for the African regional nationalists. The fear by smaller ethnic groups of the Luo-Kikuyu dominance meant a shift of contestation of power, from Africans against the colonialists to Africans against each other. It therefore became critical that the nationalism agenda be fostered beyond regional balances. However the voting pattern of the 1963 elections divided the country along ethnic lines.

Various individuals emerged as nationalists during and after independence, as demonstrated by the different authors in this volume. For example, Pio Gama Pinto, an Asian journalist, activist and trade unionist contributed immensely to the African liberation struggles. His ties with China and the Soviet Union helped him to facilitate a student airlift to Russia. He also used his ties to organise a secret meeting between nationalists and the Eastern Bloc, which was against colonialism. As a journalist, he ran the pro-radical Pan-African Press that advocated for self-determination of Kenya (Hornsby, 2012). Susan Waiyego Mwangi and Felix Kiruthu highlight the roles played by nationalists like Bildad Kaggia, Jaramogi Oginga, and Jomo Kenyatta. Bildad Kaggia was one of the proponents of nationalist liberation. He was involved in the mobilisation of the *Mau Mau* war struggle of 1952-1954, and was a strong advocate against independence land deals and critical of the use of the "willing buyer, willing seller" arrangements to transfer large white settler farms into African hands (Hornsby, 2012). According to Kaggia, the white settler lands were supposed to be confiscated to settle the landless Africans. This was a realistic expectation because the white settlers did not buy the land from Africans but forcefully evicted them. Hence, the Africans wondered why the local people were being obliged to buy land from the white settlers yet the same land belonged to the Africans.

Josiah Mwangi Kariuki (popularly known as JM Kariuki) held similar sentiments as Bildad Kaggia. He was actively involved in the *Mau Mau* war that contributed to the country's self-determination. Just like Kaggia, J.M. called for "expropriation of the remaining white-owned land, the abrogation of the British loans, ceilings on land holdings, and the nationalisation of industry" (Hornsby, 2012). He had a large political following and was famously known for the statement: "We do not want a Kenya of 10 millionaires and 10 million beggars" (*National Assembly Official Report*, March 13, 2008). Ramogi Achieng-Oneko also promoted African liberation struggles. As Kenya African Union (KAU) Secretary General, he was involved in advocating for the country's self-determination. Nonetheless, as the editor of Oginga Odinga's *Ramogi* and *Nyanza Times*, Achieng-Oneko used the two publications to agitate for independence through his weekly columns that were always critical of the colonialists (Hornsby, 2012). Many women also played an important role in the struggle for political freedom in Kenya. Such women included Grace Onyango, Grace Ogot, Chief Mang'ana of Kadem in Migori, and Chief Wangu wa Makeri in Murang'a.

In the post-independence period, nationalism took a different twist, with political parties competing for control of power and national resources. KANU asserted its dominance and made several amendments to the constitutions in order to increase the powers of the president. Members of KANU successfully convinced those of KADU to join the former, which happened in 1964. This turned the country into a *de facto* one party state. In his speech following the merger of the two parties, Kenyatta said: "[t]he wrangling, the opposition for opposition's sake have now died forever. We shall work as one team for the sake of Kenya alone" (Kenya Official Report, 1964). However, in 1966 Jaramogi Oginga Odinga resigned both from KANU and as vice president, and formed Kenya People's Union (KPU). Some members of parliament from the western region also resigned and joined Odinga in KPU. According to Adar (1998), Oginga's resignation culminated into what was called 'Little General Election 'in 1966 in which Members of Parliament who resigned with Odinga, particularly from Luo Nyanza, were re-elected into parliament, reinforcing his dominance in Luoland. The main point to emphasize is that President Kenyatta began to be increasingly uncomfortable with those directly challenging his leadership.

Following an ugly stand-off between Kenyatta and Odinga in Kisumu in 1969, KPU was banned and Oginga detained without trial. Kenya then became a *de facto* one-party state for the rest of Kenyatta's reign (until 1978), and similarly later during the era of Daniel Arap Moi, the second Kenyan president. There was a strong clamour for multi-partyism and citizen participation in governance. Moi instituted a heavy-handed governance style, leading to wide political dissent. A new wave of nationalism emerged calling for a second liberation by political leaders such as Martin Shikuku, James Orengo, Charles Rubia, Kenneth Matiba, and Wangari Maathai, as several chapters in this book demonstrate.

According to Bethwell Ogot (1995), the pro-democracy movement during the second liberation in Kenya was led by politicians such as Jaramogi Oginga Odinga, Masinde Muliro, George Anyona, and Martin Shikuku, the clergy, lawyers and academics (p. 240). Kenneth Matiba and Charles Rubia joined the opposition to drum up support for reforms following their expulsion from KANU (Ogot, 1995; Murunga, 2014; Hornsby, 2001). Their joining calls for political reforms added impetus to the already existing agitation for reforms. They organised the famous 7th July 1990 public rally (commonly referred as *Saba Saba*) at Kamukunji in Nairobi. Many people turned up to the venue of the rally despite its cancellation. There were other series of demonstrations across the city. Increased political activities against the government indicated the need for political reforms and in December 1991, the government allowed a multi-party system; and the first multiparty elections under Moi were held in December 1992. Ten years later, the 2002 elections saw the end of the 40-year KANU era, and subsequently, the widely taunted second liberation dawned. However, the voting patterns, just like at independence, continued to be regional with a clear lack of national outlook for the country.

The third liberation can be related to the constitutional review that led to the promulgation of a new constitution in 2010. The Constitution of Kenya (2010) reduced the powers of the presidency, devolved governance to the counties, and called for political accountability in leadership and governance. Currently, a new wage of nationalism is one based on the demand for accountability on the part of the government, fare distribution of resources, and broader inclusion of different regions and ethnic groups in the governance structures.

From this discussion, we see that nationalism ought not be limited to self-determination and claim to sovereignty. It needs to be incorporated into the diverse levels of freedoms; from oppression, dominance, marginalization (political and economic), insecurity, hunger, and denial of basic civil rights. In this line, five main pillars of nationalism emerge: inherited legacy grounded on political leadership and ideology; inclusive governance systems; security of persons and property; integral economic development; and constitutionalism and the rule of law.

The inherited legacy grounded on political leadership and ideology largely depends on the inspiration of the founding fathers and mothers. The early African leaders developed political ideologies that gave a national identity to their respective countries. Julius Nyerere's *ujamaa* (socialism based on communal unity) spirit in Tanzania emphasized brotherhood and sisterhood in a broader sense, calling on citizens to commit themselves to the good of the country and unite as one nation. Kwame Nkrumah of Ghana not only called for the unity of Ghanaians but of all Africans in a spirit of Pan-Africanism. Jomo Kenyatta introduced the *Harambee* spirit that called on communal support to build the country. However, these leaders were faced with the enormous challenges of being founders. Such challenges included the eventual resistance to and subsequent assassination of Nkrumah, entrenchment of negative ethnicity during Kenyatta's tenure, and retirement of Nyerere in 1985 with the admission that *ujamaa* had failed because of his compatriots' failure to fully embrace the philosophy behind the ideology. Africa continues to suffer from a lack of committed leaders who can propel the continent forward.

The second pillar of nationalism is inclusive governance systems. The traditional African structures of governance were destroyed during the colonial period through a divide and rule mechanism. The multi-ethnicity of countries in Africa implies that the governance structures must be as inclusive as possible in order to enhance national identity. Political manipulation of ethnic identities for control of power and resources has perpetuated the divide-and-rule practice of the colonialists, leading to the ethnic nationalism under political kingpins. Nyerere attempted to develop a supra-ethnic nationalism that drew attention more to national identity rather than ethnic identity. Subsequent presidents in Tanzania continue to apply the same ideology of nation-building.

Closely connected to an inclusive governance system is the integral economic development pillar in nationalism. During the colonial period, Africans were denied access to economic opportunities, for example, one needed a license to grow coffee. In the post-independence period, the Kenya government introduced the quota system in employment in order to allow different ethnic groups to access employment in the public service and trading sectors, among others. This was carried out through Africanisation policies. The Kenya government adopted Sessional Paper No. 10 of 1967 to address development demands that revolved around political equality, social justice and the provision of equal economic opportunities. Article 8 in the Paper states that: "[c]reating more jobs for the unemployed must take precedence over increasing the incomes of those already employed; raising the rural living standards is a more urgent matter than raising industrial wages; and within the public service, the needs of the lowest income earners must be given priority over those more fortunate" (Kenya Government, 1967). The government also aimed at increasing exports and improving wages and living conditions for its citizen.

The fourth pillar of nation-building is grounded on security of persons and property. The stability of the nation depends on its own security. Citizens need to feel secure and not unfairly threatened by the police, military, armed groups, and external threats. In order to cultivate a national identity, the population needs to feel that the government does not discriminate against or expose specific communities to external threats. For example, the economic and security marginalization of northern Kenya, which is constantly prone to armed cattle rustling activities, has often led to negative sentiments against national identity. Ethnic identities and community organizational structures take priority over national identity.

The last pillar is constitutionalism and the rule of law. Since independence, many African leaders disregarded the constitution and accumulated political powers with minimum separation of powers between the different arms of government (Amutabi, 2009). The judiciary and parliament became extensions of the executive. At independence, Kenya had a constitution that balanced the powers of the executive, legislature, and judiciary. However, over the years, there were many amendments to the constitution that increased the powers of the president and diminished the rights of the citizens. The Constitution of Kenya (2010) provides for the Bill of Rights and diminishes the powers of the president, while increasing the powers of the legislature and judiciary in order to effect the rule of law.

Hence, a critical analysis of nationalism in Africa today should take into account the above pillars with a strong projection into a more prosperous, politically and economically independent Africa. Nationalism ought to engender a sense of belonging and ownership of the country's resources. Hence, the future of Africa's nationalism depends on accountable leadership focused on ending corruption, creating more employment opportunities, ensuring national and regional stability, and developing mechanisms of inclusivity in governance and distribution of national resources.

The authors in this volume highlight some of the key historical aspects described above. Peter Wafula Wekesa examines the subject of disputes around boundaries within eastern Africa. He observes that disputes arising from boundaries and the emerging issues around boundary revisions in the region are significant developments that have direct implications on governance structures and inter-state relations. Although disputes over trans-boundary resources have drawn more attention previously, border security and debates on inclusion and exclusion have been the main focus in border relations throughout East Africa since independence.

Bethwell Ogot discusses the historiography of nationalism in Kenya. He gives two divergent views of Kenyan nationalists. The freedom fighters, *mashujaa,* who believed in social justice and the care of the poor, the landless and the marginalized. On the other hand, the new government after the 1963 political independence, who instead believed in personal accumulation of property and wealth for themselves. He concludes that both politicians and citizens are sceptical about nationhood and a sense of belonging to one country. Political elite use citizens as their property and vehicle to win elections and control national resources.

Ephraim Wahome advocates for the conservation of the *Mau Mau* heritage. He observes that the *Mau Mau* campaigns of 1952 to 1960 left a legacy in antiquities and monuments, which has been largely ignored by the government and by the communities which bore the brunt of colonial aggression. He suggests the potential socio-economic benefits that can be realized through the protection of the *Mau Mau* heritage.

Christian Thibon interrogates the historiographical aspects of the fifty years of independence for many African nations, and particularly for Kenya. He highlights the diverse historical moments for Kenya, particularly in relation to the review of the key moments in history such as independence, the arrival of multiparty system and the various commissions that unveiled new chapters in the country as well as the promulgation of the Constitution of Kenya (2010). He sees these historical moments as revealing identity memories and collective expectations of the citizens while putting emphasis on the role that historians can play in enhancing debates on implications of such memories and their historical experiences.

Susan Mwangi, Felix Kiruthu, and Francis Muchoki on their part explain the diverse aspects of nation-building in Kenya, particularly in the post-independence period up to 2014, covering the reigns of four presidents. Further the discussions bring to fore political dynamics and challenges experienced between 1963 and 2014. Since the unity forged by African elites was mainly geared towards the struggle against colonialism, once political independence was achieved fractures began to appear between different communities particularly due to poor governance. Chacha Kerata gives details of such challenges with a focus on tortures and assassinations that took place before, during, and after Moi's era. There was need for a different perspective to nationalism, one that claimed back the freedom of the land.

Susan Waiyego Mwangi and Albert Okinda discuss an old but nagging issue on the nexus between the International Criminal Court (ICC) and nation-building in Africa. They argue that the debates around the engagement of the ICC with Kenya could be understood under the rubric of criticism that has been raised against the court. Despite the noble cause for which the court was established, it has been perceived by some African leaders as a biased institution that aims at punishing the same African leaders. In Kenya, the ICC cases after the 2007 Post-Election Violence (PEV) had an influence on the dynamics of the 2013 General Elections. Those who voted for the Coalition for Reforms and Democracy (CORD) led by Raila Odinga, the two authors argue, were generally perceived to be in support of the ICC, while those who voted for The National Alliance Party (TNA) were similarly seen to be opposed to the court. Two principle leaders of TNA were named suspects of the 2008 Post=Elections Violence (PEV) in Kenya. The authors thus discuss the relevance of the ICC in relation to prevention of impunity and gross violation of human rights on the one hand, and its systematic targeting of leaders from African countries on the other. They also caution against labelling the court as anti-African, noting that such debates only emerge when corrupt, dictatorial leaders or those who violate human rights are targeted.

Zarina Patel and Gordon Omenya immortalize neglected political actors who have been at the core of the national building in Kenya. Patel and Omenya note that suppression, marginalization, and outright distortion of the social context of Kenya's South Asian community was contiguous with the advent of colonial rule. The role played by the Asian community has been ignored by historians for a long time. It has taken fifty years to begin to politically and economically recognize the *Mau Mau* Movement and its armed wing, the Land and Freedom Army, and to address the gross injustices and human rights violations perpetrated against the *Mau Mau* heroes. The authors argue that recognizing marginalized national heroes is fundamental to the nation-building process.

Dorothy Nyakwaka and Mildred Ndeda discuss the lingering question of women's struggle against political marginalization in parts of Luo Nyanza in western Kenya. They argue that that regardless of women's background there is one common component, gender, which relegates them to a secondary status in politics. Accordingly, the women in Luo Nyanza have to execute their political agendas within a historically entrenched patriarchal paradigm; not only is power and privilege held by men, but it is also men who define that power and its distribution. In fact, the women have to adjust to their double roles in the public and domestic spheres.

Washington Ndiiri and Albert Ochieng discuss the critical role that Joseph Martin Shikuku, a political legend in Kenya, played in the making of Kenya's history. Shikuku served in parliament for long but he never rose beyond the position an assistant minister, despite representing the underprivileged people of Kenya. According to Ndiiri and Ochieng, in retrospect, the best person to be the President of Kenya in transiting from the old to new era could have been Martin Shikuku because what Kenya needed was a true patriot who would only have one agenda – to put a clear stop to corruption.

Chacha Kerata discusses political assassinations and extrajudicial killings in Kenya. Within the framework of memorialization, the author examines and locates areas of scars in Kenya's history while proposing the kinds of interventions that can be used to repair such scars. Further discussions focus on how assassinations and extra judicial killings have altered the patterns of Kenya's cultural and political history. The different presidents bear, at different levels, the responsibility for these assassinations and extrajudicial killings. Stories of assassinations of individual victims have been differently framed, and consequently some narratives of attendant memory and pains of the same have been documented using the TJRC reports on oral submissions and reports of investigations and commissions of inquiries.

Ultimately, this book has outlined and engaged with some of the challenges that impeded the successful forging of a nation out of the Kenyan nation-state. Some of the challenges – negative ethnicity, hard economic times, and an all too recurrent culture of political violence and assassinations – nonetheless yield a promising future for nation-building. This prospect is anchored in the progressive Constitution of Kenya (2010), which emerged after the 2007/08 political violence and was widely endorsed by Kenyans in a referendum in the mid-2010. With provisions on the Bill of Rights, Devolution, and independent institutions, it is a document that promises greater national inclusivity in terms of gender, racial groups, and regions. In a sentence, this book demonstrates that although the country has experienced challenges in its post-independence era, Kenya also holds great promise for a unified and prosperous future.

Chapter 2

The Nation-State and the Border Question in East Africa: Old Issues, Challenges, and Opportunities

Peter Wafula Wekesa

Introduction

Within eastern Africa, like elsewhere in the world, internal and international boundaries remain important definitive forms of statehood, sites of citizenship and arenas of development. As territorial organizations of political, cultural, and economic power, boundaries have become, as Lord Curzon (1907) notes, the razor's edge on which hang suspended modern issues of war or peace, of life or death to nations. Two related issues amplify the centrality of the border question in the region, perhaps also signifying the emerging trend that needs to be interrogated as the countries march past the fifty-year mark since they attained their independence in the early 1960s.

The first issue relates to the fact that in the last five years there have been heightened tensions and increasing potential for intra and inter-state conflicts in the region due to inter-ethnic animosities usually fanned by political differences, growing discoveries or rumours of existence of natural resources on borders or in borderlands. Some of the key regions, especially those with shared borders and shared resources, are quickly emerging as conflict hotspots. Okumu (2010) observes that the disputes around the key border hotspots are mainly over territorial claims that are frequently caused by lack of clearly defined and marked boundaries, the availability of trans-boundary resources, and security-related matters. The proximity of East Africa to the conflict-prone neighbouring countries of South Sudan, Ethiopia, Democratic Republic of Congo (DRC), and Somalia also creates an important dimension in the discussion around state borders, security, and other related concerns including immigration and refugee flows.

The second issue relates to the fact that the wider eastern African region seems to contrast rather strikingly with other parts of Africa in regard to the nature and transformation of its international boundaries since the countries in the region attained their political independence in the early 1960s. Apart from the conflicts mentioned above, the boundaries in the region have received more revisions than in other parts of Africa Such revisions have not only resulted in new territories but have more specifically created new nation-states and solidified various forms of identities both at the cultural and national levels. Since 1993 when Ethiopia and Eritrea agreed on a mutual separation after several years of conflict, there has been a series that seems to overstate an occasional occurrence. In addition, there are emerging debates and contestations on whether the boundaries should continue to be retained or revised. Touval (1999) notes that apart from Ethiopia and Eritrea, boundary revisions have been made in Somalia, Sudan and South Sudan.

Although disputes over trans-boundary resources have drawn more attention in the past, border security and debates on inclusion and exclusion have been the main focus in border relations throughout East Africa since independence. With the impact of globalization taking shape everywhere, the region remains alive to attendant cross-border security challenges such as cattle rustling, drug trafficking, human trafficking, gun smuggling, and auto theft that continue to impact the economy of the borderlands. Other security issues relate to terrorist activities, illegal and undocumented immigrations through illegal border points by communities that have relatives on both sides of the border, and illegal cross-border activities, such as the use of herds boys as informers for human traffickers and monitoring the movements of the patrol teams (Wekesa, 2010).

The above issues are important in understanding the dynamics around and about the border question in East Africa. As Khadiagala (2010) observes, although boundaries are creatures of human contrivances, their history and evolution reflect intricate compromises that seek to stabilize human habitation within territorial spaces. The question of boundaries remains at the centre of the nation-building enterprise. Thus, as we reflect on fifty years since independence in East Africa, the struggles by the states to domesticate the borders inherited from colonialism, the constant drive towards permeability and flexibility in their functionality raise important implications for local, national and regional redefinitions of space. It is, however, useful to draw on the history of boundary making in the region in order to understand the nature of the debates and the dynamics around their functionality.

A history of boundary making in East Africa

The making of boundaries in East Africa, like elsewhere on the continent, was a product of long-drawn historical processes whose dynamics are located in the local and European economic and political rivalries, besides competitions prior to the onset of colonialism in the late 19th Century. The boundaries specifically presented interesting paradoxes since their demarcation involved several European powers and local African communities. By the time the borders were being demarcated by the latter half of the 19th Century, until the time when the countries in the region attained their political independence in the early 1960s, a series of negotiated settlements came to converge in defining the nature and meaning of the boundaries that we have today.

By 1894, for instance, when the British declared a protectorate over Uganda, which at the time included parts of present astern Uganda and western Kenya, a systematic process of colonial rule was put in place. A gradual but consistent transformation of the pre-colonial social, economic, and political structures of the various African peoples was instituted. Colonial patterns of boundary making were thus also instituted that came to reflect the superimposition of physical and political limits on the African socio-economic, cultural, and linguistic continuities. The making of the boundaries in the region thus came to be a product of both the activities of the specific African communities living within the border territories, and those of the European powers whose political and economic rivalry had culminated in the 1884 – 1885 Berlin Conference.

In the conceptualisation of borders in Africa, however, little attention is often paid to the dynamics involving African communities within the pre-colonial setting. This oversight is often justified on the premise that Africans in the pre-colonial period did not have their own traditions of mapping (Nugent, 1996). A distinction is usually made between frontiers and boundaries and argued that in the pre-colonial period there were no boundaries but frontiers. Be that as it may, these two positions do not imply that Africans lacked a conception of territoriality, but rather that political space was mapped mentally rather than cartographically. As is clear among several border communities in the region, their political dynamics were underpinned by different systems of production and expropriation of surplus. Since boundaries were always about the regulation of people and goods, one would expect a corresponding variation in the way in which boundaries were constructed and maintained (Kopytoff, 1987).

It is useful to take cognisance of pre-colonial African conceptions of boundaries in order to appreciate the nature of their evolution during the colonial and post-independence periods. The debate on the existence and nature of boundaries in pre-colonial Africa before the Berlin Conference has attracted diverse perspectives from several authors (Kopytoff, 1987; Mbembe, 1999). The most compelling argument from previous studies is that before colonialism, the attachment to territory and to land in Africa was entirely relative. In several cases, the political entities were not delimited by boundaries in the classical sense of the term, but rather by frontiers that had an imbrication of multiple spaces constantly joined, disjoined and recombined through wars, conquests, and mobility of goods and persons (Mbembe, 1999).

In eastern Africa, the history of the relations between the various border peoples including the Maasai, Somali, Babukusu, Bagisu, Iteso, the Sebei, in the pre-colonial period reveals that there was a fluid boundary zone through which various social, economic, and political interactions were transacted between the two groups. By the time the Berlin Conference was being convened, several areas were ethnically complex regions characterised by intense inter-community relations (Ogot, 2002). People of different ethnic groups from a given region and beyond interacted intensely through trade, intermarriages, and other activities, some cultural, across the fluid boundary zones.

Colonialism and the colonial patterns of boundary making created continuities and discontinuities that have come to define the nature of the boundaries in the independence period. With colonialism came the Westphalian model of territoriality and statehood that has remained dominant in the region. This entrenched a process whereby boundaries were defined on maps, delimited by treaties, and demarcated on the ground by colonial officials. As Brownlie (1979) aptly observes, the geographical delineation of territorial boundaries in the region followed a wide spectrum of experiments ranging from mathematical and astronomical criteria to physical and topographical features such as rivers, streams, watersheds, mountains, and valleys. The result of this process was the seventeen major boundaries in the eastern African region stretching from Sudan to Tanzania (Khadiagala, 2010).

Lacking precise data on topography, demography and socio-cultural patterns, the colonial powers consequently created and maintained boundaries that were both unnatural and artificial. Taking account of the legacy of fragmentation, the colonialists' goal encouraged the emergence of new representations of identity and territory that transcended historical identities that had existed between the various regions. In several contexts, the colonial governments embarked on the creation of new ethnic identities based on what came to be characterized as 'tribes', 'sub-tribes', and 'clans'. The latter had to be placed under the newly formulated and coinciding provinces, districts, divisions, and locations under the various colonial agents. That ethnic identities in the colonial period were strengthened by both internal and international boundaries of the state is at the heart of the current question on boundaries in the region. The centrality of internal and international boundaries were and continue to be emphasized as key instruments in facilitating the divide and rule strategy that is a legacy of colonialism. Colonial rule did not just lead to the fragmentation of African spaces, it also re-defined the notions of political and physical space and altered the socio-economic and political structures of Africans.

The fact that most of the boundaries in in East Africa did not delimit traditional historical-political processes specifically lends a challenge to both colonial and postcolonial regimes. Although the artificiality thesis has been critiqued by scholars including Herbst (1989) who note that all borders everywhere are products of social convention, it is true that throughout the colonial period pre-existing socio-cultural contexts were interrupted by the new partition lines. In this regard, the colonial boundaries epitomized the arbitrary character that has come to explain some of the major challenges around border problems in post-independence East Africa.

Independent state and the border question: Issues and debates

The partitioning of cultural areas and groups has saddled independent African states with two major problems. The first relates to whether, looked at in terms of the nature of their evolution, such partitions should be accepted and boundaries that were inherited from the colonial period be respected or revised. The second issue relates to the nature of policies that need to be adopted in regard to trans-border transactions between partitioned cultural groups, and whose impact transcends individual nation-state entities. Though related, the two problems have generated diverse debates among researchers.

On the nature and evolution of boundaries of independent African states, there seems to be little disagreement among scholars that such boundaries were arbitrary as a result of their largely colonial origins (Touval, 1969; Davidson, 1992; Nugent & Asiwaju, 1996). A few scholars, however, insist that the history of boundaries needs to be located in pre-colonial Africa since boundaries also existed then (Mbembe, 1999). The latter scholars insist that since boundaries generally depend on convention, the fact that African boundaries were inherited from colonialism does not necessarily make them arbitrary. There is also no consensus as to whether the creation of African borders was a liability for African states. Some scholars argue that borders everywhere are artificial and that the case for African exceptionalism is weak (Clapman, 1996). Other authors do not dismiss the relatively erratic nature of African boundaries, but suggest either that this has had few deleterious consequences (Touval, 1969); that they actually represent opportunities for Africans (Nugent, 1996); or that they are an asset for state consolidation (Herbst, 2000). Still others agree that Africa has suffered from its partitioned nature, but see the cost of reshuffling states as greater than the hypothetical benefits (Bayart, 1996). Finally, a few authors believe that at least some African states would gain from territorial reconfiguration or through efforts towards regional integration (Herbst, 2000).

Diverse and lively as these perspectives are, they suffer from several shortcomings in relation to the issue of borders and territoriality in Africa. First, most of the works have received little systematic treatment, with much of the literature proving anecdotal, opinion-based, or dependent on few and possibly biased cases. Secondly, the studies have tended to subsume African states into a single category without distinctions in the degrees of arbitrariness. In reality, however, the particular conditions of each state vary widely. Without accounting for these variations, inferences about the consequences of arbitrariness have been vague and difficult to estimate. Finally, the debates have also been limited by their emphasis on international conflicts. Given the apparent lack of inter-state conflicts in many areas of Africa until the 1990s, the argument that artificial borders 'do not matter' has gained prevalence (Bayart, 1996). Whatever its validity, this claim misses a crucial dimension of the nature and consequences of boundaries. For, if borders determine who the other is, they also define the self and confer membership to the polity.

Given the foregoing discussions on the nature of boundaries, it is important in our context to examine the issue of the question of borders in East Africa, not only within its specificity but also emphasising its implications to inter-state relations fifty years after the states in the region attained their independence. It is useful to analyse both the international and domestic dimensions of the question of borders, and how it is emerging as a critical factor in the social, economic, and political dynamics of the region. This approach should not merely be focused on conflicts, but needs also to extend to other, harmonious issues related to regional integration among especially cultural areas that traverse common boundaries in the region. In any case, as is evidently clear, a fluid cultural zone informed by strong historical ties has consistently shaped the nature of long-term, intense interactions between the various border communities and thereby minimised any possibilities of major conflicts. As international boundaries delineate and separate several border communities, there has also been the development of other cross-frontier transactions that are not only cultural but also economic and political. It is useful, therefore, to take cognisance of the fact that the borders between different countries and different communities also affect the likelihood of other non-violent patterns of inter-state relations often described variously as informal, unrecorded, underground, and also as smuggling. It is useful to emphasize that since the attainment of independence in the region, the evolution of boundaries has continued to define patterns of territories that facilitate control from the centres of the respective countries and neglect the border peripheries. Smugglers, for example, as people who possibly have double loyalties, can benefit from undermining state regulations and even threaten states at their centres as they take advantage of opportunities at the border spaces (Barth, 2000).

Domestically, the borders in the region have continued to challenge the stability of the administrations or their quests for hegemony, control and nation-building, to dictate policy choices, and to influence the quality of institutions and the degrees of allegiance of citizens, resulting in different levels of political participation and disengagement, varying propensities for repression and diverse development fortunes. Yet, as Donnan and Wilson (2015) observe, other questions relate to the identity of the persons experiencing the restrictions created by the international boundaries, and their various responses towards the border and the regimes that limit peoples' movements and fruitful cross-border transactions and communication. It is obvious that the roles of the independent nation states in East Africa have remained in their push to use boundaries as key definitive forms for their individual sovereignties.

The push by the states to solidify the sanctity of the boundaries in the region has been sustained both at the individual state level and through the continental African Union (AU) platforms. In these efforts, the legitimacy of the former colonial partition lines, with minor alterations, has remained one of the most enduring colonial legacies in East Africa. The patchwork that was left behind by colonialism has generally continued to be reinforced through the artificiality maintained at the boundaries. It must be recalled that by the time most of the countries attained their independence, they were by no means nations but rather they represented the shells of territorial independence in which different regions and ethnic communities co-existed with each other. The major task of the various East African governments thus remained the provision of the soil in which the seeds of their national sovereignty could grow.

Moreover, the process of political consolidation has over the years ensured territorial stability as the most viable means of maintaining national integrity and engendering nation and state building.

Central to the process of creating a national sovereignty and state has therefore been the issue of boundaries and how they have to differentiate national groups from others. But this process has not been easy since, as Benedict Anderson (1983) has observes, ethnic groups, or nations as he calls them, are 'imagined political communities', imagined as both inherently limited and sovereign. Most of the nations in the region have remained imagined because, as Anderson emphasizes, their members will never know most of their fellow members, meet them, or even hear of them, yet in the mind of each lives the image of their communion. The nations have continued to maintain elastic and artificial boundaries beyond which lie other nations. Even in contexts where border communities like the Maasai, the Luhyia, the Iteso and the Somali have maintained a fluid cultural zone informed by strong historical ties, the dominance of the national question has consistently shaped the nature of long term inter-group interactions in the border areas (Wekesa, 2007). In a way, therefore, regardless of the constant internal strife, inequalities, conflict and exploitation that prevail in most of the nations, there has been a loosely maintained notion of deep and horizontal comradeship.

The boundaries in the region thus have become important components in instituting patterns of territorial control and differentiating one nationality from another. The political class has not made the regional integration work since they have equally been compelled to look inward and to rank as their first priority the political, economic, and social developments of their own polities. The immediate concern, then, has always been to build viable national groups based on their traditions and customs (Wekesa, 2007). The greater the extent to which national consolidation has tended to receive high priority, the less the attention that has been paid to relations between regions and communities that have strong inter-state or regional bonds. As Nugent and Asiwaju (1996) observe, there seem to be an inherent tension between the new ideology of 'nationalism', which assumes that people belong to one nation or another, and the reality of borderlands where communities merge into each other in spite of official lines of demarcation. The result of this is that there is some procrastination in dealing with challenges posed by borders, especially those that require a regional input to address. The border dispute between Kenya and Uganda over the ownership of Migingo Island in Lake Victoria is a classic example (Wekesa, 2010). Regional efforts only succeed in contexts where they are not in conflict with the considerations of national security, prestige, or economic advantage of the national entities involved.

The border, the nation and regionalism: The contested terrain

The different developmental strategies that have been adopted by the various countries in East Africa have made relations between them and the prioritization of addressing emerging border challenges problematic. Having defined their national priorities and emphasized the sanctity of their respective national boundaries, it has generally become difficult for the various countries to adopt any supra-national unification policies that have a regional context. What therefore seems to emerge is the contest between the national and the regional domain in the social, economic relations of the various states. Yet in reality the entire region cannot socially, economically, and politically meet their national objectives without actively incorporating inter-state integration arrangements within their development agendas.

The contest between the national and the regional spaces manifested itself immediately after independence when the countries in the region inherited colonial integration arrangements that dealt with economic aspects of production of goods and exchange of services (Ochwada, 2004). Though replete with various deficiencies, the new leaders have been keen to further their integration efforts through their various economic structures. The economic justification for regionalism has overwhelmingly been emphasized almost at the exclusion of other possible intervening explanations across the region. Imbued with the western developmental arguments and conjured within theoretical assumptions of modernization, regionalism as opposed to nationalism has been conceptualised as a mechanism for ensuring economic development. Used rather loosely, regional integration came to characterize various broad social, economic and political initiatives that were hoped to

24

increase the bargaining power of the respective countries within the international political economy (Clapham, 2001).

From 1967, leaders in East Africa embarked on various treaties that formalized the operation of regionalism first through the East African Co-operation (1967 – 1977) and now the East African Community (1999 onwards). The signing of the various regional treaties has signalled a major development in the inter-state relations in the region. From a state-centric point of view, the member states have committed themselves to an economic course that is destined to benefit the peoples of the region. Yet it is not lost on many that regional spirit has been mirrored with inherent contradictions that have continued to dictate the nature of the commitment of the leaders to any supranational body. Essentially, the unwillingness of the leaders to forfeit their national political and economic sovereignty has posed a major challenge to the survival of regionalism. In terms of its broad impact on the lives of most ordinary citizens, however, the deep involvement of the states and the over-emphasis on economic arguments for regional integration has continued to provide a series of contradictions, accounting for the dismal performance of the East African community.

The state-centred economic arguments for regionalism have hardly paid attention to the particular social and political histories that inform the evolution of various peoples who are meant to benefit from the EAC integration initiatives. Integration, as Adetula (2004) argues, represents much broader and detailed arrangements which require states to make certain social, political, and economic sacrifices, commitments, and concessions, and demonstrate their will towards a redefinition of their individual and collective participation in the international economy. Thus, by conceiving the EAC in purely economic terms, its operation tends to ignore the wider realities happening within and across the boundaries of the region. For instance, while the official rhetoric emphasizes the economic gains of EAC, other social, cultural, and political dimensions of this process are usually conflated within the individual political and ideological rivalries of the power elites in the region. To the ordinary people within the different national sovereignties, the boundaries between them continue to define their insertion into the power interests at play. The boundaries basically remain lines of contact

25

between different sovereign states, each jealous of its territorial integrity and national autonomy. In a sense, contacts at borderlands have remained more often than not contacts of conflict rather than harmony (Asiwaju, 1985).

The crossing of boundaries by the nationalities of either state has remained a challenge that needs to be monitored within the context of each state's policies and interests. This is especially important for the cross-border movements of persons who have and continue to have close historical and socio-cultural ties and who continue to view the border as a great impediment to their daily transactions. As Baubock and Rundell (1998) observe, the crossing of the physical boundaries by these people blurs three kinds of boundaries: the territorial borders of the states, the political boundaries of citizenship, and the cultural boundaries of national communities. When such people move from one international location to another, as individuals or as groups, their activities affect the immediate and future development prospects both at the source of their movement, the place of their origin, and also the place of destination (Gould, 1995).

Beyond the borders: The question of the informal economy

The manner in which the national and the regional contexts have played out in East Africa in regard to the border question has equally generated important reflections around and about the various responses to border restrictions. These responses, which take place beyond the formally recognised institutions under which the border and its management is conceived by the states, continue to define the nature of its evolution and transformation over time. As Nugent (2002) argues, borders are shaped as much by the everyday activities of ordinary people, in ways that sometimes undergird but at other times may bypass the formal structures of politics.

The nature of response generated by the various peoples in East Africa and beyond through their regular interaction across regional boundaries, on the one hand, works against the logic of national integration. It also tends to reinforce a sense of commonality between these groups that is supranational in nature. On the other hand, the various peoples, in collaboration with others in similar situations elsewhere, have sought to take advantage of their unique location to participate in the daily cross-border activities that seem to challenge the national restrictions espoused by the leadership in the region. The emergence of the informal economy along the common regional borders and the increasing participation of the various peoples in it need to be conceptualised within broad dynamics.

The proliferation of the informal economy, which some scholars have called variously 'unrecorded trade', 'underground', 'smuggling' or within the context of East Africa '*Magendo*'[1], is due to cross-border interactions which have their own distinctive features but which, as Bach (1999) observes, combine elements of inter-state and trans-national regionalism. Although the informal economy generally, and informal trade specifically, comes in different forms or is known by different names, it is characterised by not being entered in national accounts. Since it operates outside the official national networks, it challenges the restrictions and tax policy frameworks put in place, as its participants are viewed in opposition to established norms. The informal cross-border activities between the various groups can be seen as constituting the subversion of the official constraints that the border has laid on their daily interactions, and which continue to hamper their activities that obviously go beyond obvious statist definitions of the border.

The proliferation of the informal economy across the East Africa's regional borders and its various categorizations unmasks the constant reality of the ordinary people's struggle to make a living outside the formal state-defined economic networks. The context of whether these activities are legal or illegal is arguably dependent on what Nugent (2002) has distinctly categorized as the divide between the national and local discourses of morality. Within the national, most of the activities may be noted as being illegal since the states have historically arrogated to themselves the right to distinguish legal from illegal activities. From the local point of view, on the other hand, cross-border informal activities, or what is often described as smuggling, is basically an exchange of goods and services over the boundary. In essence, therefore, the definition of smuggling and indeed other informal cross-border economic activities boils down

---

[1] A Kiswahili term for illegal trade

to whose point of view, between the national and local, arrogates the morality issues.

Scholars have generally observed that the restrictive policies followed by many countries create incentives for the rise of the illegal cross-border informal economy (Ackello-Ogutu, 1997). Restrictions such as import tariffs, quotas, exchange controls, state trading monopolies and export restrictions create incentives to beat the system. Together with the restrictive national policies, past historical linkages and the semi-convertibility of currencies in border areas facilitate 'illegal' cross-border informal activities. Import licensing, often a response to an overvalued currency, restricts the supply of imports and raises their domestic price which in turn provides incentives for a parallel market in smuggled goods (Ackello-Ogutu, 1997). Relative price differentials between countries and shortages in a particular country also encourage border informal trade. Scarcity and shortages in some of the neighbouring countries create effective demand and high profits, thus making it extremely difficult to control smuggling.

The limited presence of state-actors at the borders coupled with the uncertain political climate that has disrupted the traditional forms of interaction between the various groups is mainly responsible for the rise of illegal trade within the common borderland areas. The range of commodities that pass through the regional borders in East Africa include agricultural commodities (coffee, maize, maize meal, sugar, milk, rice, wheat flour, beans, groundnuts, simsim, bananas, and others), industrial goods (cooking fats and oils, petroleum products), fish and forest resources (charcoal and timber). Also important is that there have been cattle rustling, drug trafficking, human trafficking, and gun smuggling, among other activities. The border is also providing a fertile ground for terrorist activities that are threatening the security of the states in the region.

Whether with agricultural or industrial commodities, there was a clear effort through informal trade by several groups to mould the border into something that benefits them. There have certainly been various categories within the informal participants in the cross-border trade. They could broadly be delineated into three: the small-timers, or what Nugent (2002) identifies elsewhere as armpit traders, the commission workers and the rich bulk traders. The first and

28

second categories comprise mainly the local borderlanders, and are distinguished by the nature of their transactions and the volume of goods transacted. While arm-pit traders deal in petty or small quantity items, the commission workers, whether on foot or on bicycles, work for the rich to smuggle bulk goods across the border in order to earn a commission. Their success highly depends on the discrete nature of the operations and on their ability to develop good working relations with the police and border personnel. The bulk traders involve many rich merchants and companies from the countries in the region and outside.

There is, therefore, no doubt that the propitious nature of the informal economy together with the rapid growth of the border trading centres attract myriad other participants and activities beyond the region. It is significant to also emphasize that owing to the discrete and contraband nature of this trade, there has always been a real constant threat of being infiltrated by criminal elements. Following the degenerated security situation in the region and the lack of appropriate border policing mechanisms, small arms and light weapons find their way into civilian hands and are equally transacted across the borders (Okumu, 2010; Mkutu, 2007). In addition, the issue of women engaged in prostitution within the main border trading centres is real. And the degenerated security situation is reflected in the increase in the number of refugees, especially those fleeing from the conflict prone areas in the region such as South Sudan and Somalia.

Perhaps what needs to be emphasized is that whereas there is no doubt that the networks which are being exploited across the countries' boundaries during the various informal activities reflect long-established, primordial links among the various people in the region, it is also not difficult to see these activities benefiting from the new trends in globalization and more specifically improvements in information technology. The critical border question that emerges from such activities for the various nation-states in the region is that the statist border management strategies need to be revisited because they are majorly unworkable in the current context. The informal activities can easily be seen as being a resistance to the statist models and, largely, to the embodiment of the states' power which the border represents. The states in the region need to embrace more vigorously the emerging trends towards regionalism in order to deal with the negative economic and security subversions inherent in the informal economy. Deliberate policy decisions on the part of the political leadership need to convert the informal economy and generally the boundaries in the region into veritable spaces for contact and cooperation, and not for division, conflict and insecurity.

Conclusion

This chapter has generally reflected on the centrality of borders in the debates around the political economy of the East African states fifty years after their independence. We have argued in the chapter that the nation states in the region cannot afford to ignore the history and dynamics shaping the evolution of their common borders. Whether inherited from colonialism or revised within contemporary imperatives, the boundaries represent intricate social and political spaces delimiting the external reach of the state power and delineating citizenship. The boundaries in the region are thus emerging as critical centres of intense social, economic, and political interactions between states. The initial view that they are peripheral to the centres of power lodged in the capital cities is no longer tenable since they are power centres in their own right. The struggles by the states to construct a national community and the intractable debates around regionalism are important issues related to the question of borders. The constant challenge to the nationalist project, coupled with the economic attempts towards broader regionalism, has seen the emergence of inter-state tensions and conflicts across common boundaries. While this is happening at the state level, a vibrant informal economy seems to be evolving within the common borderland areas and challenging the statist restrictions on the economic, social and cultural levels. This volatile scenario is increasingly generating inter-state rivalries, especially in contexts where there are shared resources. Contestations over new forms of statehood and resources draw attention to three central dynamics: the need for cooperation between economically and culturally linked border regions as a mode of strengthening regional cooperation; the demand for the management of common resources in the border areas such as rivers, lakes and forests; and the recognition by border populations of their role in addressing their own survival and development problems. These are critical border issues that the nation-states in the region can only ignore at their own peril.

Chapter 3

The Kenyan Nation and the Historiography of Nationalism

Bethwell A. Ogot

Introduction

The modern nation-state would hardly exist without the ideology of nationalism to sustain it, a doctrine that was born early in the 19th Century and that, by the middle of the 20th Century, had become one of the most powerful and dynamic social forces in history. In the anti-colonial struggles in Asia and Africa, for example, nationalist ideologies proved to be powerful weapons (Seton-Watson, 1977). In countries such as India, Nigeria, Uganda, Ghana, and Kenya, among many others, the early nationalist ideologies attempted to unite diverse peoples under the banner of a single national idea without raising the question whether the concept of nationhood which had evolved in Europe and the Americas was suitable for the ethnically pluralistic societies, with different histories and values, that were soon to become independent within the boundaries of former colonial territories. To the majority of Africans, for example, nationalism meant the removal of colonialism.

But the acceptance of the concept of nationhood by the African leaders unquestionably influenced the way the Africans defined themselves. They became Nigerians, Kenyans, Ugandans, and so on (Paden, 1980) But we now know, given the problems of an ethnic nature that the post-colonial states subsequently ran into, anti-colonial movements were, in fact, the product of a temporary convergence of various sectional, economic, regional, and ethnic interests in getting rid of the colonial masters. Hence, many Africans did not have a strong sense of attachment to the emergent nation in which they found themselves. Thus the initial cohesiveness that sustained national identity in Europe was absent in many African countries at the moment of independence.

In contrast to the nationalism of the anti-colonial struggle, there is the nationalism of the post-colonial states, as expressed in the ideology of the state, which encompasses and subsumes all prior and partial identities. Its proponents argue that the integration of the new nation requires the demise of the pre-existing ethnic groups. This kind of nationalism usually denies all subnational ethnic loyalties and requires unconditional allegiance to the state, considered as the embodiment of the nation. It also tends to be illiberal and anti-democratic. As Zolberg (1966) reports:

> Sekou Toure stressed that the most important task of the state was 'the definite reinforcement of the Nation by means of the elimination of the sequels of the regional spirit – How can the unity of the Nation be forged if there remains in the political and electoral domain irrational elements to be exploited or which can influence a part of society.

In this case, Sekou Toure only succeeded in destroying the pristine basis of morality – the colonial societal forms – in the vain hope that a new national moral order will emerge. In the same way, African leaders including Kenyatta and Moi in Kenya, argued that a one-party state has the distinct advantage of leading to the creation of a national order and a new national moral order that would be co-extensive with this national society. Walter Connor referred to such processes as state-building and nation-destroying (Connor, 1972).

The concept of the nation-state

In order to understand state nationalism, it is important that the concept of the nation-state which assumes equivalence between the state (which is a political term) and the nation (which is essentially a sociological concept) should be discussed. The model of the nation-state developed in Europe in the 18th and 19th centuries. In the majority of cases it was initially cultural or ethnic. It crystallized around an existing cultural or linguistic community that desired to free itself from foreign domination. Language was a necessary defence against alienation, against loss of identity, and against domination. The Hungarian nationalists under their leader Lajos Kosuth, modernized Magyar to become an official language and turned the writing and speaking of Magyar into a test of patriotism. Can we develop a link between European idea of the nation-state and its transposition to Africa? Perhaps Julius Nyerere may be viewed as a latter-day Kosuth: he turned the writing and speaking of Kiswahili into a test of patriotism and nationalism. The same applied to the Serbians who developed written Serbian to express their nationalism.

Moreover, some Western European states succeeded in fusing disparate ethnic groups into nations through the absorption by "ethnic cores" of peripheral ethnic groups into the state they controlled. Such absorptions were done either peacefully or through conquest. For example, expanded English nationalism absorbed first Wales and, later, Scotland and imposed English as the language of the state. The same applies to the beginning of the French state, where a Frankish core absorbed other ethnic groups into a French-speaking state. Eugene J. Weber's noted study, *Peasants into Frenchmen* (1976), shows how, at the time of the French Revolution (from which the French nation in the modern sense stems), few folks in the largely rural society of the ancient regime thought of themselves as being distinctively "French" – indeed many of them did not even speak French (Weber, 1976). Thus, the development of pre-modern ethnic communities into modern nation-states had always been mediated by historical contingencies and conscious political effort. Hence, modern nations are political constructs.

The few "nations" which were able to create their "nation-state "through political unification were France, Germany, Italy, England, and Spain. Others did so through separation from larger entities: Norway, Belgium, and Poland – sometimes by war and violence. Then came "the period of nationalism "in Europe (19th Century to 1918). The French Revolutionary wars started a process that forever changed the core political culture of western Europe. Along with "Liberty, Equality and Fraternity", the armies of the revolution spread the notion that borders of liberal democratic "nation" were somehow sacred. The idea of an innate, "enlightened" sacredness about nations and their borders was commencing its successful rise to prominence in Western European political consciousness. From there it spread to Eastern Europe, and subsequently, to Africa. In Poland, Hungary, Croatia, Slovenia – most of them under Napoleonic France – people gained heightened awareness of their own *ethnonational identities*. In the Ottoman Balkans, nationalist concepts spread from Serb emigrants in Habsburg Slavonia to the Serb Ottoman subjects, transforming a local uprising that had begun in 1804 in the Belgrade area into a nationalist Serb movement by 1815.

The national revolutions of the Greeks and Serbs in the Balkans were breaking up the Ottoman Empire. The Czechs and the Serbs were up in arms against the Hapsburg – Austrian Empire. In the end the struggle between the Hapsburgs and the Serbians mushroomed into the First World War. In April, 1917, the United States entered the war on the *Entente's* side, and President Woodrow Wilson issued his fourteen-point declaration of American war aims, which called for the right of national self-determination for all ethno-national groups within the borders of the Central Powers.

By September 1918, Austria – Hungary had collapsed and the various ethno-national groups in Europe (such as Czechs, Slovaks, Croats, Slovenes, and Romanians) declared their independent national existence along the lines of Wilson's Fourteen Points. The Entente Powers (Britain, France, and the United States) decided to redraw the map of Europe and Africa at the Treaty of Versailles in 1918. The maps were based on their own political and economic self-interests, and they made states borders inviolable through a set of international laws institutionalized in the League of Nations.

By placing their own political interests into the forefront of their map-making, the Western Great Powers at Versailles sanctioned the creation of new states which were as arbitrary in national make-up as the states they dismantled in the name of the nation-state principle. The new state of Czechoslovakia, for instance, included the Czechs, Slovak, Germans, Hungarians and Ruthenians; Yugoslavia comprised Serbs, Croats, Bosniaks, Macedonians, Albanians, Bulgarians, and Turks; and Poland included Poles, Germans, Lithuanians, Belorussians, and Ukrainians. The West glibly spoke of "Czechoslovaks" and "Yugoslavs" as if such creatures existed as authentic nationalities. This is similar to what the European imperial powers did to Africa in 1884-1885 at Berlin: they placed their own political and economic interests into the forefront of their map-making, and created new states, which artificially and arbitrarily encompassed disparate nationalities. And from then onwards they glibly spoke of "Anglo-Egyptian Sudanese", "Rhodesians", "Belgian Congolese" and "French Congolese", "Ugandans", "Kenyans", as if such creatures existed as authentic nationalities. But whereas the people of East Europe: the Croats, Slovenes, Serbs, Macedonians, Montenegroes – have all broken away to form their own nation-states, in the 1960s the independent African states declared inviolable, the borders of the artificial states they had inherited through a set of resolutions passed by the Organization of African Unity (OAU).

While the whole world has continued to redefine the "nation "as a concept, Africa has resolutely refused to answer this basic question: what is a nation? Africans have accepted as given the definition imposed on them by the colonial powers, and they have continued to ignore earlier precedents of ethno nationalism in the continent, on which they could have based meaningful nation-states. This may require regional as contrasted with state histories. The histories of the Luo-speaking peoples of eastern Africa, for example, show that they are transnational, traversing several ethnicities, states, and polities over the centuries without being confined to any single one of them. Hence, there was a Luo-nation and cultural sphere well before the incursion of the colonial state in the 20th Century. Their sense of multiple belongings to the various postcolonial states in the region suggest an alternative paradigm for writing regional rather than state history in the long perspective than the Western historical practice. What is needed is a historical narrative that moves beyond the state into an understanding regarding explanations.

Several European countries such as England, France, Portugal, Spain, Holland, Germany, and Italy, established their own overseas multinational colonial empires in which the "nationality principle" did not apply. These empires eventually broke up after the 2nd World War, leading to the multinational and polyethnic states of today, with a few nation-states such as Lesotho, Botswana, Swaziland, and Somali. The majority of the peoples of Africa and Asia, for example, are still nations without states – Yoruba, Zulu, Igbo, Asante, Luo, Baganda, Kikuyu, Mossi, Mandingo, Barotse, Kurds, Tamils, Tibereans. In western countries, ethnic minorities and non-dominant nationalities have continued to subsist since 1918, resisting incorporation or assimilation into the dominant "nation-states."

Hence, one of the basic unresolved issues in many parts of the world today is the apparent contradiction between the conception of the modern nation-state and the pervasive reality of multinational and polyethnic states.

Theories of nations and nationalism

There are at least five major theories of nations and nationalism that are of particular relevance to the contemporary world. These are: nationalism as a primordial phenomenon based on rational or objectively valid criteria on the basis of which the world can be divided up into different national communities; nationalism as the subjective consciousness of the members of the community; nationalism as a functional requirement of the modern state; nationalism as a specific form of politics that groups use, under certain historical circumstances in opposition to state; and finally, the Marxist interpretation of nationalism (Akzin, 1964; Fredrick 1944; Elie, 1985; Ernest, 1983; Hans, 1948).

First, there are those political scientists who view the nation as an objective fact, consisting of people who share a certain number of objective traits such as language, customs, history, religion, culture, economy, and territory. They hold the opinion that the nation-state that we know today is simply the political expression in its purest form of the nation. In the words of Kedourie,

> [w]hat is beyond doubt is that the doctrine divides humanity into separate and distinct nations, claims that such nations must constitute sovereign states, and asserts that the members of a nation reach freedom and fulfilment by cultivating the peculiar identity of their own nation or by sinking their own persons in the greater whole of the nation (Kedourie, 1985).

The nation, according to the theory, is seen as a non-historical entity directly rooted in some transcendent or natural order. Since Kenya is a historical entity, this doctrine is obviously not applicable.

Secondly, some scholars have contended that it is not a series of objective traits that define a nation but the subjective awareness of it by its presumed members. A nation thus becomes the expression of a common consciousness, a common will to be a nation, and not the other way round. Gellner, for example, defines nations as "groups which will themselves to persist as communities (Ernest, 1983). He states categorically that "it is nationalism which engenders nations, and not the other way round (Ernest, 1983). Kenyans have never had a common consciousness, a common will to be a nation. And Kenyans have never generated enough nationalism to engender a nation.

Benedict Anderson, writing in the same year as Gellner, goes even further in his definition of a "nation". He writes that "[a] nation is an imagined political community and imagined as both inherently limited and sovereign. It is imagined because the members of even the smallest nation will never know most of their fellow members, meet them or even hear them, yet in the minds of each lives the image of their communion" (2006).

For Anderson, it is the literates, the lexicographers, philologists, folklorists, artists, publicists, composers and other professional intellectuals, including museum curators, that fathered the imagined communities that were to become the nation-state of the modern world (Anderson, 2006). There is no evidence that the Kenyan intelligentsia have ever fathered such an imagined community which could become the Kenyan nation-state.

Antony Smith, on the other hand, explains the rise of nationalism in terms of what he calls the "ethnic revival" that has taken place in the world since the 18th Century. He also attributes to the intelligentsia a pivotal role in the process: a project which must be realized by transforming the components of the ethnic community they have rediscovered and seek to regenerate. It is not the community as such which draws the zeal and activity of the intelligentsia, but the community transformed according to a particular blueprint, in short, "the nation." Smith, however, maintains that the intelligentsia plays this crucial role not for the betterment of the state or for the general welfare of the nation, but for their self-interests. Again, historical evidence indicates that the Kenyan intelligentsia has not transformed the community according to any particular blueprint (Smith Anthony, 1981). To the works of Gellner, Anderson, and Smith, should be added those of Eric Hobsbawm and Terence Ranger. Their work, *The Invention of Tradition*, contributed to the demystification of nationalism by demonstrating that nationalist mythologies were historically contingent creations (Hobsbawm & Ranger, 2012).

A third school of thought gives a more prominent role in nation-building to communications, instead of the intellectuals or the printed page. The school links the development of national consciousness with the communication revolution which began in the 19th Century with railroads, telegraph, and widespread secular public education system. It is through effective communication that people lose their local, parochial identities and loyalties, in order to identify themselves with a larger economic and political unit, the nation (Deutsch, 1953). This functional approach to nationalism seems to be an aspect of the larger theory of modernization, which sees the nation as an essential ingredient in the process of modernization and the ideology of nationalism as its necessary concomitant. According to modernization theory, the process of nation-building and development of the modern state entails the transformation of agrarian, pre-industrial societies into industrial, market-oriented economies. In such a process, the nation, or better still, the nation-state, replaces the clan, the tribe, the ethnic group as a focus for the individuals' loyalty and as a claim on the individuals' social and political, and ideological, commitment. Today, we know that modernization, in itself, is not a sufficient condition for breaking down ethnic identities. If anything, there is sufficient evidence to suggest that in some cases it leads to a strengthening rather than a weakening of ethnic identification. In any case, Kenya is yet to undergo communication and industrial revolutions.

Fourthly, there is the theory which regards nationalism as a specific form of politics that groups practice under certain historical circumstances in opposition to the state. The advocates of this theory argue that the historical significance of nationalism as a movement arises only when it is used for political ends with the objective of controlling or possessing the powers of the state. Nationalism, thus understood, can be expressed in three different ways (Breuily, 1982), when:

- Groups wish to secede from an existing state in order to form their own state
- Nationalist political groups wish to introduce major political and constitutional reforms as happened in Turkey under Ataturk; and

- Politically fragmented but ethnically similar groups struggle to create larger states or supra-states as has been the case with Arab nationalism.

A version of this theory, which sees nationalism as a form of politics, has been developed by J. Rothschild in *Ethnopolitics* (1981). The core argument here is what he calls politicized ethnicity which, according to him, is not the expression of some form of primordial attachment, but rather an instrument in the struggle for power, directly linked to the process of modernization. He argues that in certain societies, "politicized ethnicity has become the crucial principle of political legitimation and delegitimation of systems, states, regimes and governments" (Rothschild, 1981). In his conceptual framework, politicized ethnicity is not absolutist, it is a variable, it is invented, it is utilitarian and may be used or discarded by an ethnic group in accordance with the group's economic and political interest. Hence, much of what is usually considered as nationalism is nothing but political ethnicity. Perhaps, this concept of politicized ethnicity may help us to understand the meaning of so-called Kenyan "nationalism."

The fifth and final theory of nationalism relates to the Marxist interpretation of the "national equation." Orthodox Marxists were more interested in the class struggle under capitalism than in the national question. They argued that whereas the bourgeoisie is nationalist, "the proletarians have no fatherland." In practice, however, the masters Marx and Engels, developed the controversial and almost racist concept of nations with history and nations without history. The former represented by Germany had developed state structures that enabled them to progress economically and expand their territory. The latter groups, who according to Engels included the Slavs, were destined to disappear, because they had failed to become "nations with history."

For many decades, nationalism was considered by the Marxists as a purely bourgeois ideology, a false consciousness. In the multinational federation of the Soviet Union, it was expected that national differences would co-exist harmoniously, within the socialist economic and political structure, to the extent that all objective reasons for national oppression and separatism – as may exist in capitalist countries – would have disappeared. A new historical community, the "Soviet people" was to evolve. Events in 1989-1990 in the Soviet Union shattered this illusion. As a result of the *perestroika,* nationalists movements were on the rise, leading to the collapse of the Union and the subsequent declaration of independence by several states.

National issues and problems of national identity became dominant in the political discourse of the post-Cold War era in Eastern Europe. The violent eruption in Bosnia, Croatia, Moldova, Georgia; the abysmal way in which the newly independent Baltic states treated their Russian and Polish minorities; the break-up of the Czech and Slovak republics; the future of the 25 million ethnic Russians who lived outside Russia; and the Hungarian minorities in Slovakia, Romania, and the former Yugoslavia – all these examples, and many others should be enough to convince anyone who believed that post-communist political discourse would concentrate on the issues of democratization and the development of the market economies to think differently. This is partly because issues which most Western societies settled through trial and error, accommodation, or drastic forced adjustment, in the course of their histories, are still open questions that the people of Africa, Asia, and Eastern Europe must grapple with. Among these issues, are conflicts that are engendered by nationalism which threaten the body politic.

The Kenyan nation

Between 1952 and 1963, strong nationalism winds were blowing in most parts of Kenya, thanks to the *Mau Mau* and constitutional Freedom Fighters Movements. In early 1954, among the issues being discussed by *Mau Mau* fighters in the forest was that of electing a Kenya central council or parliament that would co-ordinate the leadership of the struggle. On the qualifications needed, one fighter, Karari Njama, said:

I would like us to elect the best twelve persons we have in this forest so that we have the best [g]overnment possible: Apart from education, we should look for the person's wisdom and ability, his courage and incorruptible character. It does not matter whether the twelve members are all real brothers or from the same village or district, what we would count on would be that they are the best we have, who will make the best we all want. We are not fighting for regions, or clans or tribes. We are fighting for the whole Kenya, including our enemies as Home Guards.... For they will enjoy the freedom which will be so abundant that even if we imprison them, they would still enjoy the freedom we are fighting for in the prisons, for [we] have a song demanding freedom (from colour bar) in prisons which you all always sing (Njama, & Barnett, 1966).·

The forest fighters were looking for leaders who would serve all Kenyans, not tribal or regional leaders. Njama saw the struggle as one for the benefit of all Kenyans and not for the benefit of only a small exclusive group. He continued:

Be sure that freedom would be so abundant that there would be no competition of some people trying to get more freedom than the others. Just as the rain pours to the rich as to the poor, to the good ones as to the bad ones, to the lazy person's garden as to the industrious one's, the same will happen to the freedom. Some of us may seek privileges, but by the time we achieve our freedom you will have learned to share a grain of maize or a bean amongst several people, feeling selfishness as an evil; and the hate of oppressing others would be so developed in you that you will not like to become another class of "Black Europeans', ready to oppress and exploit others like the system we are fighting against (Njama, & Barnett, 1966).

On the attainment of independence, these were exactly the failure of the Kenya leaders – leaders with more freedom than others, leaders who did not learn to share anything, leaders who did not hate oppression but instead oppressed others, and leaders who did not feel that selfishness is evil but instead practiced it continuously.

Mau Mau detainees on Manda Island, near Lamu, had important debates. The list of the detainees included Achieng' Oneko and Pio Gama Pinto. In 1965, Achieng' Oneko wrote about these debates:

> We had great hopes for the future of our country. We pledged to carry on the fight after our release to help create a society based on African traditions, a society in which one is his or her brother's keeper, a society of devotion and love for one another, a society of self-sacrifice and self-denial as opposed to selfishness, personal ambition and greed (Pheroze Nowrojee. Nairobi: *The Star Articles* 2012 – 2013).

It is therefore, evident that the freedom fighters, the *mashujaa*[1], believed in one set of national values, and the independent government in another. The *mashujaa* believed in social justice and the care of the poor, the landless and the infirm first. But the new 1963 government believed instead in personal accumulation of property and wealth for themselves by any means.

This means that the Kenyatta government of 1963 decided to break the promises of the national struggle and its own earlier promises to the freedom fighters. It punished those who spoke up against this; and the harshest punishment was reserved for the freedom fighters. They were pushed out of national politics; land was denied them; and they were impoverished, financially, like Bildad Kaggia. Elections were rigged against them, many were detained, like Jaramogi Oginga Odinga, and some were killed. *Mau Mau* General Baimungi was killed on January 26, 1964 together with General Chui, General Ikiugo and others (Mrs. Baimungi, October 22, 2011). On February 24 1965, Pio Gama Pinto, himself a former *Mau Mau* detainee, freedom fighter and MP, was assassinated. Pinto was also a writer, and after his release from detention, he was an important political worker in KANU, both out of parliament as a key campaigner and in parliament as a KANU backbencher, and a powerhouse in the political constellation around Jaramogi Oginga Odinga. On July 5, 1969, Mboya was assassinated; and on March 2,

---

[1] This a Kiswahili word used to describe heroes. In the Kenyan context, it generally implies the *Mau Mau* fighters, among others, who fought to restore the independence of Kenya.

1975, J.M. Kariuki, another former *Mau Mau* detainee and MP, was also assassinated.

Kenyans were generally prevented from remembering and respecting these freedom fighters. These fighters' acts of heroism were omitted from school textbooks, not taught at universities, not even seen on TV or in newspapers. The truth about them was not to be told. The Jomo Kenyatta regime thus chose to turn its back on Kenya's great political past. The fundamental question which has not been satisfactorily resolved is: why did the Jomo Kenyatta regime decide to betray the freedom fighters? Why didn't it fulfil the stated promises of the independence struggle? And why didn't it share power and government with the returning freedom fighters? Was it greed? Was it pressure from the British government? Or was it both? There cannot be a nation devoid of nationalists. And without a nation, it is meaningless to talk of a nation-state.

A related basic issue is that of the massive oathing campaign, following the assassination of Tom Mboya, in which almost every adult Kikuyu male was forced to swear in mass ceremonies at Gatundu, Kenyatta 's home, and on pain of death, to keep presidency in the House of Mumbi. Oath-takers pledged, ominously, to maintain Kenya "under Kikuyu leadership ... No uncircumcised leaders will be allowed to compete with the Kikuyu leadership. You shall not vote for any party not led by a Kikuyu. If you reveal this oath, may this oath kill you (*Daily Nation*, April 10, 2001). Njenga Karume, who was one of the people who was forced to take this oath at Gatundu, has confirmed in his book, *Beyond Expectations*, the content of this pledge (Njenga, 2009). A similar account of the oath was given in an article published in *Time* magazine of August 15, 1969. One recent estimate suggests that over 300,000 people were transported to Gatundu (Knighton, 2009). Using an ethnic oath to unite the Kikuyu and establish their ascendancy and dominance was a total negation of everything Kenya as a nation was supposed to stand for. Ethnic polarization became total; and as Branch has stated, by 1971 "[t]he President abandoned all but the most perfunctory pretence that his was a government for all Kenyans (Branch, 2011).

The Jomo Kenyatta regime consolidated its state power, including the police, the army, the judiciary, and the public service, to serve its class and ethnic interests. It did so through coercion and co-optation: dissenting voices were jailed, exiled or killed; resource allocation became grossly inequitable; the public sector was increasingly ethicized; contracts were awarded according to ethnic or political affiliation. State power, previously coloured by colonial racialism, now took an ethnic shape. The Kikuyu returned to the Rift Valley in large numbers, and the Kikuyu reserves now reached socially and politically into the Rift Valley – South, Central and even North Rift areas of Nandi, Uasin Gishu, and Trans-Nzoia.

Kenyatta's ethnicity was defining the state and the direction of Kenyan politics. In 1970, his decision to centralize most power in his hands increased this tendency, leading to disunity, corruption, a bloated and inefficient public service and economic marginalization of some groups. The 1970s saw Kikuyu hegemony or ethnic sovereignty expand over economic and political life. It could truly be said that they owned Kenya and controlled its state. Jomo Kenyatta became an Imperial president, a true successor to the departed British Governor. In effect, the new rulers had established a kind of internal colonialism, with the rest of Kenya citizens being treated as their subjects. The resentment of the marginalized and alienated groups grew in intensity by the day. They took little pride in a Kenyan identity, a Kenyan nation. Indeed, people's primary loyalty now did not lie with the nation called Kenya, since Kenya patriotism meant nothing to those excluded from power. Kikuyu nationalism, one of the oldest anti-colonial movements, was now being used by Jomo Kenyatta to kill Kenya nationalism, and by extension, Kenya nation.

The Kalenjin ascendancy

Daniel Arap Moi became President of the Republic of Kenya in August, 1978 on Jomo Kenyatta's death. Moi was confronted by entrenched Kikuyu elite who had tried to change the constitution in order to prevent his succession of Jomo Kenyatta. Moi decided to replace the Kikuyu hegemony with a Kalenjin one; and consolidated his executive powers further by introducing the notorious Section 2A which turned Kenya into a *de jure* one – party state in 1982. By 1991, the constitution had been amended thirty-two times (Odhiambo-

Mbai, 2003), resulting in the establishment of an autocratic state. Dissenting voices were detained, jailed, tortured, and killed.

By the late 1980s, Kenya had become an artificial state, controlling an unstable amalgam of ethnic enclaves through satellite barons created, sustained, and controlled by state patronage. By 1990, Moi felt strong enough to embark on ethnic wars of conquest. History had to be reversed in the Rift Valley Province, his home-base. All ethnic groups that were perceived not to be indigenous to the area were to be forcibly evicted. Organized militia and gangs killed, maimed, raped, robbed the Kikuyu, Luo, Luhyia, and Kisii. Over 1,500 people died in the 1992 election period and over 300,000 others, mostly Kikuyu, were displaced. The situation was the same during the 1997 elections. The casualties of the two elections in the 1990s totalled 2,000 killed and 500,000 displaced (Boone, 1992). The Rift Valley's political landscape changed permanently. Moi had accomplished his mission of recolonizing the Rift Valley, but at the expense of balkanizing the Kenya state and nation.

President Mwai Kibaki succeeded Moi after the 2002 election, one that was acclaimed as a national victory. But he soon succumbed to the ethnic pressures resulting in the disputed or "stolen" elections, during which ethnic violence erupted again, along ethnic lines. The 2007-08 violence revealed that all this time we had been living a lie that there was a Kenyan nation. Individuals, who had lived their whole lives in different parts of the country, fled for safety fearing former friends and neighbours as well as organized militia and youth gangs. They were expected to go back to so-called "ancestral homes", which in many cases never existed. Organized gangs patrolled urban slums, raping women and destroying property. By February, 2008, over 1,000 were dead and about 350, 000 had been displaced. The idea of a nation had been fractured and Kenya appeared on the brink of a major collapse.

The Report of the Commission of Inquiry into the Post-Election Violence (CIPEV) which was chaired by Justice Philip Waki, established that 1,133 people were killed in the first three months of 2008, that rape and sexual violence were rampart; that the property of unknown value on over 117,000 sites was destroyed; and that over 300,000 people were displaced from their homes. The report further revealed that the security forces were the leading cause of death, accounting for a shocking 35.7% of all deaths. The report showed that ethnic citizenship enjoys greater legitimacy and exercises more persuasive authority over Kenyans than the weak and incoherent civic citizenship and nation.

Conclusion

Since 2008, Kenya's balkanization into ethnic chiefdoms has gathered pace. The notion of Kenya as a nation whose citizens can live and work anywhere in the country has fewer supporters today than it had at independence in 1963. Worse still, scepticism over nationhood is most pronounced among the political elite who see the citizens of various ethnic groups as their property, to be used in bargaining for royalties. Ethnic barons continue to dismember Kenya, perpetuating disunity and exploiting their clients – the masses. The Constitution of Kenya (2010) constitutes a gallant attempt to respect social pluralism. Its preamble states the national message, and the messengers are the people of Kenya. The message present a vision of the development of a just society in which big ethnic groups do not push small ones to the periphery; and proclaims the possibility of Kenyans living together in harmony, while appreciating national diversity. The Constitution of Kenya (2010) has set the country on the right course in terms of representation, justice, ethnic relations, equitable wealth distribution, a threefold separation of powers, and respect for human rights. Its full implementation will provide Kenyans with the only hope of recreating a meaningful and desirable nation.

Chapter 4

Tourism and Liberation Struggles in Kenya: Ensuring Sustainability in the Conservation of *Mau Mau* Heritage

Ephraim W. Wahome

Introduction

Conservation of the *Mau Mau* war heritage has been one of the controversial issues in the history of post-independence Kenya. Increase in population, the need for agricultural land and never-ending political squabbling have overshadowed conservation activities. This has meant that less attention and time have been devoted to preservation of heritage and historical relics on a national scale. Defining what needs to be urgently protected or left to natural attrition without hurting the other forms of socio-economic aspirations in the post-independence governments has been a major challenge. The *Mau Mau* heritage and colonial escapades of 1950s and 1960s need to be defined in this light. Other countries like Rwanda and the Republic of South Africa have conserved the most difficult moments in their socio-political history, including genocides, while Kenya lags behind in protecting its dark heritage. The *Mau Mau* campaigns of 1952 to 1960 left a legacy in antiquities and monuments, which have been largely ignored by the government and by the communities which bore the brunt of colonial aggression. This chapter explores the extant types of heritage and reasons behind this blatant neglect. We conclude that potential socio-economic benefits can be realized through the protection of the *Mau Mau* heritage. This chapter also proposes a model cultural heritage circuit for the sustainable protection and promotion of the *Mau Mau* legacy. It also provides a comparative model from Robben Island to conclude that the *Mau Mau* heritage can be conserved profitably.

Mau Mau was a war intended to counter the evils of colonial domination in Kenya. The movement started in 1952 and ended in the 1960s after intensive campaigns. The war left behind a legacy of a war-heritage which has been largely ignored. Time and population explosion since independence to date have aggravated the rate of deterioration of these forms of heritage, which are important elements of 'dark tourism'. Dark tourism is drawn from our unfortunate experiences like war, genocide, tsunamis and landslides which, if properly conserved and appropriately branded, embody our values and memorialization of the past (Lennon & Folley, 1996). In this chapter, the term dark tourism encompasses diverse forms of relics including detention camps, prisons, places of punishment, trenches, monuments, and artefacts of war which offer a sense of wonder, mystery, excitement, recreation or leisure. In a nutshell, dark tourism involves the commodification of locations and occasions associated with death and destruction (Stone & Sharply, 2008).

This chapter explores potential dark tourism sites in Kenya that warrant immediate attention, while opening up a discourse on the potential for conservation, associated opportunities and challenges. The study explores the dark aspects of the *Mau Mau* heritage and offers strategies for its conservation and promotion as a tourist product. The branding of such sites has been a popular way of attracting tourists and ensuring sustainability as has been documented in Robben Island.

Heritage encompasses a combination of materials, social memories and socio-cultural differentiation in its broad definition (Bessiere, 2013). Placing the war heritage in Kenya into this definition is hampered by the bitter rivalries created by the divide-and-rule political orientation of the colonial regime which polarised communities into perceptual divisions of freedom fighters and loyalists. The divisions were further enhanced by post-colonial regimes which rewarded the loyalists at the expense of the real fighters in the name of unfounded fears of disunity. In the process, the contribution of the *Mau Mau* to the independence of Kenya was overshadowed by heated discourses, in both academic and political circles, on whether the movement was 'tribal' or national in character.

This environment of contestation paralysed the protection of heritage which no one wanted to be associated with. It also redefined the concept of heritage from a process of association to one of dissociation. The Jomo Kenyatta and the Daniel Moi regimes of independent Kenya opted for unity rather than confrontation in solving this impasse. This was the main challenge in the conservation of the historic monuments of war (Maloba, 1994). However, the turning point of this history came with recognition of *Mau Mau* as a nationalist movement by Kibaki's regime in 2003, followed by the compensation of torture victims by the British government in 2013. This chapter also attempts to identify this heritage, document its state and propose a viable heritage tourism promotion strategy for its sustainable protection within the existing legal framework.

The study conforms to the contemporary conservation mode which acknowledges the importance of stakeholders, or those affected by conservation, as participants in the process. By so doing, the sustainability of the heritage is enhanced as stakeholders are obliged to take up some conservation responsibility. This contravenes the traditional conservational model which is primarily driven by the scientist. The traditional model has failed as the *Mau Mau* heritage has been systematically destroyed since the 1950s. To achieve this objective, data collection involved field observation, extant literature review, and oral interviews.

It is, therefore, necessary to incorporate the contemporary theory of conservation which accommodates communities in the identification of heritage and the conservation process. Identified values are exhaustively discussed through stakeholder participation encompassing individuals or groups that may be impacted by proposed conservation. Beside the virtual lack of a participatory conservation process in the past, tangible economic benefits were never considered as possible sources of motivation for sustainability. This chapter further shows that proper packaging and marketing of *Mau Mau* heritage through tourism could positively change our perceptions of conservation and enhance sustainability.

Identifying *Mau Mau* heritage

Mau Mau, as a military outfit, challenged the colonial government in many ways, which were countered aggressively. The subsequent conflict created a wide range of heritage forms before the onset of the country's independence. Keeping the movement intact in the face of colonial might led to the administration of different types of oaths of allegiance. The two popular oaths were *Githaka* (land or forest oath) and *Mbatuni* (platoon oath) (EAS, 4/6/1960). An often cited example of an oath is given by Muriithi and Ndoria (1981):

> I swear that I will fight for the African soil that the white man has stolen from us. I swear that I will always try to trick a white man and any imperialist into accompanying me, strangle him, take his gun and any valuables he may be carrying. I swear that I will offer all available help and further the cause of *Mau Mau*. I swear that I will kill, if necessary, anybody opposed to this organization.

The sites where these oaths were administered qualify as heritage sites because of their significance to the success of the war. One such site is Kiburi House in Nairobi, which also served a communication hub and the former Head Office of Kenya African Union (KAU), which was patronized by *Mau Mau* luminaries like Field Marshall Kimathi and General Mathenge Mirugi (EAS, 23/12/1960). Other oath-taking sites include Ruthigiti Village in Ndeiya Location, Kiambu County, and various spots in the Aberdare and Mt. Kenya forests. One major challenge for conservators is that most of the sites, including buildings like Kiburi House, which constitute an important part of the heritage, cannot be located. The long line of communication from Nairobi to the forest, which included mail delivery, weapons, and food, must have generated different forms of heritage.

There were clear indications that more people were being convicted in connection with oath-taking in areas like Kericho by 1959 (EAS, 6/5/1960).This led to the fear of continued resistance among the settlers as the movement spread beyond the traditional areas of Aberdare and Mt. Kenya forests, and adjoining Kikuyu reserves. Confrontation also took place in concentration camps and prisons, spurred by the emergence of the combative *Kiama Kia Muingi* (KKM) organisation, which seemed to take the place of *Mau Mau* in the reorganisation of resistance forces (EAS, April 14, 1958). After *Mau Mau* was systematically weakened, KKM continued with the struggle until 1960, when it was proscribed by the colonial government and replaced through the formation of two political parties, Kenya African National Union (KANU) and Kenya African Democratic Union (KADU) (Maina wa Kinyati, 2008).

The fighters also used the Mount Kenya and Aberdare forests as perfect hideouts from which they effectively launched surprise attacks. Being more familiar with this terrain, the *Mau Mau* was able to outmanoeuvre their adversaries for an extended period of time before their eventual defeat. On their part, the Europeans resorted to heavy artillery of The Royal Air Force Bombers, Full Infantry Division of the Six Kings African Rifles (KAR) Battalions, the Kenya Police, tribal police, and armed loyalists to ensure systematic isolation of the *Mau Mau* along forest fringes and out of settled areas (Lonsdale, 1990).

Operation areas fringing the forests were cleared to ease the scouting of the movement of the fighters between forest and settled areas. Areas to the East of the Aberdare Forest and the South and East of Mount Kenya Forest had a stretch of one kilometre cleared as an operation area for this purpose (Clayton, 2006). Police posts were also erected in such areas and populations from the areas relocated into fortified villages (See Figs. 1 and 2 below).

Guns were freely used in operation areas including the forests, while anyone remotely associated with the movement was detained without trial in one of the detention camps, spread throughout the country, while oath administration and gun possession translated into an automatic death sentence (Clayton, 2005; Smith, 2005). The 'pipeline' system of punishment for presumed 'hardcore' (ZI) criminals, who were relocated to camps, outside Central Province, followed by intermediate (YI) and works camps (Y2) within the province, were meant to deter any kind of resistance by keeping the combatants away for an extended period of time (Clayton, 2006:16). With the onset of Operation Anvil from 1954 to 1956, there were concerted attacks targeting *Mau Mau* hide-outs on the slopes of Mt. Kenya and the Aberdares (EAS: 5/11/1954). There are indications that *Mau Mau* hideouts, including the Naromoru Cave (Fig. 3) on Nairobi River, were shelled and extremely damaged (EAS: 5/11/1954). Many other sites were also shelled indiscriminately as a way of cowing the freedom fighters into submission. The sites targeted in this indiscriminate aggression, including the caves, war trenches and operation areas, should be identified and conserved as war heritage (EAS 27/1/1955).

Figure 1: Watch Tower

(Source: Kenya National Archives)

Fig. 2: Fortified Villages

(Source: wa Kinyatti, 2008)

Fig 3: *Mau Mau* cave in Naromoru: Note the ledge shattered by bombing

(*Source:* Author)

The *Mau Mau* leadership organised battalions in forests and fairly isolated environments against a well-equipped force. In the ensuing encounter, some of the movement's luminaries like Mathenge disappeared from the Aberdare Forest without trace while others were captured in their quest for replenishment. A number were killed in combat. The leader of *Mau Mau*, Field Marshall Kimathi, was captured on October 21, 1956 near a trench, or so called stop line, at the Aberdares and later executed on February 18, 1957 (EAS: 26/10/1956). His burial site, a form of heritage, has remained mysterious to date. Some of his lieutenants, including General Kennes, (Kirinya s/o Wamahiu), Brigadier Chui and General Sheikh Abdalla (Gitonga s/o Muthui) faced a similar fate. General China was wounded and captured in 1954 (KDM 22/1/1954). To survive under such attacks, the movement successfully managed facilities for the sick and injured in the forest hide-outs, including fully equipped mobile and fixed hospitals of up to 150-bed capacity which form part of this tangible heritage (Kenya Committee, 1954). While most of the actual facilities have disappeared, model ones can be constructed and popularised in their place.

In the hide-outs, workshops with elaborate equipment for the manufacture of home-made guns existed. The gun-making materials included piping, spring and bolts and gun oil (EAS, 6/7/1955). Some of the materials from these factories have been conserved at the Nairobi National Museum, but the factory sites including Karura Forest, Shauri Moyo, Kanjore Village and Pumwani, and the Meru Forest gun factory, should also be properly identified and conserved as part of a repertoire of indigenous knowledge (EAS, 6/7/1955).

The war courts, like the one documented in Nyeri, should be conserved as a constant reminder of *Mau Mau* elaborate justice system (KDM, 18/11/1952). Similarly, the colonial courts which represented the tilted justice system, which were disliked by luminaries like Jomo Kenyatta, Dedan Kimathi, and General China, should be protected for posterity. Anderson (2005) cites a number of colonial sites within Nyeri Town, including the early colonial 'block and concrete buildings' that 'line the main highway' used in counter-insurgency, besides the Agikuyu Peace Museum. The infamous public gallows used for condemned prisoners which were conspicuously placed to scare prisoners and potential criminals in places like "the Thomson's Falls prison camp...and...Nyeri golf course" are an important heritage that could be re-created for the sake of history and posterity (Clayton, 2006).

For the captured combatants and suspects, detention camps and prisons became their new homes. They became prime sources of labour in government construction projects like the Embakasi Airport (current Jomo Kenyatta International Airport), which is the second largest airport in Africa after Oliver Tambo International Airport (Mathenge, 2008). Other projects included Lamu water projects and the Hola desert irrigation scheme. On Hola, "[i]t was the work of these detainees to irrigate the desert land from the Tana River" (EAS, April 17, 1959). Some of these projects should have some form of acknowledgement of the contribution of the liberation movement. A plaque containing a short history of their experiences and a list of those who perished during the project is a good starting point.

The Jomo Kenyatta International Airport (formerly Embakasi Airport) is interesting because the Director of Public Works requested for 3, 000 prisoners to provide labour which would save the country over £500,000, remarking that "convict labour....represents a big saving of public money" (EAS, 21/5/1954;

EAS, 28/1/1957). According to the Commissioner of Prisons, J. H. Lewis, "Embakasi [P]rison was established for the sole purpose of supplying labour for building the new Nairobi Embakasi Airport" which echoes Mr. Michael Blundell sentiments that "[w]e do not detain people for what they have done, we detain them for what they may intend to do" (EAS, 21/12/57). In confirmation to the sentiments expressed by Blundell, and on completion of the Airport in 1957, the prisoners were relocated. To the colonial government, therefore, these punitive acts of slavery were good for the economy in lieu of expensive machinery needed for construction works (KDM; 21/5/1954). In his judgment on the case, Judge Cram stated that

> [t]here exists a system of guard posts ... these are interrogation centres and prisons to which the Queen's subjects, whether innocent or guilty, are led by armed men without warrant and detained – and as it seems tortured until they confess to alleged crimes and are then led forth to trial on the sole evidence of these confessions – naked oppression (Cited by Clayton, 2006).

Detention camps and prisons like Embakasi were constructed strategically for labour exploitation purposes, and in some cases the number of prisons or detention camps was dependent on the labour requirements, meaning that the processes of detention and imprisonment were arbitrary. Gikandi and Mathenge (2008) capture the agony in "Monuments of Slave Labour and its Shame". This article evokes memories of the torture that prisoners were exposed to. It is a clear indication of the national importance of this heritage. Other detention camps and prisons of bad repute, included Manyani, Mageta, Kagunduini Camp, Gathigiriri, Naivasha and Athi River transit Camps, Manda Island, and Mackinnon Road.

For the rest of the population in combat zones, the Colonial War Council imposed strict movement regulations which were enforced through relocating populations into fortified villages (WAR/c. no. 468, 1955). A directive issued by the governor in 1954 proposed two main types of villages to contain potential passive supporters of the *Mau Mau*, the model village and the punitive village. The model villages proposed by the War Council were to have well-spaced huts with a garden, a social centre and a few shops. The aim of these villages was to entice the passive occupants and loyalists into accommodating their European adversaries. In contrast, the punitive villages were constructed with "a pungi moat surrounding them … [and] … left to get crowded, dirty and unhygienic as a disciplinary measure" for populations that were considered 'uncooperative' and suspected supporters of the movement (WAR/c. 468, 1955). By April 1955 the war committee had anticipated that there would be 200 villages housing some 80% of the Kikuyu, Embu and Meru population (WAR/c. 468 1955).

A combined force of regular police, home guards, and secret informers administered these villages while an observation tower at the entrance ensured a bird's eye view of the villages. To the War Council, all the villages were to be registered and the population issued with identity cards (IDs) in the form of a passbook as a form of control (WAR/c. no. 468, 1955). The construction of the villages and their management was, however, affected by disagreements between the security forces and the administration, with the former contending that the population should be tightly controlled while the latter's view was that

> [f]encing and ditching was to be based on the judgment of the local administrators. Fencing all villages would not achieve the objective of control since they could not police the full extent of the fence. A larger part of the village should also be left unfenced so that the population can disperse and escape in the event of an attack by criminal gangs. Concentrating a loyal population with ditching and fencing in punitive type villages would turn that population against the administration (WAR/c. 468, 1955).

In spite of these disagreements, the population was moved from their traditional settlements to new villages and their original homes were demolished. For example, more than 80,000 Kikuyu households were relocated from Kiambu District alone in 1954, while 17,000 squatters were ejected from the Rift Valley and forced into such villages by 1955 (Presley, 1988). Plans for the period up to April 1, 1955 were to have villages constructed in Nyeri, Fort Hall [now Murang'a], and Meru (EAS, 18th March, 1955). These villages represent the range of the *Mau Mau* war heritage in Kenya, and they should be reconstructed as model structures for posterity and memorialization. Some villages like Kiaruhiu in Nyeri County still retain some of the colonial characteristics in addition to a communal burial *kaburi*[1] used during the emergency, between 1952 and 1959, and a faint semblance of the pungi moat constructed by the colonial government. Kiaruhiu village later became home to all those who could not move back to their original homes after the war for one reason or another.

Mau Mau monuments represent a phenomenon of key domestic and international tourist attraction in view of the controversies associated with the *Mau Mau* uprising and its contribution towards Kenya's independence. As attractions, these unique features are likely to benefit immensely through conservation. Communities, as the real custodians, will also benefit as more and, hopefully, properly managed tourism is generated. Tourism expenditure has the potential of developing the regions which suffered this menace through the multiplier effect. This can be achieved through the development of circuits targeting the *Mau Mau* heritage as proposed in Figure 4 below.

The circuit should target *Mau Mau* landscapes and associated features besides cultural relics in their diverse forms, including tangible and intangible modes of communication. Libraries, museums, prisons, and mass graves are important components of this kind of circuit. Since the relics are distributed widely in geographical scope, a national circuit can be designed, though counties like Nyeri and Murang'a may decide to operate independent or joint circuits.

---

[1] *Kaburi* is Kiswahli for grave

Fig. 4: Proposed *Mau Mau* Tourist Circuits

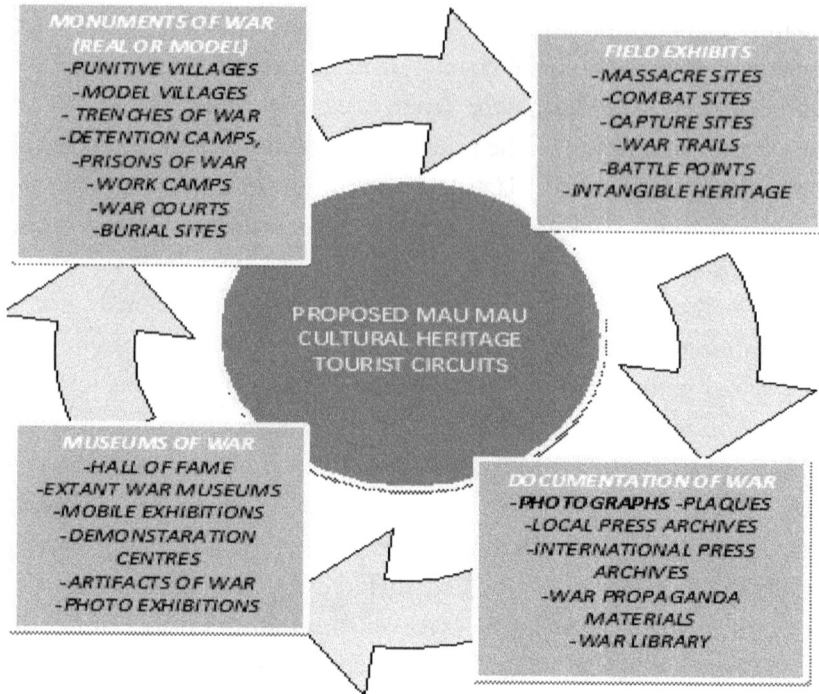

MONUMENTS OF WAR (REAL OR MODEL)
-PUNITIVE VILLAGES
-MODEL VILLAGES
- TRENCHES OF WAR
-DETENTION CAMPS,
-PRISONS OF WAR
- WORK CAMPS
-WAR COURTS
-BURIAL SITES

FIELD EXHIBITS
-MASSACRE SITES
-COMBAT SITES
- CAPTURE SITES
-WAR TRAILS
-BATTLE POINTS
-INTANGIBLE HERITAGE

PROPOSED MAU MAU CULTURAL HERITAGE TOURIST CIRCUITS

MUSEUMS OF WAR
-HALL OF FAME
-EXTANT WAR MUSEUMS
-MOBILE EXHIBITIONS
-DEMONSTARATION CENTRES
-ARTIFACTS OF WAR
-PHOTO EXHIBITIONS

DOCUMENTATION OF WAR
-PHOTOGRAPHS -PLAQUES
-LOCAL PRESS ARCHIVES
-INTERNATIONAL PRESS ARCHIVES
-WAR PROPAGANDA MATERIALS
-WAR LIBRARY

Source: Author

Currently, the push for integrated conservation and community involvement in forest protection could be effectively extended to the protection and promotion of the monuments in the Aberdare and Mount Kenya forests which were the hotbeds of the campaign. Furthermore, the Mt. Kenya ecosystem was inscribed as a world heritage site in 1997 and extended in 2013 by the United Nations (UNESCO, 2013). *Mau Mau* monuments are features that contributed to the transformation of the population socially, economically, and politically from a traditional to a multicultural way of life. It also led to the transformation of their cultural landscape in an irreparable manner.

The features described in this chapter qualify for the legal definition of cultural heritage in Kenya as

architectural works, works of monumental sculpture and painting, elements or structures of an archaeological nature, inscriptions, cave dwellings and combinations of features which are of universal value from the point of view of history, science and art [or as] ...ancient earthworks or other immovable objects attributable to human activity (NMHA, 2006).

Under the current circumstance of continued anthropogenic deterioration, the only realistic hope for the monuments lies with Sections 43 and 59 of the National Museums and Heritage Act, where heritage is assured continued protection with the benefit of police and heritage guard inspection from time to time (NMHA, 2006). The Constitution of Kenya (2010) Chapter 2 (Section 11) provides for the 'recognition', 'promotion', 'compensation' and 'use' of communal cultural heritage (GoK, 2010). In light of these legal provisions, tourism promotion targeting *Mau Mau* heritage would serve as a form of protection if the communities involved are assured direct and tangible benefits from the monuments.

Global trends

Globally, heritage sites associated with war have been developed and promoted as major tourist attractions. They include: Kigali, Nyamata, and Ntarama genocide museums in Rwanda, Canadian War Museum, Dachau Concentration Camp in Germany, Dunkirk War Museum, Anzac Cove in Turkey, Commonwealth Military Cemetery at Ari Burnu, Franco Austrian Museum, Hitler Exhibition in Berlin Museum, Auschwitz Concentration Camp in Poland, and Robben Island Museum in South Africa. *Mau Mau* heritage can benefit from similar efforts through the development of a heritage tourist circuit, in consultation with stakeholders, encompassing various combat attractions (Fig. 4). The National Museums and Heritage Act (NMHA, 2006) and the Constitution of Kenya (2010) provide the necessary framework for the protection of this heritage and its elevation to the level of other global sites.

Tourism circuits based on dark tourism and thanatourism are frequent in different parts of the world. The 1st and 2nd world wars are especially popular in this mode of tourism. In dark tourism, visitors are driven by the imagery of misery, of punishment, and misdemeanours of our society. Thanatourism is therefore a subset of dark tourism. This concept of tourism fits the broad *Mau Mau* history which is characterised by diverse forms of misery, including villigisation, grief, destruction of property, incarceration, enslavement, and death. Such atrocities were so severe that the British government conceded to a plan to construct a *Mau Mau* memorial in Nairobi in recognition of their crimes. They also compensated some of the victims of the atrocities in 2013 (Strange & Kempa (2009; 387) They conclude that battle sites and death camps are the best understood dark tourism sites which can attract high consumption if properly marketed (Strange & Kempa, 2009). However, this process of commodification of history and its aspects of misery has been challenged as unethical. "The refashioning of punishment to tourism product raises ethical questions about commodification of suffering and its evident entertainment value" (Strange & Kempa, 2009).

Dark tourism or thanatourism is mainly centred on death episodes, whether natural or anthropogenic (Seaton, 1999). Their selling point is remembrance which draws visitors who are linked to the tragedy in one form or another. There are those who lost friends and relatives who have the reason to memorialize the dead. Others are motivated by symbolism and images associated with death, while travel could be purely based on expected leisure, recreation novelty and discovery in sites associated with incomprehensible experiences like genocide and burial sites. On regular basis, people are likely to be attracted to places of death, like fatal accidents, not uncommon in Kenya, because of the curiosity and mystery factor associated with such phenomena.

Fig. 5: Robben Island showing the dark tourism circuit

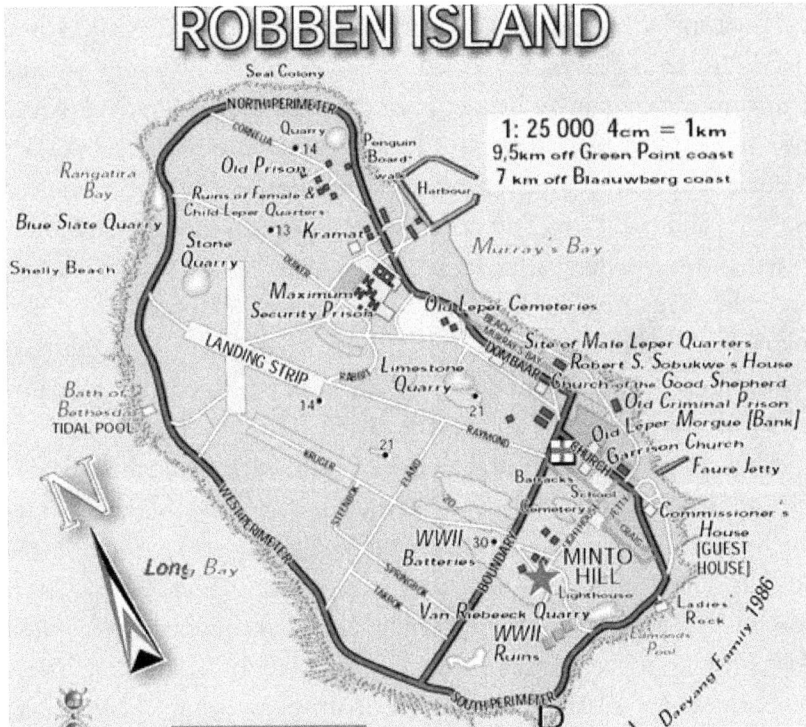

Source: The Maps available at www.themaps.co.za

Rwanda's genocide museums and sites serve as ideal dark tourism destinations with memorial sites, like schools and churches, where the atrocities were committed, being preserved and made accessible to the public. Pictures of the victims are also displayed as a process of remembrance and reconciliation. Because of the large number of people killed (approximately 900,000) in different parts of the country, many sites have coalesced into a tourist circuit close to the city of Kigali. Some of the sites in the circuit include Murambi, Gisozi, Nyamata, Ntarama, and Bisero. Photo exhibitions on the children lost in the event, a cemetery and a library on genocide make Gisozi in Kigali one of the most visited memorial sites. Murambi genocide memorial site is located in a school where many children were killed, while Nyamata and Ntarama are churches where the dead had sought refuge before slaughter. They are both about 35 KMs from Kigali. Other important genocide sites are located at Bisero and Gisenji. The circuit also encompasses the history of Rwanda in the pre-colonial and colonial period. Tourists visiting the sites also get a chance to see world attractions like the mountain gorilla. Other sites in Africa include the Gold Coast slave caves in Ghana and Goree Island House of Slaves in Senegal, which represent different aspects of torture meted out on helpless Africans during the Trans-Atlantic salve trade. Globally, other dark tourism sites include Chernobyl in Ukraine and Three Mile Island in USA, known for their nuclear disasters, and the Twin Tower terror attack site in the United States. Potential future dark tourist sites are likely to include areas of genocide, like Aleppo in Syria, and nuclear disaster sites, like Fukushima Daiichi in Japan, which were characterised by massive loss of lives, displacement, and loss of property. Recurrent tsunami and hurricane disasters also provide potential for dark tourism.

This chapter is based on the use of tourism for sustainability of heritage conservation (Smith, 2009). For the *Mau Mau* heritage, which has been largely ignored, proper packaging and marketing are the only practical avenue for sustainable conservation, especially in areas of low economic potential characterising the location of *Mau Mau* sites. With expanding human populations and concurrent competition for scarce resources, tourism becomes a viable, long-term form of motivation and sustenance. The Robben Island circuit was analysed in this chapter as offering the best inspiration for the kind of dark tourism proposed for the *Mau Mau* heritage (Fig.5). The Robben Island dark tourism circuit starts at the waterfront harbour in Cape Town, where the history of the Republic of South Africa, from the pre-colonial times to date, is exhibited in a detailed manner (Fig. 6). Visitors indulge in the history of the struggle as they wait for the commencement of a 7 Km journey to Robben Island by sea. Some of the boats used for the trip to the site were used to transport the prisoners to the Island to commence their jail terms and back after completion of their terms, thereby making them part of this dark history that led to the freedom of South Africa from apartheid. Robben Island covers an area of about 13 Km^2 and, in spite of its size, the number of tourist visiting the island at each time is high.

Buses labelled the 'Driven by Freedom' conduct a circular tour of the island from the harbour and back. The one-hour circuit takes visitors through the prison house of Robert Sobukwe, leper burial sites in honour of lepers who were once quarantined in the island,

and the famous Riebeck quarry where the prisoners worked while in prison. This is followed by a visit to the maximum prison which has detailed histories of the events and of resident prisoners. Tours within the prison are conducted by former prisoners. Nelson Mandela's prison garden is an important part of this guided tour. Finally, visitors sample the pictures of prison life before departing for the waterfront harbour for the return journey. The island site also offers a spectacular view of Table Mountain, the light house and the 2nd World War batteries (WWII). All these attractions complete the experience of dark tourism at Robben Island.

Similar circuit(s) can be packaged to give a holistic view of the *Mau Mau* history either at the counties or national level. Such sites would benefit from the natural landscape in which the war and other forms of *Mau Mau* heritage evolved, including the Aberdare ranges, Mount Kenya, Hola semi-desert, Mageta Island on Lake Victoria, Kenyatta House in a grassland eco-system, and Lamu Island on the Indian Ocean. If well packaged and embedded into the circuit, these supplementary attractions would enhance the experience significantly.

Conservation of the *Mau Mau* War heritage is justified by the suffering that the populations were exposed to, including dehumanisation in various forms like forced relocation in an unknown destination including Tanzania, demolition of indigenous homes, loss of property, and general break-up of the traditional nuclear family, especially among the Kikuyu. 'Slave' labour, economic exploitation, famine, and death were evils that violated the human rights of the local populations. While conservation is justified, it is sustainability that presents the biggest challenge. The proposed heritage circuits and sensitization provide the most reliable means of sustainability.

Fig. 6: Robben Island circuit in pictures

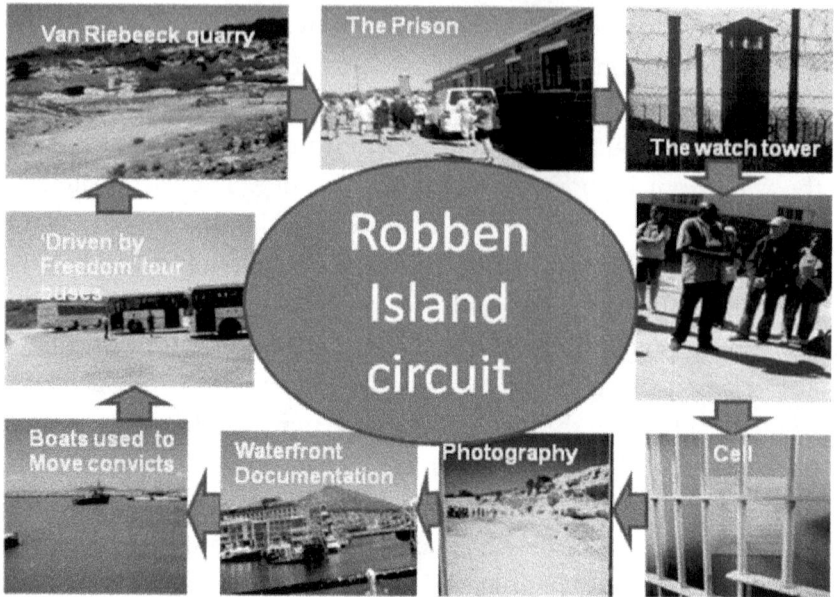

Source: Author

Conclusion

The recognition of the contribution of the *Mau Mau* movement by the Kenya and British governments, especially through London Case and subsequent reparations, is a major step towards a healing process from divisions that have existed since colonial times. Monetary compensation by the British government, however meagre, is the first step in the process. The next step should be to create an environment for integration through the recognition of their heritage as a lifetime contribution to the country's history. There exists a wealth of heritage that should be salvaged for the sake of future generations.

The *Mau Mau* image has largely existed in the shadow of poor scholarship and negative public perception. Most scholars have focused on whether or not *Mau Mau* was a nationalist movement and ignored its contributions. Scholars have also debated fiercely on whether it is the *Mau Mau* that secured Kenya's independence. There is no doubt that the *Mau Mau* factor was important, even if for the sensitization of the British government on the national plight. Now is the right time to restore the image of *Mau Mau* as a true nationalist movement and commence the restitution of their heritage to national status. This will commence a process of understanding in areas where communities have been split through incorrect perceptions of war. It will also contribute to positive economic development through the creation of national tourist circuits targeting *Mau Mau* cultural heritage in diverse areas of the country.

Controversies have negatively impacted the conservation efforts for the extant *Mau Mau* heritage. There is no doubt that promoting the heritage for tourism is a daunting task. However, it is the responsibility of national tourism organizations to develop a positive image that can sell both nationally and internationally. This image must transcend the negative colonial and post-colonial representations. Changing trends in tourism, especially through emergent Asian markets, and the changing age profiles, offer an ideal environment for this transformation. Proper and competitive packaging can significantly change the perception of the heritage. Attrition and changing age profiles within the communities involved are also likely to soften the hard stance that has traditionally characterised the image of the movement. Currently, there is no deliberate attempt to package the product, which explains its poor appeal. Haphazard conservation attempted so far has no prospect for sustainability, given the competing commercial ventures in agriculture and general infrastructural development. It is in this light that tourism becomes a viable option.

Chapter 5

Commémorer Les Indépendances Et Écrire Le Fait National Au Kenya[1], En Afrique

Christian Thibon

Les regards posés sur le passé, portés sur des faits aussi symboliques et fondateurs que sont les proclamations-temps d'indépendance, sont révélateurs autant des mémoires-identités et des attentes collectives, des demandes politiques que des lectures scientifiques, historiographiques des historiens, et en fin de compte des offres et des réponses que les historiens peuvent alors apporter aux questions que se posent les sociétés. Les manifestations commémoratives, aussi bien politique que scientifique, lors du cinquantenaire des Indépendances Africaines sont donc l'occasion de mesurer cette relation, et de s'interroger autant sur l'état de la Nation que sur celle de l'histoire, de l'écriture du fait national, et ce faisant, sur la place de l'historien.

Le cinquantième anniversaire des Indépendances Africaines ([2] et les manifestations que l'événement a suscitées, ont fait, dans les vingt-cinq pays qui sont devenus indépendants entre 1957 et 1964, soit plus de la moitié des pays africains, l'objet d'un traitement politique, public plutôt modéré bien que très diversifié selon les pays, allant d'un devoir de mémoire pour la majorité d'entre eux au désintérêt, voire à

---

[1] Cette communication propose une réflexion suite aux deux séminaires tenus à l' IFRA, au BIEA le 23-24 septembre 2013 « The 50th Anniversary of African Independances : marginalized, forgotten and revived political actors » et le 12 13 juin 2014 « Fifty years after Independence : the Nations in East Africa, revisiting nation-building between particularism and universalism », il sera fait référence aux débats lors de ces deux rencontres, voir le compte rendu de Mwongula Kamencu dans la revue Awaaz, Nairobi, janvier 2014 ; d'autres manifestations scientifiques en Afrique et au Kenya dont le colloque de Katarina University « Mau Mau et les autres mouvements de libération, 50 ans après l'Indépendance », le 6-7 décembre 2013 sont également examinées.

[2] Entre 1957 et 1964, 25 pays sont devenues Indépendants, le contexte international mais également les difficultés des premières Indépendances datant de l'année 1960, en particulier celle au Congo ex belge, vont peser sur les Indépendances suivantes, c'est particulièrement le cas au Kenya.

l'amnésie officielle pour une minorité. En raison de l'organisation publique et du patronage politique des manifestations commémoratives, mais aussi dans certains pays du rôle croissant des médias indépendants et internationaux, ces « nouveaux entrepreneurs mémoriels »[3] qui ont apporté de nouveaux témoignages et documents audio-visuels à la mémoire collective, un consensus, quelque peu nostalgique, s'est imposé avec une injonction patrimoniale autour d'un compromis, un socle mémoriel à minima, et d'une démarche inclusive. Le contexte politique a joué dans ce sens. D'une part, le renouvellement politique générationnel, quasiment terminé dans la plupart des pays, a relativisé de facto, sinon effacé les blessures et conflits internes des années de l'Indépendance. D'autre part et plus généralement, le contexte de désenchantement politique, dont les problèmes politiques actuels rappellent les ratés de la première expérience démocratique des Indépendances, et le marketing politique se prêtaient bien à ce service minimum. Plus étonnant, il en fut de même sur le plan universitaire et scientifique.

A l'ombre des commémorations officielles, des manifestations scientifiques diverses en demi-teinte.

A l'ombre des commémorations officielles, dans les Universités, les activités scientifiques (sous la forme de conférences, de colloques, d'éditions..) sont restées également entre une logique de maintenance institutionnelle et une participation mesurée des historiens. Ces derniers ont trouvé, à minima, un terrain d'ententes dans la valorisation patrimoniale d'une histoire nationale apaisée : les projets de musées et de tourisme mémoriel, comme l'essor des « heritages studies » témoignent de cette nouvelle tendance. Comment s'explique cette commémoration scientifique en demi-teinte ?

L'état des départements universitaires voire de la discipline, des écoles historiques, souvent dans un état critique dans certains pays, n'explique qu'en partie ce positionnement, sous les traits d'un service minimum. Toutefois cette faiblesse est contrebalancée par la montée en puissance de la science politique. Cette discipline mitoyenne de

---

[3] Expression de J-F. Havard « histoire, mémoire, mémoire collective et construction des identités nationales dans l'Afrique subsaharienne » dans *Cités*, 2007, 29.

l'histoire, plus discursive qu'analytique, s'impose alors plus facilement dans la mesure où le Cinquantenaire a quelque peu court-circuité la démarche historienne : le bilan des Indépendances et ses tentations comptables, hagiographiques, privilégient bien plus le décryptage des scénarios positifs et la mise en intrigue des stratégies réussies, bien plus du ressort des sciences politiques que de la démarche historienne qui privilégie le retour critique sur l'événement et sa complexité, la part de la contingence, la diversité des acteurs, gagnants, perdants et oubliés. On peut aussi voir dans cette prudence des historiens, qui en Afrique n'ont pas accès au marché de l'édition écrite particulièrement actif en Occident lors des périodes commémoratives, une position distante spécifique à la discipline. En effet et paradoxalement, alors que les historiens sont sollicités en priorité, la commémoration n'est pas leur problématique privilégiée... même si, depuis peu, l'étude critique des mémoires fait partie de leurs nouveaux terrains de recherches. A vrai dire, la mise en lumière de la complexité des événements risque souvent de gâcher la fête commémorative par nature unanimiste et de contrarier les légitimités acquises. A cette occasion, on retrouve l'ambivalence, sinon le grand écart, entre les objectifs d'une histoire officielle, publique, la mémoire collective historique nationale enseignée et les règles d'une histoire scientifique, universitaire, savante, nuancée et plus critique, bien que l'écriture de l'histoire et les historiens, enseignants-chercheurs, participent à ces deux exercices.

Plus encore, cette retenue résulte d'un bilan mitigé des travaux historiques de ces cinquante dernières années à l'image d'une expérience scientifique inachevée. Rappelons que le chantier des Indépendances imposa le défi d'une écriture d'une histoire décolonisée, autant une redécouverte qu'une découverte d'une histoire nationale et panafricaine, auquel la première génération d'historiens africains a été confrontée avec optimisme et enthousiasme. Mais cet objectif s'est avéré plein d'embuches, puis de divisions internes. Ces limites ont cultivé implicitement dans la profession le sentiment que la mission d'écrire le roman national, du moins d'y participer, n'avait pas été remplie. On peut suivre et comprendre ces difficultés en restituant les débats historiographiques successifs, qui ont impliqué les mondes universitaires africains et africanistes. Dès les années 1970, la mobilisation nationaliste de l'histoire et des historiens de la décennie des Indépendances, leurs dérives héroïsantes voire leur instrumentalisation politique, font déjà l'objet de premières critiques qui portent alors sur les écoles historiques établies[4]. Plus encore, les travaux et programmes de recherches[5], qui prennent en considération la moyenne durée des années 1935 aux années 1980, les filiations précédant ou suivant les Indépendances, qui traitent de la « décolonisation et Indépendance » et « des nationalismes en situation coloniale, des rebellions anticoloniales », ont brouillé les certitudes, puis ont ouvert des débats sur la nature des nationalismes, des régimes issus de l'indépendance, sur les modèles imposés et importés, leur dévoiement ethnique, régionaliste, tribaliste, des tribus qui déconstruisent la nations!

A cela, s'ajoutent le contexte autoritaire des années 1970-80, les cloisonnements de la guerre froide, qui pèsent sur les débats entre écoles marxistes ou non, alimentent des divisions. C'est à ce moment-là que certains dans la communauté des historiens s'interrogent sur les revers de la construction nationale et se détournent d'un tel projet, en recourant à l'histoire sociale soit d'une façon classique au travers des structures sociales, soit d'une façon originale en questionnant les liens et solidarités ethniques.

Pourtant dans un tel contexte scientifique polémique postindépendance, mais académique rassurant dans la mesure où les nouvelles universités publiques hébergent les départements d'histoire, cette crise fut en partie masquée et gérée par un repliement sur des thématiques nationalistes anticoloniales et sur de nouveaux champs de recherche : d'une part les études sur les périodes précoloniales et coloniales, suivant une démarche privilégiant l'ethnohistoire et des monographies régionales, entretiennent alors la priorité nationale d'une histoire décolonisée, d'autre part de nouveaux champs de recherche renouvellent et décloisonnent les

---

[4] Voir pour l' Afrique de l'est, B.A Ogot « Three decades of historical studies in East Africa » dans *Kenya Historical Review*, vol 6, 1-2, 1978, et les débats sur l'école historique de Dar es Salaam, dont la contribution de T. Ranger « The new historiography in Dar es Salaam : an answer » dans *African Affairs*, vol 70, 278, 1971.

[5] Sur la difficulté d'écrire l'histoire de cette période et la tentation de privilégier l'explication de la dépendance, l'impact des modèles importés, voir le Tome 8 de *l'Histoire Générale de l'Afrique, L'Afrique depuis 1935*, UNESCO, 1998, sous la direction d'A.A. Mazrui qui aborde en deux chapitres généralistes les décennies des Indépendances.

espaces nationaux suivant en cela les nouvelles tendances de l'histoire sociale et de l'idéologie développementaliste du moment. Or ces nouvelles thématiques et champs de recherche éloignent les historiens de la question nationale devenue piégeuse[6] . De facto, l'histoire nationale dans ses dimensions contemporaines immédiates postindépendances fut délaissée, tant et si bien que l'histoire politique de cette période devint le domaine réservé des historiens africanistes ou exilés ou celui de la science politique.

Ce n'est récemment, avec la démocratisation de la décennie 1990, que l'histoire politique nationale réapparait avec une nouvelle génération d'historiens ; ces derniers réinvestissent ces champs de recherche en association avec les sciences politiques. Mais le contexte d'une démocratisation et d'une décompression autoritaire qui accentue les clivages politiques et crises ethniques, met de nouveau à mal l'écriture d'une histoire nationale positive et ravive le pessimisme envers un tel projet. Au regard de cette histoire des rendez-vous manqués, la rencontre entre historiens et le Cinquantenaire des Indépendances ne pouvait être que faussée.

Cependant il convient d'aller au-delà de cette première impression générale d'une rencontre ratée, et d'examiner, en prenant en compte les programmes, les premières publications et comptes rendus de colloques et séminaires, les divers scénarios des commémorations scientifiques et leurs thématiques historiographiques retenues. On peut alors distinguer trois configurations dans les divers contextes nationaux : soit les Indépendances sont traitées comme des objets historiques, sinon « froids », du moins apaisés, soit elles restent des sujets historiques sensibles, enfin dans certains cas elles sont des non-dits.

Trois scenarios de commémoration scientifique, un bilan mitigé

Cinquante ans passés, le recul historique serait-il propice à l'âge de raison ou à la critique historique? Certaines manifestations scientifiques en ont, semble-t-il, fait l'expérience et le pari. Les

---

[6] Les nouveaux champs de recherche de l'histoire sociale, rurale, urbaine, démographique, de la santé puis culturelle et des « mentalités », et le discrédit porté à l'histoire politique sont aussi à l'image des tendances historiographiques occidentales des années 1960-70, dominées par l'histoire sociale, les inspirations Braudéliennes et l'école des Annales.

Indépendances, en tant qu'évènement, sont abordées d'une façon sereine et critique, comme un objet d'histoire totale : celui-ci dévoile sur le plan politique encore des inconnues, des énigmes quant aux stratégies et attitudes des acteurs majeurs nationaux et internationaux, sur le plan de l'histoire sociale des vécus, un climat et des ambiances, enfin sur la plan de l'histoire culturelle et des identités, des perceptions, des mémoires et des mythes, tant et si bien que l'on peut espérer que l'écriture de l'histoire puisse alors tourner la page d'une histoire. C'est le cas, par exemple, des deux colloques tenus à Alger[7]. Au demeurant l'Indépendance algérienne, un peu comme un cas d'école, se prête bien à cette démarche objective avec ses deux versants: d'un côté, elle coïncide avec la victoire d'une guerre de libération, l'association Indépendance et libération nationale diffère des autres indépendances souvent négociées, octroyées et donc plus complexes à analyser ; d'un autre côté, elle est, en tant que guerre extrême, un évènement traumatisme fondateur dont la charge émotionnelle et la résonance mémorielle sont toujours prégnantes, ce qui alimentent de nouveaux débats. Cette maturité se vérifie dans la finalité affichée des deux colloques, en association avec les médias écrits, qui était de déconstruire l'objet historique dans ses différentes dimensions (courte, de moyenne et longue durée) pour renouveler la connaissance et enrichir la compréhension de cet événement fondateur, et d'une façon critique, voire de démythifier certains de ses aspects.

On observe un pareil objectif suivi par plusieurs colloques tenus en Afrique de l'Ouest[8] : les thématiques choisies « Vivre les Indépendances » « Indépendance année zéro » portent alors sur le contexte, le vécu et les mémoires, mais aussi sur l'espérance soulevée et les modes d'appropriation populaire. Dans les deux cas, cette

---

[7] Deux colloques se sont déroulés et succédés à Alger début juillet 2012. Le Centre National de Recherches Préhistoriques Anthropologiques et Historiques (CNRPAH) en partenariat avec le quotidien national *La Tribune* a organisé, du 1er au 3 juillet, un colloque intitulé « Algérie 50 ans après: libérer l'histoire ». Puis, les 5, 6 et 7 juillet, le journal *El Watan* a été à l'initiative d'un colloque ayant pour titre « Cinquante ans après l'indépendance: quel destin pour quelle Algérie ».Voir G. Fabbiano « Algérie: 50 ans après l'indépendance (1962-2012) Permanences et changements » dans *Insaniyat*, 57-58, 2012

[8] Voir O. Goerg alii « Les indépendances en Afrique, L'événement et ses mémoires, 1957/1960-2010 » PUR, Rennes, 2013 qui aborde les indépendances en Afrique de l'Ouest et la vague des Indépendances de l'année 1960.

histoire par la bas privilégie l'étude d'acteurs longtemps ignorés, de nouvelles sources (dont les mémoires) et de nouvelles méthodes (les sources orales, les biographies et récits de vie, les ressources iconographiques.); elle se présente d'une façon décalée, sinon autonome mais complémentaire par rapport aux cérémonies officielles. Remarquons que dans ces pays, le fait et l'identité nationale, sentiment d'appartenance et socle mémoriel, sont des faits acquis et assumés, que l'on soit dans des vieux espaces historiques à caractère national, comme l'Algérie, ou dans des constructions géopolitiques récentes, coloniales, comme le Sénégal. Le fait que dans ces pays, la classe politique des pères de la Nation, de l'Indépendance ait quasiment disparu, a facilité ce regard distant sinon apaisé sur ce passé.

Ce n'est pas le cas pour un autre groupe de pays, particulièrement en Afrique centrale et d'Afrique de l'Est: cinquante ans passés, les blessures et questions de l'Indépendance restent d'actualité, ouvertes et toujours sensibles. Aussi les problématiques abordées restent essentiellement politiques, centrales; les thématiques périphériques, culturalistes, sociales, en vogue en Afrique de l'Ouest, ne sont pas ou peu traitées. Aussi l'histoire et les pistes historiographiques tendent à se répéter, tant et si bien que les axes affichés continuent à s'interroger sur les questions des années 1960, la construction nationale et l'unité nationale, comme le dévoilent les intitulés du colloque d'Antananarivo « Construire, déconstruire et reconstruire la Nation » ou du colloque de l'Université de Tchang au Cameroun sur la « Réunification », ou du Pole institut de Goma en R.D.C « repenser l'Indépendance Indépendance cha ! cha ! Danser enfin sur un bon pas »[9]. Pourtant ces pays partagent avec le reste des pays africains devenus indépendants à pareille époque la même trame politique et des environnements internationaux identiques, mais ils se distinguent par des points communs qui pèsent encore sur leur vie politique, dont la mitoyenneté des rébellions paysannes anticoloniales (rébellion de 1947 à Madagascar, de l'UPC au Cameroun, que l'on peut rapprocher du mouvement *Mau Mau* au Kenya) et des conflits-guerres civiles postcoloniales (rebellions congolaises) de l'Indépendance, alors que

---

[9] Les actes sont sous presse mais plusieurs de ces conférences comme celles de Goma ou d'Antananarivo se sont déroulées sur fond de crise politico-militaire ouverte.

pour certains d'entre eux, le fait d'avoir été des colonies de peuplement (comme pour le Congo Belge, le Kenya et Madagascar) a brouillé les cartes politiques et les alliances au moment de leur indépendance.

Reste le cas de quelques pays qui, autorités gouvernementales et communautés scientifiques confondues, n'ont pas abordé la question n'y trouvant aucune légitimité historique ni intérêt scientifique : c'est particulièrement le cas au Rwanda et en Ouganda qui ont effacé toute commémoration officielle et dans une certaine mesure du Burundi, des pays où les crises postcoloniales ou néocoloniales majeures de la décennie de l'Indépendance, guerres civiles et génocides, apparaissent comme des revers, des moments fondateurs de césure nationale.

Pour d'autres raisons, on retrouve ce mutisme dans les organisations internationales, à l'exception des agences de coopération économique qui se sont penchées sur le bilan économique et social ou de l'Union Africaine qui est revenue sur le projet panafricain. Enfin dans certaine ex-puissances coloniales (France, Grande-Bretagne) la question a été abordée, en raison de la sensibilité des problèmes postcoloniaux internes.

Cette réserve politique et académique tranche avec l'attitude des médias audiovisuels internationaux qui ont abondement traité du sujet, un trait également observé dans les médias nationaux.

Commémorer les Indépendances et écrire le fait national au Kenya

De prime abord, le Kenya s'apparente à la deuxième catégorie de pays, pour lesquels la commémoration reste problématique, tant les questions soulevées au moment de l'Indépendance et au cours des dernières cinquante années restent toujours d'actualité. La commémoration de l'Indépendance est révélatrice de la difficulté d'écrire le fait national, et de fortes singularités, voire des pesanteurs qui agissent sur le débat historiographique et l'opinion publique. Nous nous pencherons d'une façon classique historiographique sur cet exercice, l'écriture de l'histoire du fait national, puis nous aborderons le vécu et le quotidien national au travers du patrimoine national en construction qui est une autre façon d'écrire l'histoire, en paraphrasant la vision d'E. Renan pour qui « la Nation est un plébiscite de tous les jours »[10], une sorte d'écriture de tous les jours.

Les discours à la nation des historiens Kenyans

Il convient de signaler en premier et à la différence d'une majorité de pays africains où l'histoire, en tant que discipline universitaire, est sinistrée, qu'il existe une forte communauté d'historiens, bien établis dans les mondes universitaires public et privé ; pourtant à l'occasion des commémorations nationales, celle-ci est restée distante, du moins ne s'est guère mobilisée et a été peu sollicitée[11]. Certes les réserves générales disciplinaires et méthodologiques déjà signalées envers des commémorations ont joué d'autant plus que, hasard du calendrier politique, l'anniversaire coïncide en 2013 avec une campagne électorale présidentielle, une compétition entre les fils des pères fondateurs de l'Indépendance. Mais l'explication de cette retenue scientifique est plus profonde et elle nous oblige à revenir sur l'école ou les écoles historiques kenyanes et sur certains débats qui les ont animées concernant l'histoire du fait national.

---

[10] Conférence donnée à la Sorbonne, Paris en 1880, « Qu'est-ce que la nation ».
[11] Les deux conférences de l'IFRA BIEA le 23-24 septembre 2013 « The 50th anniversary of African independences : marginalized, forgotten and revived political actors » et le 12 13 juin 2014 « Fifty years after Independence : the nations in East Africa, revisiting nation-building between particularism and universalism », et le colloque de Katarina University « *Mau Mau* et les autres mouvements de libération, 50 ans après l'Indépendance », le 6-7 décembre 2013.

Difficile dans un pays dont la culture est générationnelle, de ne pas voir des générations d'historiens et ce faisant des seniors et des cadets, on préfèrera se contenter d'une appréciation froide, celle d'écoles-cohortes qui ont suivi les aléas des universités kenyanes : une première cohorte historique, celle des mentors et de leurs pairs, bien établie et reconnue sur le plan international comme dans le paysage national intellectuel, à l'image de la figure emblématiques B.A. Ogot[12] ; une seconde cohorte quelque peu orpheline apparue dans une période difficile de restrictions des libertés universitaires et de divisions, les années 1980, souvent dispersée à l'étranger à l'image de E.S Atieno-Odhiambo , sinon emprisonnée à l'image de Maina wa Kinyatti[13]; enfin à compter de la décennie 1990 une nouvelle vague de professeurs et «senior lecturers » qui bénéficient de l'expansion universitaire des années 2000[14]. Autre spécificité, le renfermement des années 1980, qui a divisé cette communauté, ne l'a pas mise en difficulté : s'engageant peu dans la vie politique, sinon épisodiquement, et gardant un cap professionnel, les historiens ont cultivé, comme d'autre corps professionnels kenyans dans les médias ou la justice, une distinction et une impertinence qu'ils ont su entretenir par une activité éditoriale soutenue, d'abord collective puis individuelle[15].

Mais cette communauté va connaître deux épreuves. Dans un premier temps, les dérives autoritaires des régimes postindépendances ont ébranlé la confiance collective, positiviste, mise dans une construction identitaire nationale et bien plus dans le nationalisme. Rappelons pour mesurer cette désillusion que le projet

---

[12] A titre d'exemple, B.A Ogot est le directeur scientifique de l'Histoire générale de l'Afrique de l'Unesco, d'autres historiens contemporanéistes kenyans vont participer à la rédaction de plusieurs chapitres. Sa génération se compose des premiers historiens universitaires kenyans à l'image de G. Muriuku, W.R. Ochieng, H. Mwanzi, G. Were, B. Kipkorir…

[13] Historien de KU spécialiste des *Mau Mau*, sur cette période et la fuite des universitaires voir le témoignage de Celia Nyamweru dans son blog.oup.com/2016

[14]Dont les départements d'histoire de l' UoN, de KU, de Moi University, d'USI, de Maseno University, de JOOUST, de la CUEA…

[15] Il s'agit d'abord de revues (Kenya historical review, Hadith…) du temps de l'association des historiens kenyans puis d'ouvrages édités ou en coédition, localement et dans des maisons d'édition internationales. A titre d'exemple, les deux ouvrages les plus marquants *Polities and Nationalism in colonial Kenya* B.A Ogot edt, Hadith 4 , Nairobi , 1972 et *Decolonization and indépendance in Kenya 1940-1993*, B.A Ogot W.R. Ochieng Nairobi Londres, 1993.

politique, résumé dans l'hymne national[16], était aussi une espérance en germe dans l'enthousiasme nationaliste anticolonial, que les images-mémoires unitaires de la proclamation de l'Indépendance[17] nous permettent aujourd'hui de visualiser.....et que les historiens kenyans, alors jeunes témoins et acteurs, ont vue, vécue et partagée[18]. Dès les années 1970-80, les alertes se multiplient pour une approche alternative ou prudente, en faveur d'une « histoire postcoloniale » selon ES Atieno-Odhiambo et d'une « nouvelle philosophie historique » selon B.A. Ogot qui alimentent un réalisme critique devant la déficience de la Nation, de l'invention de la citoyenneté et la difficulté de l'écriture d'une histoire nationale. La seconde épreuve confirme ces craintes, elle vient des ratés de la démocratisation-décompression et du multipartisme dès les années 1990 avec des violences ethniques ascendantes qui vivifient les tribalismes, la résurgence de rebellions millénaristes, plus encore les violences post électorales de 2007-08. Les historiens, majoritairement acquis à une lecture constructiviste de la nation, à l'historiographie du fait national qui privilégient les références aux thèses de E. Hobsbawm -T Ranger et de B. Anderson[19], notent la faiblesse du « projet politique imaginé kenyan », de la construction idéologique du nationalisme et de son revers à succès les tribalismes. Bien plus que les rebellions anticoloniales et le mouvement nationalisme de l'indépendance des décennies 1950-60, les violences et cette guerre civile froide, qui s'instaurent et se répètent à compter de la décennie 1990, apparaissent alors comme des évènements structurants sinon fondateurs ; ces violences qui s'accentuent pour culminer en 2007-

---

[16] Comme le montre une des strophes de l'hymne national « Notre pays le Kenya que nous aimons, Soyons prêts à le défendre Et bâtissons notre nation»

[17] Les medias kenyans lors du cinquantenaire ont diffusé ces photos des événements, de la mobilisation populaire et « l'état de grâce », les moments heureux de fraternité partagée par J. Kenyatta, O. Odinga, T. Mboya, P. Murumbi....

[18] Lors du colloque de l'IFRA Nairobi, plusieurs historiens ont témoigné de leur entrée en politique, et plus généralement des mobilisations, dans un climat national non entaché de ressentiment ethnique, entre Luo et Kikuyu en particulier (cf.. les témoignages-remarques de G Muriuk, B. Kipkorir, P Ndege) et de la nécessité de collecter, conserver ces récits individuels.

[19] B. Anderson *Imagined communauties, reflections on the origin and spread of nationalism*, Londres, 1983; E. Hobsbawm *Nation and nationalism since 1780*, Cambridge 1990, E Hobsbawm T Ranger (ed) *The invention of the tradition*, Cambridge, 1983.

08, sont un peu à l'image des crises nationalistes et de la première guerre mondiale pour les nations occidentales, car elles figent douloureusement les mémoires et cristallisent les identités sur l'ethnicité. Finalement le réalisme critique des décennies 1980-90 s'efface devant un pessimisme mature résumé dans les analyses de B.A Ogot dans la synthèse « Kenyans, Who are we, Reflections on the Meaning of National Identity and Nationalisme » paru en 2012[20], un peu à l'exemple d'un « discours à la Nation »[21].

Au demeurant cette prudence, ce pessimisme des historiens devant le cours d'une histoire nationale ni prévu ni souhaité et en raison des manipulations identitaires qui ont souvent piégé leur carrière universitaire, sont renforcés par l'expérience de recherches incomprises, voire le sentiment d'avoir été défaillants. Trois chantiers historiographiques illustrent bien cette déconvenue : ils concernent « l'histoire du temps présent »[22], au travers des champs de recherche suivants mais essentiels pour l'histoire du fait national : l'histoire régionale, l'histoire du mouvement *Mau Mau* et du tribalisme-ethnicité.

La question régionale est abordée en premier dès les années 1960 ; les sujets des premières thèses des historiens kenyans sont des monographies régionales, qui empruntent les méthodes de l'histoire sociale (la monographie régionale), de la longue durée et les ressources de l'ethnohistoire (l'histoire orale), elles suivent une objectif commun et classique à bien des écoles historiques africaines naissantes : la valorisation des apports régionaux et leur contribution à l'histoire nationale. Un des mérites de ces thèses, est d'avoir mis en évidence la fluidité des identités et la perméabilité des frontières et

---

[20] B.A Ogot, *Kenyans, Who are we, reflections on the Meaning of national identity and nationalism*, Kisumu, 2012, et "Rereading the History and Historiography of Epistemic Domination and Resistance in Africa" dans *African Studies Review*, Vol 52, 1, April 2009.

[21] Un peu à l'image des discours de J.G.Fichte (conférences à Berlin, 1807) qui visaient au lendemain de la défaite d'Iena à éveiller un sentiment national mais avec une différence, une approche constructiviste de la nation.

[22] La définition de « l'histoire du temps présent » s'attache à une séquence historique délimitée par la présence d'acteurs vivants, donc porteurs d'une mémoire, de souvenirs, d'un témoignage qui peut aider à la connaissance du passé. Mais le champ couvert par cette partie de l'historiographie se raccourcit en amont et s'allonge en aval. Aussi la distingue-t-on de l'histoire immédiate qui traite de l'actualité.

constructions ethniques, dénonçant l'instrumentalisation politique des tribus, de la période coloniale aux décennies de l'Indépendance. Mais cet apport des recherches sur la complexité et l'hétérogénéité des ethnies, des nationalités, sur l'importance des échanges, des transferts, ni les débats sur les nationalités entre historiens[23], ne sont pas retenus par des opinions publiques et des élites de plus en plus ethniques ; celles-ci s'arrêtent aux titres, ignorent les contenus de ces travaux et leur préfèrent des « traditions » déjà écrites et diffusées depuis la période coloniale, des mises en intrigue des traditions culturelles souvent embellies par des mythologies essentialistes ou des écritures religieuses [24], tant et si bien que B.A Ogot, G. Muriuki, W.R. Ochieng, H. Mwanzi, G. Were, B. Kipkorir et bien d'autres encore ont été perçus, étiquetés comme des porte-paroles ethniques et de leurs universités respectives.

Pareille mésaventure se renouvelle au sujet de la question des *Mau Mau*. Cette question centrale des études historiques sur le nationalisme kenyan et sur ses racines historiques (dont les prémices nationalistes des rebellions paysannes et de la contestation urbaine), mais complexe (une guerre anticoloniale et civile), cristallise la recherche historique tant kenyane qu'internationale, et au-delà les témoignages et les analyses des acteurs-témoins, des militants et intellectuels, en autant de versions érudites, populaires, mémorielles. Ceci se traduit par une bibliographie et une historiographie impressionnante : aussi dénombre-t-on du premier ouvrage de L.S.B Leakey aux plus récents ouvrages de D. Anderson et C. Elkins une dizaine de trames-interprétations, toutes révisionnistes, ce qui est en soi un indicateur positif sur le plan scientifique même si les expertises historiennes doivent être débattues ; ces analyses renvoient à presque

---

[23] Par exemple le débat sur la nation luo dans DW Cohen ES Atieno Odhiambo « Ayany, Malo and Ogot ; historians in search of a luo nation » dans *Cahiers d'études africaines*, 107-8, XXVII, 1986 et J.R. Campbell

"Who Are the Luo? Oral Tradition and Disciplinary Practices in Anthropology and History" Reviewed work(s), dans *Journal of African Cultural Studies*, Vol. 18, No. 1, Jun., 2006.

[24] L'importance de l'invention des traditions ethniques, du moins les premières écritures déterminantes car elles font souche en raison de cette primauté, datent de la période coloniale, y compris dans des formes non conventionnelles. Voir à ce sujet les travaux de D R Peterson dont *Ethnic patriotism and the East African revival, a history of dissent 1935-1972*, Cambridge university press, 2012 et *Creative writing*, Heineman, 2004.

autant de lectures-périodisations nationalistes[25]. Mais comme dans le cas précédent de l'histoire régionale, cette histoire dramatique « qui ne passe pas » a aussi un second versant sur lequel les historiens n'ont aucune prise. Elle est devenue une ressource pour des instrumentalisations et des marketings politiques, de la part aussi bien du Pouvoir que des oppositions, de la période du Président Moi, durant la transition politique des années 1990 à la présidence de Mwai Kibaki qui est alors confronté à un mouvement similaire, les Mungiki ; elle est aussi une source d'inspirations et d'inventions littéraires, d'imaginaires. Ces deux lectures trient et récupèrent l'héritage, la légitimité ou l'inspiration des mythes, des mémoires et anti-mémoires associés aux *Mau Mau*: dans ce cas, l'enjeu n'étant plus la connaissance historique mais les usages, les filiations que l'on peut en tirer. Or le couple politique-littérature et histoire entretient une relation inégale désavantageuse pour les historiens qui le plus souvent sont trop nuancés pour se plier à une lecture simpliste puis qui sont pressés de choisir leur camp. En 2003, ES Atieno Odhiambo caractérise alors la question comme un « bourbier », un état de connaissances et problématiques non closes, qui appelle à des nouvelles recherches avec une multitude d'interférences qu'il faudra alors dénouer.

Le troisième chantier historiographique, l'analyse du fait ethnique est une constante des recherches historiques et d'une discipline qui, tout en se démarquant d'une anthropologie culturelle très présente au Kenya, ont inscrit la construction des ethnies-tribus-nationalités dans la longue durée. Mais dans les années 1980, ce champ de recherche prend une nouvelle dimension, une seconde orientation historiographique ; celle-ci s'interroge sur l'évolution récente du fait ethnique, sa valorisation culturelle et son instrumentalisation politique, le tribalisme. Alors que le Kenya est à la recherche d'un souffle moral, autant communautaire qu'un leadership, puisé dans les ressources nationale et locales de l'*Harambee* puis de la Nyayo

---

[25] L'historiographie des *Mau Mau* est abondante, on retiendra les synthèses de R.Buijtenhuijs « Essay on *Mau Mau* » dans *Research reports* 17, 1982, African Studies Center Leiden ; de G. Prunier « Mythes et histoire, les interprétations du mouvement *Mau Mau* de 1952 à 1986 » dans *RFHOM*, tome 74, 277, 1987 et d'A. Odhiambo dans A. Odhiambo J. Lonsdale *Mau Mau Nationhood*, J Currey, Londres, 2003.

philosophie, et que s'expérimente un nationalisme pluriethnique, le « majimboisme », la recherche va s'enrichir de deux contributions majeures, initiées par J. Lonsdale et B.J. Berman[26]. D'une part, les travaux sur les ressorts de l'ethnicité, de sa mobilisation dans les luttes sociales et dans le nationalisme, et de son inscription dans « la politique par le bas », un concept venu des Sciences politiques, l'importance de la culture et du concept d'économie morale, séduisent l'histoire sociale accoutumée à la reconstitution des cadres économiques, sociaux, mentaux et des négociations du bas. Or l'histoire kenyane, avec ses singularités, ses résistances sociales anticoloniales et son absence de royaumes « féodaux » souvent alliés au pouvoir colonial, sans compter les clichés anthropologiques, de la démocratie pastorale à l'ethos capitaliste paysan qui angélisent les sociétés locales, se prête bien à cette redécouverte, à cette vision valorisante du fait ethnique. D'autre part, l'analyse du tribalisme, décrit comme un « nationalisme incivique », restitue en deca du système décrit (des identités ethniques, un patronage des big-men et des clientélismes, l'autoritarisme d'état), des acteurs, des paysages et des dynamiques politiques, des terroirs politiques, ces espace-temps qu'affectionnent la micro histoire politique et la sociologie historique du politique. Des recherches, plus africaniste que kenyane, plus anthro-politiste qu'historienne, vont alors approfondir la connaissance de ce patriotisme ethnique et de sa modernité avec la tentation optimiste de voir la diversité culturelle, sinon la pluriethnicité comme fondement institutionnel de la nouvelle démocratie[27].

Une fois de plus, cet optimisme se heurte aux faits, toujours têtus. La reconstitution historique et plus encore le cours de l'actualité, les violences et manipulations des identités ethniques, dévoilent une ethnicité essentialiste et exclusive comme le rappelle B. Ogot[28] . La

---

[26] Les publications de J. Lonsdale et B. Berman dont en particulier *Unhappy Valley conflict in Kenya and Africa* tome 2, James Currey, Londres, 1992 et B. Berman « ethnies, patronage and african state, the politics of uncivil nationalism » dans *African Affairs*, 97, 1998

[27] Voir cette question débattue dans la thèse d'Andria Kenney, *Multi-ethncity and Democracy in Kenya: ethnicity as foundation of démocratic institutionalization*, Aalorg University, Denmark, 2006.

[28] Voir B.A Ogot *Kenyans, Who are we, reflections on the Meaning of national identity and nationalism*, Kisumu, 2012

frontière entre ethnicité et tribalisme est poreuse, alors que l'ethnicité morale n'est pas si morale, du moins elle est morale entre soi et immorale hors de soi, et alimente des divisions internes, tant et si bien que le concept relevant de l'économie morale, pertinente analyse ou prédiction créatrice, mériterait selon son auteur d'être plus justement requalifié d « ethnicité patriotique »[29] ; mais comme les concepts font chaine et passent dans le domaine public, son usage a mené à une contre-sens. Le mariage des petites patries ethniques et de la grande nation kenyane, pour reprendre une imagerie politique française, reste en chantier, bien plus un défi du présent, du futur qu'un héritage du passé !

Ainsi les batailles historiographiques de l'histoire du temps présent, le décryptage des trois dialectiques-clés de la construction de la nation kenyane comme ailleurs, entre centre et périphéries (la question régionale), entre le nationalisme des champs et celui des villes (la question *Mau Mau*), entre communauté nationale et communautés ethniques (la question ethnique), bien que gagnées en partie sur le papier, ont été perdues au sein de l'opinion publique, voire sur un plan académique. Au demeurant la démocratisation et ses régimes politiques successifs, ses changements politiques, n'ont pas modifié la donne, n'ont pas facilité la tâche, bien au contraire les violences tribales extrêmes et croissantes ont sacralisé le sentiment d'appartenance bien plus à l'ethnie, à la région qu'à la nation, et dans ces cas, il ne s'agit pas de l'estime de soi des petites patries ethniques mais de la haine de l'autre que ces violences ont intériorisées.

Ainsi la crise de la nation et du nationalisme politique et citoyen, l'invention de la Nation, résonne dans la fragilité de l'écriture du fait national, du roman national. Certes l'écriture de l'histoire reste toujours un projet académique en devenir mais l'histoire, en tant que discipline structurante, si elle est restée une voie, est devenue une voix peu audible : les constats faits par B. Ogot et plus récemment par Munene Macharia[30] le reconnaissent. Une situation paradoxale car cet

---

[29] Voir J. Lonsdale, « le nationalisme, l'ethnicité et l'économie morale: parcours d'un pionnier de l'histoire africaine, entretien avec D. Conan » dans *Genèses*, 83, 2011-12.

[30] Cette crise de l'histoire en tant que discours national est décrite par Munene Macharia dans *Historical reflections on Kenya, intellectuals adventurism*, Nairobi University Press, 2015.

effacement de l'histoire en tant que discipline, peut être conjoncturel en attente de nouvelles figures, tranche avec l'usage et la publicité dans les débats politiques et dans les chroniques des médias donnés à l'histoire de la nation, du nationalisme et à ses théories historiographiques. Ces polémiques médiatiques qui recoupent les débats politiques[31], répondent à une demande populaire, à une préoccupation des élites, d'une société qui vit la Nation au travers de ses drames et aussi dans son quotidien, et qui l'écrit en quelque sorte mais qui s'interroge sur son devenir.

La commémoration de tous les jours, le nouveau roman national, le kenyanisme, entre fondations patrimoniales et modernisation

Si l'écriture de la Nation n'est pas, n'est plus du seul ressort des historiens, il s'agit alors d'examiner le roman national, pas dans le sens communément entendu comme un récit historique structurant, une pédagogie consciente et critique, mais au travers d'une manière d'être et de se distinguer de ses voisins nationaux sans accéder à la conscience, à la manière d'une autochtonie, une sorte d'habitus, au travers d'une identification mimétique et psychologiquement rassurante en œuvre, un imaginaire, que nous pourrions qualifier de « haute identité »[32] associée et se superposant aux identités culturelles, sociales, ethniques.

Quels sont les signes de cette évolution silencieuse, de cette « haute identité » qui a déjà un nom, le kenyanisme, et qui se construit au travers de fondations patrimoniales ? Quels sont ses monuments, ses médiateurs, ses usages, son socle mémoriel, c'est-à-dire ses forces et son impact identitaire ?

Ce faisant, ce déplacement dans l'analyse du fait national kenyan suppose de changer d'échelles et des sources, comme de grilles de lecture. Autant dans l'analyse du roman politique national, de ses succès, comme ses dévoiements et échecs, il s'agit d'un bilan critique des élites, de leurs stratégies, de leurs idéologies, y compris des héros

---

[31] Comme l'illustre la double commémoration de la fête nationale en 2016, l'officielle et celle de l'opposition.

[32] Haute identité, en copie décalée du concept de Haute culture avancé par A Gellner.

ou collectifs oubliés[33] qui a comme échelle le temps présent....autant dans l'analyse de la construction d'une identité nationale banale et de masse, à laquelle les historiens participent également[34], prime l'observation du présent, des pratiques et des mémoires[35], et de leurs tendances sérielles ; que celles-ci soient fortes ou superficielles, seul l'avenir nous le dira. Cette histoire du bas suppose de faire la biographie du peuple, des gens communs, de la vie quotidienne, de sérier de nouvelles données, de fabriquer ainsi de nouvelles archives[36]. Tout en gardant une approche constructiviste, la reconstitution et l'analyse historique se déplacent alors du projet politique collectif, discours et stratégies politiciennes, au quotidien et aux identités collectives, la production de l'identité nationale et sa réception-appropriation. Les références historiographiques, les outils conceptuels changent également: ce sont plutôt les travaux d'E. Gellner sur le couple nation/modernisation, ceux des historiens sur les nations inachevées européennes et l'étude d'E. Weber[37], dont le titre français de sa thèse « la fin des terroirs » est plus percutant, qui servent d'hypothèses et de guides. Bien plus que le scénario de la vie politique, le décor, et dans ce cas la modernisation de la société, la fabrique de l'espace-temps kenyan et la construction de l'Etat-Nation, devient un acteur historique à prendre en compte. Toutefois le développement proposé ci-dessous repose sur une inconnue, une hypothèse: l'état d'avancement de la fin des terroirs au Kenya, un effet d'annonce ou une réalité en œuvre[38]. Or la moyenne durée si

---

[33] Cet aspect a été abordé lors du séminaire de 2013 au travers des quatre thèmes-panels suivants : « Forgotten heroes », « Mobilization without gain » « An embattled community, the East African Asians » « The fighting women of Independence ».

[34] Comme le prouvent leurs contributions à l'histoire mémoire collective, leur investissement dans les « heritages studies », dans les projets de conservation, de protection et de valorisation du patrimoine (circuits d'interprétation et musées).

[35] Des mémoires conflictuelles fut l'objet d'une séance lors du séminaire de 2013: « Conflicting memories ».

[36] Cet aspect est plusieurs fois revenu dans les débats lors des séminaires dont les remarques de W. Ochieng, B. Kipkorir, F. Kiruthu et la défense des « subalternes studies » par E. Wahome.

[37] E. Gellner, *Nations and nationalism*, Cornell univ press, 1983, E Weber *Peasants into Frenchmen, the modernization of the rural France*, Stanford, 1976.

[38] L'hypothèse à travailler serait la fin des terroirs, leur ouverture ; voir la lecture opposée à cette vision de J Klopp dans sa thèse *Electoral despotism in Kenya : patronage and resistance in the multiparty context*, McGill univ, 2001.

facilement reconnaissable par l'historien dans le passé, ne l'est pas dans les conjonctures du présent: c'est un des paris ou une des inconnues de l'histoire immédiate.

Si l'histoire et le discours politique n'arrivent pas à écrire la nation, les fondations patrimoniales en tant que discours culturel et politique patrimoniale, mais aussi en tant que messages et usages, peuvent-elles le faire, pourraient-elles remédier à cette carence?

Effectivement à la différence de l'histoire qui pose des questions souvent laissées sans réponse et qui fait débat, le message patrimonial, qui est un tout globalisant à la fois historique de longue et de courte durée, culturel, naturel, paysager et immatériel, possède la vertu apaisante de répondre sans trop poser de question, faisant silence et laissant à voir avec un communication et médiation souvent consensuelle. Certes l'abus de mémoire existe souvent le temps des fondations patrimoniales, mais il s'estompe sous l'effet des registres psychologiques convoqués par la médiation patrimoniale : la participation et l'identification émotionnelle, la quête de valeurs, de sens et d'esthétique, le sentiment valorisant d'héritage et de filiation, comme les modes de communications et d'interprétation privilégiés dont l'importance de la vision, du regard, qui ne sont pas ceux de la critique historique, une culture de l'écrit. D'une certaine façon, le patrimoine quand il n'est pas sursignifié, permet aux sociétés d'oublier et de vivre avec le passé, ce qui est aussi une fonction souvent méconnue de l'histoire, dans la mesure où le passé est alors clôturé, enfermé et protégé dans des espaces clos sacrés, mémoriels ; de cette manière, les sociétés peuvent faire leur deuil des drames du passé, au risque d'en oublier certaines parties, mais en se satisfaisant d'un socle mémoriel à minima.

Cette montée en puissance du discours patrimonial national, sous la forme de fondations patrimoniales et de politiques culturelles, est bien réelle même si elle reste périphérique et demeure silencieuse: on peut en distinguer divers temps, du moins saisir les impulsions majeures. Comme toute construction nationale patrimoniale, par nature régalienne, la première fondation patrimoniale s'affirme dans les années 1970-80. Si elle a hérité de la vision naturaliste coloniale qu'elle entretient pour une mise en tourisme, sa contribution originale ambitionne de valoriser la culture nationale et ses différentes cultures régionales, selon les registres classiques de la conservation, de la protection de la culture matérielle et immatérielle suivant les recommandations de l'Unesco et de l' OUA : avec le relais des musées, des festivals et des institutions scolaires, des écomusées, la trame folklorique, la culture des peuples, deviennent alors dominante. La deuxième fondation, durant la transition et plus encore, la Présidence de Mwai Kibaki, est une impulsion politique mémorielle qui modifie le calendrier mémoriel et le panthéon national. D'une façon symbolique, avec parfois des calculs politiciens, le patrimoine politique et l'espace public, longtemps associés aux Présidents (dont le journées en hommage des Présidents Kenyatta puis Moi) s'élargissent aux héros des luttes anticoloniales mais aussi aux politiciens déchus ou écartés de l' Indépendance, aux vétérans *Mau Mau* puis à certaines et nouvelles figures de la société civile[39] qui sont honorés. Cette réhabilitation symbolique de nature monumentale bien que limitée[40], muséographique, urbaine, spatiales au travers de quelques lieux de mémoire s'accompagne parfois de mesures de compensation. Cette seconde fondation qui se poursuit de nos jours[41], a été relayée par les médias qui lui donnent alors de l'ampleur et contribuent à dessiner un imaginaire national au travers d'un espace médiatique national.

La contribution des médias, d'abord écrit puis audio-visuel, est originale et décisive. Originale, car faute de saint-patrons laïques artistes, scientifiques et alors que les noms des grands entrepreneurs nationaux sont entachés de scandale, la presse écrite, quotidiens et hebdomadaires, met alors au-devant de l'espace médiatique les sportifs, et en l'absence d'équipes nationales, les athlètes, ces nouveaux héros se substituant aux guerriers, peu nombreux dans l'imaginaire national[42]. Cette contribution perceptible dès les décennies 1980-90 dans la presse quotidienne et hebdomadaire devient décisive dans les années 2000 et plus encore au lendemain des violences post électorales de 2007-8, dans une société traumatisée, le processus s'accélère alors. Les deux fondations

---

[39] Comme le prix Nobel décerné à Wangari Maatha.

[40] Le nombre de monuments historiques inscrits « gazettés » reste limité.

[41] A l'image de l'hommage fait à J. Murumbi, du procès intenté par les vétérans *Mau Mau* à la Couronne Britannique.

[42] A l'exception des chefs militaires *Mau Mau* et de certains chefs de la période coloniale.

politiques patrimoniales sont alors relayées par un communication de gestion et de sortie de crise, par de nouveaux messagers issu du marché, de la société civile et de nouvelles institutions : elles se renforcent via la communication des mass-médias audio-visuels et leurs techniques performantes, leur marketing, leur scénographie, puis via internet au fur et à mesure que la couverture des réseaux téléphoniques puis numériques s'étend, alors que les associations et les institutions culturelles, les agences nationales (KWS, NMK, NEMA) et leurs programmes de conservation marquent le paysage national, en autant de sites majeurs que la publicité privée et la mise en tourisme rendent emblématiques. La Nation s'affiche alors, non plus uniquement dans le décorum et le protocole du pouvoir, les timbres postes et les manifestations officielles mais dans les images en boucle des mass-médias. La décentralisation devrait poursuivre cette mise en scène d'un patrimoine national et la décliner avec ses variantes régionales alors que les universités se positionnent sur les nouveaux terrains-marchés des heritages studies, de la médiation patrimoniale et de la communication.

Bien plus que la teneur des messages ou les performances des messagers, le fait décisif de ces dix dernières années, est que ces fondations patrimoniales, un nouveau discours national relayé par les mass-médias, gagnent de nouveaux publics, de nouveaux récepteurs. La modernisation et dans une certaine mesure la construction d'un état-nation expliquent cette progression de la réception, cette patrimonialisation, cette appropriation. Les enquêtes statistiques nationales[43] suivent l'émergence de cette modernisation au travers d'indicateurs, comme les taux d'alphabétisation, de scolarisation, d'accès aux médias, aux réseaux sociaux mais aussi la mobilité, l'urbanisation ; les sondages d'opinion dévoilent le nouvelles sensibilités cosmopolites et valeurs individualistes, les nouveaux modèles familiaux ; enfin la géographie des services publics et les nouvelles offres des politiques publiques témoignent d'une état-nation, toujours autoritaire mais qui présent localement redistribue des services voire des biens. Ainsi au fur et à mesure que l'espace-temps kenyan se construit dans les imaginaires, il s'expérimente dans

---

[43] Les données statistiques suivies des enquêtes démographie santé (EDS DHS), en particulier.

les nouvelles pratiques, les mobilités ville-campagne inter-régionales, les usages administratifs, les pratiques quotidiennes, le tourisme domestique...... selon un mode spatial concentrique, des villes vers les campagnes et un mode social sélectif, les jeunes et les générations démographiquement majoritaires. Tout ceci est supporté par la diffusion d'une langue nationale, bien plus le swahili que l'anglais, un bilinguisme voire un trilinguisme d'abord au sein des élites et les classes moyennes, ce qui correspond à la « haute culture » de E. Gellner, ensuite dans la population agissant comme une « haute identité » en association avec les identités ethniques régionales.

Sommes-nous à la veille de la « fin de terroirs » ou de la formation de nouveaux territoires, national et régionaux correspondant aux comtés? La réalité semble plus complexe car les changements structurels contextuels nationaux presque linéaires, peuvent, en fonction des conjonctures politiques, être contrecarrés par des identités ethniques qui se réveillent. En effet les identités associées des sociétés plurielles, de facto sous tension, ne sont pas à l'abri de crispations identitaires exclusives, aussi bien nationale, xénophobe, que régionale ethnique. La classe politique peut et sait instrumentaliser ces ressources en situation de crise nationaliste ou ethnique, mais elle peut également les négocier : la vie politique actuelle illustre bien cette revendication, régionale, sectorielle voire séparatiste de la part des élites périphériques désireuses de participer au pouvoir national et à ses redistributions, en fin de compte la possibilité d'une institutionnalisation nationale des conflits régionaux.

Toutefois aussi performante, du moins aussi séduisante soit-elle, la construction nationale patrimoniale, entre fondations patrimoniales et modernisation, ne peut faire l'économie d'une construction politique citoyenne comme d'un devoir de mémoire et d'histoire; l'imaginaire a besoin d'une idéologie et de vérités et de se projeter dans un futur. Si la construction et la vision du futur est du ressort du politique, la connexion entre l'écriture de l'histoire et la construction d'un patrimoine national, entre devoir de mémoire et devoir d'histoire, reste un chantier de l'histoire, voire un objectif stratégique académique pour la discipline mais elle suppose une critique historique renouvelée, de nouvelles finalités et méthodes.

Conclusion: quels préalables pour une écriture du fait national?

Cette tache démystificatrice de l'histoire comme finalité, cette entreprise de déconstruction intellectuelle comme méthode[44] reposent sur deux préalables. D'une part, elles ont besoin d'une volonté politique pour débloquer les pesanteurs, libérer la parole et ouvrir des débats : ce fut déjà le cas au travers des travaux des différentes commissions vérité et réconciliation, le rapport Waki (2008), le rapport sur les populations et les communautés autochtones (2010), le rapport Vérité Justice Réconciliation (2012) qui s'apparentent à un devoir de mémoire consensuel préliminaire, peut être insatisfaisant pour la critique historique, mais qui ciblent des questions tout en apportant des sources. D'autre part, elles supposent tout un ensemble de prérequis propres à la méthode historique dont l'accès aux sources, le jeu du recul historique et de la multiplication des témoignages, le croisement de ceux-ci.....avec un dégradé de possibles et d'impossibles. D'ores et déjà, certains champs ou certaines questions peuvent faire l'objet de synthèse[45], d'autres sous la forme d'approfondissements sont nécessaires à la lumière des problématiques posées par l'actualité comme la place des femmes, dans certains cas le retour sur événement et sur certaines zones d'ombre apparait nécessaire[46], enfin d'autres territoires de l'historien dont la question des droits de l'homme mériteraient d'être explorés.

Ces recommandations, entendues lors des deux séminaires de Nairobi de 2013 et 2014, laissent entrevoir des recherches, des projets qui visent à dépasser, transcender les blocages entre histoire et patrimoine, devoir de mémoire et devoir d'histoire, particularisme et universalisme tout en étudiant ces clivages en œuvre et en tension dans l'histoire kenyane, alors que l'actualité ou l'histoire immédiate

---

[44] Cette exercice qui vise à démythifier l'histoire nationale, et en particulier l'histoire du mouvement *Mau Mau* pour mieux « nationaliser » ce mouvement anticolonial, est défendu par C. Musembayi Katumanga et suppose des recherches indépendantes comme le souligne M. Rutccre.

[45] C'est au sujet du mouvement *Mau Mau* que W. Ochieng estima qu'il est désormais possible d'écrire cette synthèse, avec toute la prudence car « la vérité est approximative », comme le remarque G Mutiuki.

[46] Dont la nature, l'étendue des négociations entre la puissance coloniale et le nouvel Etat à l'exemple des travaux de G Wasserman *Politics of decolonization Kenyan europeans and land issue 1960-65* , Cambridge university press, 1976.

91

mettent en évidence la complexité ou la paradoxe kenyan en œuvre, entre la construction, l'apprentissage d'une identité nationale, le sentiment d'appartenance à la Nation, et les difficultés d'un projet politique citoyen sinon communautaire du moins consensuel, le nationalisme ou l' Etat-Nation .

Chapter 6

Nationalism and the Nation-Building Project in Kenya, 1963-2014: An Appraisal

Susan Waiyego Mwangi, Felix Kiruthu, Francis Muchoki

Introduction

Recent tensions and conflicts between and among African nations, especially in countries considered to be in peaceful zones, have led to a renewed focus on nationalism. This is a phenomenon that entails a great feeling of patriotism and pride towards one's nation. Therefore, it is one form of identity within a multiple set of identities. Of importance is to recognize that since identities are constructed, they can also be deconstructed. Snyder (2000) defines nationalism as a doctrine where people believe that their culture, language history, institutions and religious beliefs are distinct and aspire to self-rule under a political system that expresses and protects those distinct characteristics.

Generally, the roots and character of modern African nationalism are traced to colonial experience in Africa. Prior to colonialism, African communities enjoyed their social, economic, political, and social independence in the form of small "nations". However, after the Berlin Conference in 1885, multiple African communities were lumped together in artificially created territorial entities, regardless of their ethnic affiliations and other affinities. This then led to attempts at forging a broader sense of national identity based on Western European societies' sense of national identity. Nevertheless, the need to fight for political liberation would eventually motivate development of nationalism among these different ethnic groups in Africa, geared towards eradication of colonialism (Kersting, 2009). As such, modern African nationalism was part of the decolonization process (Ake, 1996).

Nation-building, on the other hand, is the deliberate effort towards forging a nation constituting of several different ethnic groups. In Africa, respective colonial powers unwittingly contributed towards this effort in their bid to control their colonial possessions under one central administration. African elites used the process of nation-building to their advantage against colonial rule. Indeed, unity between different ethnic groups was seen by the African elite as a panacea towards the eradication of tribal conflicts in the continent after independence. This chapter examines the quest for nation-building in post-independence Kenya up to 2014, covering the reign of four presidents. The efforts at nation-building are examined, besides the political dynamics and political challenges experienced from 1963 at the onset on independence up to 2014.

In Kenya, a country which until 2008 was perceived as a peaceful nation neighboured by conflicting countries, incidence of ethnic related violence[1] (GoK, 2008), coupled with acts of terrorism dating back to the 1998 bombing of the US embassy in Kenya, have left scholars questioning the perceptions of 'oneness' expressed in the country's national anthem, and the constant rhetoric by political leaders about the need for unity of the diverse ethnic groups.

In order to understand and appreciate the attempts at, the limitations, successes, and the prospects of nation-building in Kenya, it is important to interrogate two related questions. First, what efforts or energies have Kenyan consecutive leadership put in place in trying to forge and build national consciousness of its citizens? What (dis)continuities in the building of Kenya's national consciousness have been observed? Nation-building involves the processes of national integration and consolidation, often initiated by state leaders with an aim to unite and develop a sense of national consciousness as opposed to localized primordial ties[2]. According to Ogot (1995), nationalism is founded on the premise that the individual's loyalty and devotion to the nation-state surpasses other individual or group interests. Enloe (1990) rightly adds that a nation is composed of people who believe that their common past shapes their present as it helps them build their future together. Such a people are also bound

---

[1] The 2007 PEV, the worst of its kind left close to 1,300 people dead and over 200,000 displaced.

[2] See Carl J. Friedrich, "Nation-Building?," in Karl Deutsch and William Foltz, eds., *Nationbuilding* (New York: Atherton, 1963): 28; Charles Tilly, ed., *The formation of national states in Europe* (Princeton: Princeton University Press, 1975).

together by such things as an ideology, a language, religion, and or a common history. How they remember their past experiences then becomes an important aspect of the nation-building project. The custodians of such a past, either in the form of national holidays, national anthems, national identities, daily flag-raising ceremonies at all administrative headquarters, and the use of a national *lingua franca* often embedded in the country's constitution, must thus be guarded. The extent to which such emblems succeed in uniting Kenyans merits interrogation. It is, however, the times and purposes for which such are whipped that we also seek to interrogate. Remembering is a political act and what we remember is dictated by times, context, and place. Political leadership is also an important aspect in the remembrance/forgetting processes. It determines what aspects of history and historians are to be remembered and for what reasons. In this chapter, thus, we also seek to understand how such memories and the politics of selective amnesia have continually influenced nation-building in Kenya since 1963.

Second, we focus on the dynamics that have shaped the nation-building process. The fight against colonialism played a significant role in unifying Africans from all walks of life. It also helped create a heterogeneous African nation whose sole intent was to drive out the common enemy, imperialism. The strong cultural and ethnic bonds were, for some time suppressed especially in the late 1950s as Africa communities forged forward to welcome *uhuru*.[3] In Kenya, where the various ethnic groups amalgamated around two main political parties; KANU and KADU the national leadership though from diverse ethnic groups agreed that they had to wait for Kenyatta to take over leadership after the departure of the colonial governor[4]. This unity and nationalism was, however, short-lived after independence as there appeared no other common threat to the development of the nation state. The neo-colonial tendencies after independence saw disillusioned citizens scatter and coalesce around their ethnic groups as patrons of the ruling elites shared the national cake among themselves, their families, and cronies. This is what has been called the imperial state building project whose major aim was not to

---

[3] Kiswahili for freedom
[4] By the time Jaramogi Oginga Odinga was at the helm of the political group fighting for independence while Kenyatta was in jail.

benefit the population (economically, socially, and politically) but to ensure control of the state and its resources by a small clique around the executive. Raftopoulous (1999) sees this as "a case of authoritarian nationalism which utilised state violence to repress dissidence in the name of building the nation". In this chapter, we explore the impact that this tendency towards self-aggrandizement and the manipulation of the moral ethnicity card has had on national consciousness and nation-building in Kenya.

Some scholars have argued that nations only exist in so far as we imagine them (Anderson, 1991; Ranger, 2004). Such scholars thus advocate for the use of the term 'nationalisms' in place of nationalism as an indication that national consciousness is subjective and is dependent on one's environment and place of origin (Ranger, 2004). The extent to which this statement is valid is, just like the first presupposition, not debatable. It is these spatial-temporal circumstances that we seek to question in this chapter, noting that for nation-building to bear fruits and for Kenyans to appreciate their 'Kenyanness' without necessarily being reminded by politicians and those given the responsibility to brand Kenya, the constitution, the myriad of emblems and slogans occasionally harped on during specific times for specific reasons, leadership must be at the core of such a project. The leaders' dedication and determination to inspire Kenyans to uphold justice as Kenya's 'shield and defender' fifty years after independence is important and should therefore be nurtured.

Nation-building in Kenya has been shaped by diverse economic, social and political developments that we may not wish away, although some scholars have argued that the period of colonialism was too short to influence anything.[5] The history of colonialism and its attendant forces has also not only been instrumental in dictating development (and underdevelopment), as Walter Rodney (1972) argues, but it has influenced how we perceive and interpret nationalism and we must thus first interrogate British imperialism before discussing the various developments that have shaped the building of the nation.

Colonialism and the birth of a Kenyan nation

---

[5] Jeffrey, Herbst

Kenya gained her independence after almost seventy years of colonial rule, which was largely characterised by exploitative and domineering of local Africans' economic, political, and cultural systems. Young (1994) argues that within the rubric of British economic exploitation, land was expropriated and large inequalities created through racial exclusion of the Europeans, Asians, and Africans. Indigenous populations were also confined into reserves and others forced to work for long hours in settler plantations with a meagre salary. Despite the conditions in the plantations, many able-bodied people especially men could, however, not resist the temptation to work in the White Highlands and other settlement schemes because it was from here that they acquired funds to pay for the imposed hut and poll tax; imposed to cater for the administrative costs of the colony. Many moved from the rural to urban areas while some walked for long distances to live with relatives as *ahoi* (squatters), all in the effort to get funds for familial and government needs (Zeleza, 1989). Locals were also denied the opportunity to grow cash crops and to rear exotic animals; the colonial government gave the excuse that local cattle breeds were weak and tsetse fly infested, capable of spreading diseases to the high-yielding grade settler animals. However, the real reason was that to allow Africans to grow cash crops and rear exotic animals, could have diverted labour from settler farms to African agriculture. It could also have provided the Africans with an alternative means of earning cash and it would be no longer necessary to work in the settler plantations to pay taxes. Women on their part were, unless labour demands dictated so, required to remain at home as their migrant husbands toiled under the harsh working conditions of the *mbeberu*,[6] Kiswahili for colonial agent. Though engaged in home economics and within the Marxist conception of productive labour, women were, however, not rewarded and when they were forced to work in the settler farms their labour was lowly paid, due to what the colonial supervisors considered long resting hours while they took care of infants and/or pregnancies.

---

[6] Kiswahili term for colonial agent

The incorporation of Kenya into the Western capitalist system thus led to the emergence of colonial economic and political institutions. The most important development was the emergence of new class divisions and the elite. The new class of elites used the patronage of the colonial state to accumulate wealth, while the peasants were pauperized as a result of land alienation and other factors. Under the prevailing conditions, discontented Africans had few opportunities to form political groups to fight against colonialism. Indeed the colonial government denied Africans this opportunity for fear of reprisals. This did not, however, dampen the spirit of Africans who used their religious antics to organize prayer and worship meetings which were eventually transformed into the earliest resistance movements. The *Dini ya Msambwa*, *Mumbo* and *Sakawa* should be seen in this light. Communities also joined hands and came up with ethnic associations out of which national liberation movements were drawn. Harry Thuku founded the Young Kikuyu Association (YKA) in Central Kenya, while the Young Kavirondo Association was launched in Western Kenya (Kanogo, 1989). There was also the Kisumu Native Chamber of Commerce (KNCC). In northern Nyanza, there emerged the North Kavirondo Central Association. Joseph Kang'ethe and James Beautah later formed the Kikuyu Central Association (KCA) in 1924 in Murang'a. KCA concentrated on local grievances. At the coast emerged the Young Nyika Association (YNA) among the Mijikenda to protest against land alienation, *Kipande* system, forced labour, taxation, and the harsh economic conditions brought about by the depression in 1929. The Kamba formed the Ukamba Members Association to protest against the impending destocking policy or decree. The Taita Hill Association was formed in 1939 to protest lack of land after large scale alienation of land to create room for European sisal plantations at Mwatate and Taita Hills (Maloba, 1989). The emergence of ethnic politics in Kenya can be traced to the colonial period. The colonial government encouraged the formation of ethno-based associations as a way of defeating African nationalism. Attempts by Africans to form nationwide associations were thwarted by the colonial government and they were ruthlessly suppressed or crushed.

These associations addressed local grievances, but calls for a national movement saw such groups mobilize people with a national representation. Between 1940 and 1946 when the Kenya African Union (KAU) articulated the aspirations of all Kenyans by stressing the need for African unity, a national ideology of unity in diversity was crystallizing. KAU eventually became the national voice of Kenyan Africans and later associations endeavoured to have members from diverse ethnic groups, a sign that nationalism was slowly taking shape. Mboya (1970) observes that after the 1940s, all Kenyan citizens were united for the single struggle for independence under the rubric *uhuru ni sasa*.[7] It was under such calls for nationalism that when KADU emerged in 1962 to counter KANU's ideology for a centralized Kenyan state, consultations saw a merger of the two parties, after KANU formed the independent government in 1963 under a colonially designed constitution. Kenyatta, supported by members of diverse ethnic groups, became the founding president of the new nation – Kenya.

Post-independence developments and nation-building in Kenya, 1963-1978

Mazrui (1972) notes that after colonialism, Kenyans were ready to bring in the right political leadership into the country. Political independence was expected to give Kenyans and Africans elsewhere an opportunity to unite and engage in development projects that had long been left to settlers and a few elites. The 1960s and 1970s were thus a monumental period for the nation as it had to reorient into a path of development engineered by and for Africans. After more than fifty years of colonialism President Jomo Kenyatta announced that the immediate problems that bedevilled the nation were poverty, disease, and ignorance (Kiruthu, 2001). Other challenges included political inequality, illiteracy, and unequal economic opportunities as stipulated in Sessional Paper No. 10 of 1965 (Republic of Kenya, 1965). Kenya after independence wanted to shake off the colonial legacy and promote African socialism. How this socialism was to be realized, however, became problematic because after independence Kenyan leaders lacked a common goal, as illustrated by quarrels between those who advocated for a *laissez faire* or capitalist economic

---

[7] An urgent or immediate agitation for political freedom

orientation, including Kenyatta and Tom Mboya, and those who favoured a more socially oriented economy, such as Oginga Odinga and Bildad Kaggia (Elkins, 2005). Kenyatta surrounded himself with former loyalists who got access to powerful positions in government, and this could explain why Western investments continued to dominate the country's economy after independence. Some scholars (McWilliams, 1996; Leys, 1975; Ogot *et. al.* 1995) argue that the idea of nation-building in Kenya required visionary leaders whose role in the drawing and drafting of the desired ends of the nation-building would steer the country into a unified front (Gertzel, Goldschmidt and Rothchild, 1969). The task also required a working nation that could not easily be called upon to demonstrate and destabilize the government. This could only have happened if the founding president steered the economy in the right direction. Politically, he needed to appoint government and parastatal bosses on the basis of merit as opposed to favouritism. Socially, he needed a common agenda for the revival of African cultures not only through uncoordinated folk music, but a clear blue print that would allow Kenyans to appreciate their socio-cultural diversity while at the same time respecting different ethnic opinions. All these, however, became mere rhetoric as exigencies of politics led Jomo Kenyatta to consolidate his hold into power. There were accusations against Kenyatta's government of tribalism, patronage, political assassinations, and skewed economic development.

Given the prevailing situation, nation-building became a mirage. Citizens began 'othering' competing communities as they considered themselves victims of these other ethnic groups. Ethnic bashing and suspicion became entrenched in work places and unity became a word only enshrined in the constitution, the national emblems, and in political speeches. The realization that there was no shared sense of history apart from colonialism began to crystallize as ethnic groups pursued conflicting agendas all aimed at building the Kenyan (or was it a pan-ethnic) nationalism (Samper, 1997).

Jomo Kenyatta devised ways to galvanize the citizens and assure them that his government was willing to assist every Kenyan. He thus officially launched the political philosophy of 'Harambee[8]'. In spirit the citizens were to help each other regardless of ethnic group, religion, and or race. By introducing *Harambee* socialism, the Tanzanian way was the ideology that the president was envisioning. He hoped that the *Harambee* movement would not only enable citizens to pool resources together and by so doing, integrate citizens from all corners in the country. In practice, however, *Harambee* events were presided over by wealthy businessmen, senior civil servants and politicians. In the process, areas which had the advantage of such powerful individuals benefitted more than other parts of the country in terms of development. Critics of the *Harambee* philosophy, however, observed that rather than promote equal development and integration, relatively rich regions, or those perceived thus, held more *Harambee*s and contributed better than poorer regions thereby leaving a huge gap between the more developed and less developed regions of the country (Barkan & Holmquist, 1986). Nyerere's socialism was different in the sense that he was not only willing to pull the resources of the former Tanganyika together, but to also walk the talk by ensuring that *ujamaa*[9] took root in the economic, social and political sectors. Kenyatta unwittingly helped to establish a system through the *Harambee* movement, where the rich politicians got an opportunity to win more votes than the poor counterparts during general elections by virtue of their economic prowess during *Harambees*. Consequently, politicians simply called on the rich to attend fund-raising events and invite the people to vote them into office come the next general elections. The politicians quite often attended such *Harambees* with an amount reportedly from the president himself as a wise way of showing how connected they were to the president (Barkan & Holmquist, 1986). Widner (1992), Throup and Hornsby (1998) note that there was nothing as important, at least at the time, as being known as close to the president and his men. This is because it would be easy to get the benefits that accrue from such neo-patrimonial relations. Land, employment, and business

---

[8] This is the Swahili word for pooling and pulling together. The word was actually engraved in the national court of arms to show its centralitnya to Kenya's national imagination.

[9] This is aconcept under the ideology of socialism that advocated for togetherness among all peope of diverse groups

opportunities were easily available for such people and their relations. In return they would vote in such a leader, regardless of his policies or lack of the same. Widner (1992) calls the people around President Kenyatta the "Family" to underscore the fact that they were not necessarily blood relations. They benefited from the presidency to acquire land in the Rift Valley, which had been bought off from the departing settlers, plum jobs in parastatals, and government ministries (with no or limited academic qualifications) and strategic business ventures. A majority of them, as Widner (1992) notes, were from the Kikuyu ethnic group. According to Murunga (2004), by the time of Kenyatta's death, four out of eight provincial commissioners were Kikuyu. In 1974, seven out of the twenty cabinet ministers were Kikuyu. Similarly, Ogot (2003) also shows how the Kikuyu monopolized top positions at the University of Nairobi where they held all the top administrative positions. The provincial administration and civil service were also ethnicised and even the Permanent Secretary in Charge of Provincial Administration was a Kikuyu. In short, the Kikuyu were the majority in the civil service, headed the police, controlled banks, had the lion's share in the cabinet, had many permanent secretaries, and one of their own also headed the University of Nairobi.[10]

This marked the beginnings of ethnic resentment from other ethnic groups who felt left out in building the nation. While Oginga Odinga's formation of KPU[11] may have been informed by ideological difference between himself and Kenyatta, the factor of ethnicity should not be overlooked. Jaramogi had stepped down for Kenyatta to lead the nation, and rewarding Kikuyu elites to the chagrin of other communities was seen as a betrayal of the ideals of nationalism. KPU's land policy favoured the poor Kenyans and advocated for distribution of free land to the needy, including squatters and those

---

[10] However, it has been pointed out that, soon after independence, there was a shortage of personnel and there was a limited number of qualified African Kenyans available to fill the positions left vacant by the departing colonial officers and as the post-independent government implemented the Kenyanization policy in various ministries (Matiba, 2000: 63). This might have led to the dominance of the Kikuyu in the early days of independence.

[11] Miller, 1984 argues that Kenyatta betrayed nationalism further when he banned KPU in 1969.

who had lost their land in the struggle for independence either by expropriation or through land consolidation. The manifesto dismissed African socialism as a cloak for the practice of capitalism (Odinga, 1967: 304; Kinyatti, 2008: 405). The ex-*Mau Mau* freedom fighters also felt betrayed. They had expected free grants of land from the government, land for which they had gone to the forest to fight, but which they were never granted post-independence. They felt the nationalist agenda they fought for had been abandoned by Kenyatta and the elites who had joined hands with colonial collaborators to accumulate wealth at the expense of the poor masses.

Bildad Kaggia, an ex-detainee supported the KPU and denounced Kenyatta for the failure to resettle landless groups because he felt that the nationalism that they had been fighting for in the 1940s and 1960s had been betrayed. Whether his criticism of the then president was informed by genuine concerns of nationalism or personal motivation is debatable. The formation of KPU and the support that the party got from especially the grassroots was, however, a clear indication that Kenyatta and his former friends were following different paths in their attempt to build the Kenyan nation. The proscription of KPU marked a watershed moment in Kenya's attempt at bringing the nation together as some communities became, henceforth, marginalized from public political life. Kaggia and Jaramogi remained silenced for championing a different path in nation-building. Socialism was also overtaken by capitalism and primitive accumulation became the order of the day among the Kenyan elite both in civil service and commercial sector.

Kenyatta's nation-building project was focused towards undermining opposition politics as he sought to unite the different ethnic and racial groups in the country. After 1964, the KANU parliament made far-reaching constitutional amendments which increased the powers of the executive tremendously making it very difficult for the country to re-introduce devolution in a constitutional manner. Successful lobbying by Kenyatta government further led to the disbandment of elected regional assemblies and regional governments especially after the launch of Sessional Paper Number 10 of 1965 which led to the transfer of core social services such as health and education to central government ministries (SID, 2011). Other changes included the disbanding of the bi-cameral parliament and the enhancement of the Provincial Administration which played a key role in consolidating administration under a unitary style of management with a clear hierarchy from the assistant chief all the way to the presidency. This state of affairs ensured that the head of state had a free hand to run the country with little interference from political competitors.

The consolidation of power into the presidency and the declaration of Kenya as a *de facto* one party state saw detention without trial, exile of dissident voices, and assassinations reach their apex in 1969 with the death of Tom Mboya.[12] In 1975 J.M Kariuki, an ardent supporter of the poor, was also killed in cold bold. This alienated a good fraction of population in Central Kenya from the ruling elite, thereby further undermining the nation-building project. Some of the disenchanted political leaders from Central Kenya included those who provided an avenue for Dainiel Arap Moi to take power peacefully upon Kenyatta's death in 1978 (Kakai, 2010).

Kenyatta was, however, an astute politician. He declared, through parliament, Kiswahili an official language in 1969. An important ingredient in developing a national identity, Kiswahili, together with oral literature, were also included in the school curriculum and despite the earlier hiccups, played a significant role in bringing people together and building a national consciousness. Akivaga and Adagala (1982) note that education fosters a sense of nationhood and promotes national unity. Njengere (2014) emphasizes that by attaining education, people are able to tolerate divergent opinions and therefore contribute to national cohesion and integration of people of a multi-variant linguistic grouping. The emphasis on Kiswahili as a simple yet powerful tool for enhancing national cohesion can thus not be underestimated. By insisting on Kiswahili, Kenyatta allowed communities to communicate and exchange ideas regarding diverse issues and an appreciation of divergent opinions, although on a lower scale cultivated. Problems of unemployment, landlessness, corruption, and general disillusionment of the citizenry, however, remained the largest challenge to Kenyatta's leadership and

---

[12] See Kakai (2010). The assassination of Mboya created serious division between the Luo and the Kikuyu.

they became serious impediments to nation-building in the later years.

The Moi era, 1978-2002

Kenyatta's attempt to revive the national integration and cohesion of all Kenyan communities was also thwarted by a group of people around him, especially after the realization that he was sickly. Around the Change the Constitution Movement (CCM) the close group began strategizing to lock out Moi, then the Vice President, from ascending to the presidency upon Kenyatta's death. The group, however, failed and in 1978, Daniel Arap Moi succeeded Jomo Kenyatta as president when the latter died of natural causes. His first announcement was that he was ready to work with every citizen and in accordance with the footsteps of his predecessor. He moved around the country championing for peace, love, and unity, perhaps in recognition of how divided the nation had become. His move to introduce free milk to all schools and the quota system in education benefitted students across the country in the name of ensuring a united and fully integrated society. Graduates of this education system were also deployed far from their homes and the results were felt as bonds of national unity were created everywhere in the country. This move was however short-lived as the 1980s progressed. The attempted 1982 coup and the introduction of Structural Adjustment Programs that called for cost-sharing in government amenities saw a big crop of able students drop out of school or attend local schools, a phenomenon that had significant implications on Moi's attempt at integration.

It was the attempted coup that was, however, most disastrous to the nation-building project. The 1982 coup attempt was allegedly started by junior members of the now defunct Kenya air Force. Political tribalism, which had matured during the Kenyatta regime, intensified as Moi established a dictatorship characterized by a personal rule. Moi attempted to restructure the political economy of Kenya to benefit his Kalenjin community and to establish new patronage networks in order to reward his allies elsewhere. In his neo-patrimonial state, he distributed jobs and other material benefits to the Kalenjin and other loyal supporters, including South Asians in an elaborate patron-client system (McWilliams & Cowen, 1996). Things were made worse by the ethnic clashes which started at the end of 1991 in which over 1,500 people perished and more than 300,000 were forced to flee their homes (KHRC Report, 1998). Ethnic clashes started after the Rift Valley meetings which called for *Majimboism*[13] during the first three months of the new multi-party era. At first, the clashes seemed to confirm Moi's predictions that multi-party democracy would ignite ethnic animosities, discrediting opposition leaders and advocates of multi-party politics. The government was involved in provoking the ethnic violence for political purpose. Among the so-called warriors, were junior military, police, General Service Unit (GSU) officers and ex-servicemen (KHRC Report, 1998). A Parliamentary Committee appointed to investigate the clashes popularly known as the Kiliku Report (named after the chairman of the committee, Kennedy Kiliku), in its report, indicated that there were training camps at Maasai Mara Game reserve which were funded by prominent personalities in the government (Kiliku Report, 1992). The clashes were designed to secure KANU domination of the whole Rift Valley. In the Rift Valley, violence was meant to alter the political demography of the multi-ethnic province ahead of the multi-party elections to the advantage of Moi and KANU (KHRC Report, 1998). The ethnic clashes and the harassment of the opposition communities was meant to ensure that no opposition candidate would receive 25% of the presidential vote and as many as 1.5 million voters in the clash-torn areas did not register to vote in the 1992 elections (Kagwanja, 2003; Wanyande, 2006). The architect of the violence wanted to ensure that the forty-four parliamentary seats in the Rift Valley Province went exclusively KANU's (Kagwanja, 2001). The bloody

---

[13] *Majimboism* in Swahili means "regionalism. *Majimboism* had emerged in the 1960s and at the eve of independence and was aimed at protecting territorial claims of small pastoral and agricultural communities in Kenya. Thus, unlike in the Constitution of Kenya (2010) where regionalism refers to devolvement of governance, *Majimboism* was initially promoted by KADU between 1960 and 1963 as a basis for protecting smaller or "minority" communities from the dominance of larger communities. *Majimboism* in the 1990s, as interpreted by some and especially the Rift Valley politicians, was a federal system based on the notion of excluding other ethnic groups in what was claimed to be territories of particular ethnic communities referred to as "indigenous". See Muchoki (2012: 272-3); Anderson (2005: 548-64).

clashes in the Rift Valley and parts of Western and Nyanza provinces in 1992 caused bitterness among the non-Kalenjin ethnic groups and further scattered the nationalist agenda. The clashes continued in the Rift Valley after the 1992 elections. It appears that they were intended to punish those ethnic communities who never heeded Moi's warning against voting for the opposition (KHRC Report, 1998; Kagwanja, 2001).

Ideally, nation-building should be on the basis of equal distribution of resources and clear and concerted efforts by the state to initiate social, economic, and political developments of the citizens exclusively. It is for this reason perhaps that despite Moi's dictatorial tendencies, and pushed by the clergy, media, law society of Kenya, and some politicians, he opened up to the introduction of multipartyism in 1991. Corruption and poor service delivery were and they remain Kenya's biggest challenge to cohesion and integration. Some ethnic groups felt deprived of basic services which in turn bred animosity and resentment consequently resulting in violence. As Moi was retiring from the presidency, in 2002, the Kenyan nation was so divided and the feelings of Kenyanness were simply to be found in the flag, anthem and such emblems as the court of arms. How was Kibaki to revive the sense of togetherness and understanding?

Kibaki and the revival of the nation-building project

When Mwai Kibaki came to power in 2002 under a broad National Rainbow Coalition (NARC), he was very popular and Kenyans expected a lot of positive changes, earning Kenya the top rank as the most optimistic people in the world (Murunga and Nasong'o, 2006).The election results produced a euphoria and sense of national unity unlike any prior election. "Many people felt like Kenyans like never before" (Holmquist, *Finance*, 31 May, 2003).Although Kibaki was not able to fulfil all the pre-election promises given by his NARC party on becoming president, a number of measures were taken that strengthened nation-building. His first cabinet was quite inclusive, with ministers from the different parties in the coalition and showed the face of Kenya. Indeed the NARC victory was perceived by many Kenyans as a national rebirth (Branch, 2011).Free primary education was introduced, public hospitals were stocked with more medicines, corruption was reduced, and a number of reforms in public transport sector undertaken, which made Kenyans feel more empowered (Kagwanja, 2006). The Constituency Development Fund (CDF), which channelled 2.5% of the national revenue to constituency level, was also introduced by the Kibaki government and went a long way to bring equity in the nation as its impact was felt in all the constituencies across the country. With the NARC administration's ability to increase more tax collection, a number of services in general were improved, including road repairs and improvement of salaries of public servants.

On the political front, the NARC government also legitimized *Mau Mau* movement, which had remained a proscribed movement during the Kenyatta and Moi regimes (Anderson, 2005). The pre- and post-independence national heroes and heroines were also given special recognition by government and monuments were established in different parts of the country in their honour. A statue of Tom Mboya, for example, was built in the city centre of Nairobi. Also built was Dedan Kimathi's monument. This move greatly energized the struggle by the *Mau Mau* veterans in pursuit of compensation by the British government in London. A number of notable achievements of both the Kibaki regime and the Grand Coalition of President Kibaki and Raila Odinga as Prime Minister, include the completion of the Thika Super Highway and a number of bypasses in Nairobi that have gone a long way in tackling the challenges of traffic jam. These projects are part of Vision 2030 project that is envisioned to transform Kenya into a middle level industrial power by 2030 based on the social, economic and political pillars.

Unfortunately, the NARC coalition was later to be plagued by an alleged Memorandum of Understanding (MOU) between NARC led by Mwai Kibaki and the Labour Democratic Party of Kenya (LDP), led by Raila Odinga. The failure to adhere to the alleged MOU became the greatest thorn in Kibaki's government as it contributed greatly to the split of NARC, the crisis in government, and the polarization of the Kenyan society leading to the 2007 post-election violence. The LDP faction complained of isolation and marginalization from the centre of power and this led to a split of the NARC coalition. Consequently, the LDP members joined KANU members especially from the Rift Valley and other non-LDP members to oppose the Kibaki government (Kanyinga, 2010).

The other problems that greatly undermined the Kibaki administration were allegations that the NARC regime, especially in its first two years, gave top public sector jobs to the Kikuyu people from the Mount Kenya region and others close to the centre of power (Kanyinga 2010). The failure to adhere to the MOU by the Kibaki regime and the alleged dominance of people from Mount Kenya region confirmed the suspicions of other groups that Kibaki and the Kikuyu elite were not after any meaningful change. Matters were worsened by allegations of corruption which was associated mainly with elites from the Mount Kenya region, the so called "Mount Kenya Mafia", majority of whom happened to be ministers in the Kibaki administration. The worst of this was the Anglo-leasing scandal which is believed to have cost the government nearly KShs 7 billion (33million US dollars). In this toxic political situation, the national referendum of 2005, where Kenyans were to vote on whether to adopt or reject a draft new constitution drafted under the Kibaki government provided an opportunity for politicians to settle their scores over the MOU controversy and other grievances against the government. Politicians fanned hostility against each other using ethnicity as a platform to securing support. Ultimately, daggers were drawn between the Kikuyu and the Mount Kenya groups on one side and the majority of other Kenyan communities on the other hand (Maina quoted in Oloo 2010). When the referendum was called, the voting was largely influenced by ethnicity. President Kibaki and Central Province, the Mount Kenya groups and pockets of supporters from Western, Coast, Eastern and Nairobi provinces voted "Yes" (Banana)[14] for the new constitution. Raila Odinga, supported by leaders of other ethnic groups led majority of the other communities to vote "No" (Orange) against the new constitution. The constitutional debate and the referendum of 2005 provided the avenue through which the frustrations and anger by non-Kikuyu elite were expressed. The tensions, political polarization and the crisis in

---

[14] Banana was the symbol for those who voted "Yes" in support of the proposed constitution while "orange" was the symbol for those who voted "No" against the proposed constitution. The symbols were chosen because they were said to be politically neutral since both are fruits

the government reflected unfulfilled promises by the Kibaki regime. Following the defeat in the referendum, President Mwai Kibaki sacked all the cabinet ministers who participated in campaigning against passing of the referendum. These included Raila Odinga, Anyang Nyong'o, Kalonzo Musyoka and Charity Ngilu. This further created more bitterness against the Kikuyu elite and the Kibaki government. It is against this polarised atmosphere that the country went into the 2007 General Elections.

The 2007 elections destroyed completely any pretence to national unity. The campaigns leading to the 2007 elections centred on issues of land, devolution of power and resources, *Majimboism* and ethnic politics. The perceived historical injustices, especially on the land questions and appointment in the public service and the skewed distribution of resources favouring certain regions are largely a product of ethnicity. The violence after the 2007 election was a product of the historical processes during the Kenyatta, Moi, and the Kibaki regimes. During the campaigns of 2007 elections, real and perceived ethno-regional exclusion deepened and generated political divisions along ethnic and regional lines. The elections were characterized by deeply divided political elite. The divisions were as a result not only of ethnic animosities but also due to perceived monopolization of state power by the Mount Kenya mafia, as they were called. The political violence was partly triggered off by the rigged elections but the causes of the violence are largely to be found in the historical grievances dating back to the Jomo Kenyatta regime.

The Constitution of Kenya (2010): a new dawn in nation-building

Kenya's current constitution was promulgated in 2010 with a lot of celebration and excitement, which expressed Kenyans' expectations that things in the country would work for the better. Kenyans expected a complete break with the past and a new beginning leading to a prosperous Kenya in which there would be freedom and democracy. The unequal allocation of resources between regions since independence has been blamed on all-powerful presidency and the absence of power-sharing which leads to a winner takes-it-all situation. The all-powerful presidency had led to those who have occupied the position to distribute the resources to their ethnic groups and loyal supporters of other ethnic communities leading to inequality. The all-powerful presidency was seen as the cause of multi-problems that have faced independent Kenya, including despotism, because it perpetuated a culture of inequality, impunity, intolerance and authoritarianism (Wanyama, 2010). One of the main motivations behind devolution was that for long, Kenyans sought for ways of reducing the wide-ranging powers of the Presidency (Muchoki, 2012). The presidency, as per James Orengo, had become a monster as the President of Kenya combined the powers of the US President and the powers of the British Prime Minister, making him extremely powerful. Consequently, the presidency had an inordinate say in the sharing of national resources. Political cronyism and corruption meant that national resources were diverted to areas that were politically favoured, besides lining the pockets of senior government officials and their friends. At the Kenyan coast, one of the factors that have fostered opposition to national government has been the issue of allocation of beach plots to selected individuals. Similarly, allocation of gazetted government forest land to well-connected individuals in areas like Mau plateau, which is an important rain catchment area, at the expense of the country's heritage, was decried by citizens (Kiruthu, 2014).

Years of inequality in resource distribution resulted in a situation where citizens were frustrated with the winner takes all perception. This could explain why general elections have been given such a high premium in Kenya. The infamous violence after the 2007 elections was caused in no small part by the fear of losing out from state largesse by the political class. Following Kofi Annan brokered negotiations between the opposition and the Kibaki government between January and February 2008, a Grand Coalition government was established with a clear mandate to govern for five years within which time it was to execute the reform agenda agreed upon during the negotiations (Nyong'o, 2015). In addition to electoral reforms, the Kofi Annan brokered negotiations also concluded on the need to undertake constitutional reforms and devolution was identified as an important aspect of the reform. Devolution was therefore seen as a solution to the challenge of inequality in the distribution of national resources in Kenya. Consequently, one of the revolutionary ideas in the constitution was the creation of two levels of government, namely national government and county governments. The forty-seven county governments were to be led by elected governors and who were to benefit from a threshold of resources so as to ensure a fair distribution of political power and economic resources all over the country, as one way of redressing the problem of skewed resource distribution. On March 27, 2013, forty-seven elected county governors were sworn in, officially signifying Kenya's adoption of a devolved system of government, by the Jubilee government under President Uhuru Kenyatta (Ghai and Ghai, 2013). This, it was hoped was a new beginning for Kenya. The fact that the government was bold enough to launch the county government is perhaps an indication that devolution has taken root in the country. Despite the many challenges facing devolution, the Jubilee government has implemented many policies that have ensured devolved governments are working. Among these, is the allocation of 40% of the national revenue to county governments against the mandatory fifteen per cent recommend by constitution. According to a recent survey, Kenyans are happy and supportive of the devolved county governments. 74% and 69% of men and women, respectively, are supportive of the devolved governments (*Daily Nation*, September 12, 2014). At the national level, the Jubilee government has embarked on many projects including empowering the youth and improvement of the infrastructure in many parts of the country. These projects, if well managed, could go a long way in nation-building.

A number of innovative projects have been initiated by the Jubilee government, one of them being the *huduma* centres[15], which are a one-stop point for accessing several government services, including national identity cards and driving licence applications. This has eased the difficulties experienced by citizens in accessing basic services, especially on-line. The Jubilee government has also done well in the expansion of transport infrastructure. The Jomo Kenyatta International Airport in Nairobi has been expanded and modernized to a very high standard. Similarly, several small airports have been upgraded so as to serve different parts of the country efficiently. Railway transport is also being improved with the Chinese built

---

[15] *Huduma* is Kiswahili for service. *Huduma* Centres were initiated to provide one-stop service centres for those who need to renew licenses and such.

Standard Gauge Railway between Mombasa and Nairobi that launched services in June 2017. The number of Kenyan roads being tarmacked has also been expanded under an ambitious programme whereby the Jubilee government has seen great improvement in Kenya. The government is reported to have built 896 km of new tarmac roads and upgraded 462 kilometres by May 2017[16].

The implementation of devolved system of government, however, faces many challenges including allegations of corruption, the struggle for power between the senate, the governors and the members of parliament. There is also a struggle and conflicts among some constitutional office holders and ministries. Already, some groups are calling for amendments to the new constitution such as the Okoa Kenya Movement led by Raila Odinga and the Moses Kuria led team[17]. The Jubilee government also encountered serious challenges since its inauguration in 2013. These include the case lodged by Raila Odinga to challenge presidential elections in 2013. CORD gracefully accepted the court's verdict perhaps as an affirmation of faith in the judiciary. Another serious challenge has been the terrorist attacks experienced in the country. In October 2013, a terrorist attack by *Al Shabaab* linked group at the West Gate Mall in Westlands, Nairobi, left over sixty seven people dead (*East African Standard*, 29th October 2013). *Al Shabaab* alleged that their attack was motivated by the need to revenge against the activities of the Kenya Defence Forces in Somalia, where the force went in pursuit of Somali-based militias who had attacked and kidnapped some tourists in Kenya (Lisa De Bode, *Al Jazeera* Media, 4th April, 2015). Similarly, in 2014, terrorists struck at the Kenyan Island of Lamu, killing scores of people, displacing many others, and destroying property worth millions of shillings. The government had to deploy the Kenya Defence Forces to restore normalcy.

Conclusion

From the foregoing analysis and discussion on nationalism and nation-building in post independent Kenya, it emerges that this

---

[16] See *The Star* Newspaper, Saturday, 20th May, 2017

[17] http://www.nation.co.ke/news/politics/-/1064/1853244/-/jx3yl8/-/index.html

process can be traced to colonial period during the decolonization process. Unfortunately, since the unity forged by African elites was mainly geared towards the struggle against colonialism, once political independence was achieved fractures began to appear between different communities particularly due to poor governance. In Kenya, KANU during early independence saw some leaders such as Oginga Odinga leave the party alongside his supporters. This undermined the nation-building process substantially. Similarly, upon the ascendance to the presidency by Daniel Moi, some communities felt sidelined and in return supported the opposition against the government. The politically sponsored ethnic violence witnessed in the Rift Valley Province of Kenya in the 1990s could be understood against this perspective. The Kibaki administration did not escape political division either. At the heart of the differences between the ruling party and the opposition was the neo-patrimonial style of governance whereby those regions and communities supporting those wielding political power seem to benefit from largesse in the form of plum positions in government, lucrative government tenders, and other rewards. Fortunately, the Constitution of Kenya (2010) is an attempt to tackle the ills bedevilling the nation-building process in Kenya. The many ways in which the current government has tried to disregard the rule of law and ignore the constitution, however, dim the hopes of many Kenyans whose faith in the constitution continue to dwindle.

Chapter 7

The International Criminal Court and the Nation-Building Project in Kenya

Albert Okinda and Susan Waiyego Mwangi

Introduction

A range of political, judicial and other expert bodies have been appointed to check states' protection of human rights, so that it is no longer difficult to assess the actual human rights situation in all countries of the world. As a rule, treaties under international law are concluded among states and contain mutual rights and duties that are binding under international law, and are overseen by the states parties themselves as a matter of principle. This generally also holds true for human rights treaties, although the beneficiaries in this case are not states but individuals. Governments are not only responsible for ensuring those human rights are respected and ensured on their sovereign territory, but that other state parties do this as well through appropriate monitoring measures. For this purpose, a permanent International Criminal Court (ICC) was set up in The Hague, but in its dispensation of duties, the court has been accused of bias against Africa.

The International Criminal Court in historical context

The International Criminal Court (ICC) is a permanent judicial body established by the Rome Statute of the International Criminal Court (1998) to prosecute and adjudicate individuals accused of genocide, war crimes, and crimes against humanity. On July 1, 2002, after sixty countries ratified the agreement, the Court began its sittings. The ICC is headquartered in The Hague, Netherlands. It was established as a court of last resort to prosecute the most heinous offenses in cases where national courts fail to act (Lee, 2000). Unlike the International Court of Justice (ICJ), which hears disputes between states, the ICC handles prosecution of individuals. The court's jurisdiction extends to offenses that occurred after July 1, 2002, that were committed either in a state that has ratified the agreements or by a national of such a state. Although the Rome Statute was widely praised with some 140 countries signing the agreement by the time it entered into force, few countries in the Middle East and Asia joined (Broomhall, 2004). By 2002, the United States, China, and Russia had declined to join, and the United States had threatened to withdraw its troops from the United Nations (UN) peacekeeping forces unless its citizens, both military and civilian, were exempted from prosecution by the ICC. However, within five years of its first sitting, over 100 countries had ratified the treaty establishing the ICC. All member states are represented in the Assembly of State Parties, which oversees the ICC's activities. The first hearing of the ICC was held in 2006 to decide whether charges should be brought against Thomas Lubanga from the DRC, who had been accused of recruiting child soldiers when he was a warlord (Cassese, 2010).

The "Road to Rome" was a long and often contentious one. The court's history can be traced to the 19th Century when Gustav Moynier, one of the International Committee of Red Cross founders, proposed a permanent court in response to the crimes of the Franco-Prussian War (Schiff, 2005). The next serious call for the establishment of the ICC came after 1st World War, with the Treaty of Versailles. Framers of the treaty envisaged an *ad hoc* international court to try the Kaiser and German war criminals. Then after the 2nd World War, the Allies established the Nuremberg and Tokyo Tribunals to try the Axis War criminals. On reflecting on the Holocaust that was one of the main features of the war, the world cried: "Never Again" (Broomhall, 2004). The call for the establishment of an international criminal court to try individuals for the most heinous crimes resonated throughout the world. Many thought that with the founding of the United Nations, the world was closer to creating a permanent international criminal court. Yet more than fifty years would pass before the leaders of the world met to prepare a treaty that created a permanent international criminal court (Schiff, 2005).

The earnest effort towards creation of the ICC began in October 1946, when an international congress met in Paris and called for the adoption of an international criminal code prohibiting crimes against humanity amid calls for prompt establishment of an international criminal court. This meeting came soon after the Nuremberg Trials that put the Nazi leadership on their defence after the 2nd World War. In December 1948, the UN General Assembly adopted the Convention on the Prevention and Punishment of the Crime of Genocide and, among other things, asked the International Law Commission to study the possibility of establishing an international criminal court (Cassese, 2010).

The end of the Cold War in 1989 made the idea of establishing a permanent international criminal court more viable. Wars in Croatia and Bosnia between 1991 and 1992, which included violations of the Genocide and Geneva conventions, led the United Nations Security Council to establish a temporary *ad hoc* tribunal for the former Yugoslavia in 1993 and strengthened the discussions for a permanent court (Broomhall, 2004). In 1994, the International Law Commission Court submitted a draft statute for an international criminal court to the General Assembly. The war in Rwanda in 1994 led the United Nations Security Council to establish a second *ad hoc* tribunal for Rwanda called International Criminal Tribunal for Rwanda. In the same year, the General Assembly established an *ad hoc* committee on the international criminal court to review the draft statute.

The processes of establishing a permanent international criminal court culminated in the signing of the Rome Statute in 1998 by a significant number of countries. Between June 15 and July 17, 1998, a total of 160 countries participated in the United Nations diplomatic conference of Plenipotentiaries on the establishment of an international criminal court in Rome, Italy. In July 1998, member states overwhelmingly voted in favour of the Rome Statute of the international criminal court, creating the treaty establishing the first permanent international criminal court capable of trying individuals accused of crimes against humanity, genocide, and war crimes. Senegal became the first state party to ratify the Rome Statute in February 2, 1999 (Lee, 2000). In 2002 the treaty entered into force, becoming binding for all countries to have acceded or ratified to the statute and for whom it had entered into force by July 1, 2002. The Court effectively began its sitting from this date (Schabas, 2004).

The International Criminal Court and nation- building in Africa

Following the referral of Kenyan cases to the ICC, there was debate about the relationship between the international criminal court and Africa. Much of the debate was about whether the ICC unfairly targets Africans. This led to a call by the African Union (AU) for the thirty-four members of the AU to withdraw their membership from the ICC. This was always advanced by the argument that African states are independent and sovereign and can handle their cases independently. Since most cases at the ICC involve Africans, does it mean that the court targets Africans?

The nexus between ICC and nation-building in Africa could be understood under the rubric of criticism that has been raised against the court. Despite the noble cause for which the Court was created, it has been perceived by African leadership to be biased. This is because out of the nine countries the Court has opened investigations about and prosecution of, seven are from Africa – including Kenya, Democratic Republic of Congo, Sudan, and Central African Republic. Therefore, the Court was accused of selectively investigating and prosecuting crimes against humanity committed by the individuals from Africa, despite the common knowledge that there are crimes committed against humanity in other parts of the world, such as Iraq (Glasius, 2006). Nevertheless, does this mean that the investigations of the court in Africa did not have a basis? The biases of the ICC as perceived by some African scholars and political leaders, led to calls by a section of African leadership for African states to withdraw from the Court.

Subsequently, during the October 2013 African Union Assembly that was mainly dedicated to Africa's relationship with the ICC, the African leadership raised many concerns about the court. The then Ethiopian Foreign Minister Tedros Adhanom Ghebreyesus noted, "[f]ar from promoting justice and reconciliation. The Court has transformed itself into a political instrument targeting Africa and Africans. This unfair and unjust treatment is totally unacceptable" (Hickey, 2013). This captured the African political leaderships' feeling towards the Court; however, it also highlighted the failure by the Court of focusing more on prosecution than on also putting mechanism for reconciliations. This created a challenge for nation-building for countries whose leadership was facing charges of crimes against humanity. A case in point is the DRC, which had many leaders facing charges of crimes against humanity in the ICC, including Thomas Lubanga, Bosco Ntaganda, Mathieu Ngudjolo Chui, Sylvestre Mudacumura, and Callixte Mbarushimana. Despite these leaders being indicted and some having been arrested, not much has changed and the challenges of nation-building continue to bedevil the country.

Libya could be the most archetypal case to show that the ICC is a challenge to nation-building and supporting case for African scholars and leadership against the ICC. Knoops (2012) argues that the referral of cases involving Colonel Muammar Gaddafi and his sons Safi al-Islam and Abdullah Senussi to the ICC was more political than fact based. Knoops (2012) presents the dynamics and intrigues leading to the referral of the cases, with possible outcomes. However, he notes that the referral of the cases to the ICC was on flimsy grounds, made in order to provide a leeway for overthrowing of Gaddafi for geopolitical considerations. The decision to launch an ICC investigation was made on 26 February 2011 and the arrest warrants were filed on 16 May 2011. This timeframe of merely three months could not possibly be enough to investigate crimes against humanity, unless there was compelling evidence already available to the prosecutor. Therefore, the ICC proceedings were misused to justify a regime change, rather than human rights protection. Hence, the ICC became a means to an end. Similarly, Charles Ble Goude and the former Ivory Coast President Laurent Gbagbo are on trial at The Hague for alleged crimes against humanity. The Gbagbo case is perceived to be associated with fact that he was considered to be a threat to the Western interests, specifically French.

Between 2013 and 2016, more African countries have threated to pull out of the ICC, with some having already initiated the process. Therefore, the ICC debate has become a threat to nation-building in many African countries. In South Africa the court reversed an earlier decision by government to pull out of the ICC, while Burundi has made a formal request to pull out from the court. Jacob Zuma's government, faced with charges in a South African court of failing to arrest President Omar al Bashir (indicted for war crimes in Sudan) of Sudan during 2015 African Union Summit, had chosen to pull out of the ICC. The South African case and, as we shall see later with Kenya, typifies cases of personalisation of the state. The personalisation of the state by African leaders could be the problem rather than the ICC itself. Neopatrimonialism of African state has created a situation in which the objectives of the state and those of the leadership are indistinguishable. Therefore, the state interest is a reflection of the regime in power and the interests of the state are intertwined with that of the ruler. As a result, the challenges to nation-building emerge within the confines of the state, which is neopatrimonialism. To interrogate the implication of personalisation to nation-building in regards to the ICC, we look at Kenya's case.

The ICC and nation- building in Kenya

The 2007/2008 post-election violence was just culmination of long history of the challenges of nation- building since independence in 1963. Since the reintroduction of multi-party politics in 1990s, violence had become integral part of electioneering process (Waki Commission Report, 2008). Nation-building remained conjured in neopatrimonial state. This particular nature of the African state, characterised by the lack of separation between the public and the private sphere, is found as fundamentally inhibiting state capability in Africa.

The 2007/2008 post-election violence epitomised the challenge of nation-building. It is only under the umbrella of African Union (AU) that the Panel of Eminent African Persons, chaired by former UN Secretary-General Kofi Annan mediated for peace. As part of the mediation, a Commission of Inquiry into Post-Election Violence (CIPEV) was set up, headed by former Judge Philip Waki to look into the facts and circumstances of the 2007 post-election violence. The Commission suggested to the government to create a Special Tribunal to prosecute those responsible. Taking considerations of the prevalence of political impunity, the Commission recommended that upon failure by the government to establish the special tribunal, the sealed envelope containing the names of those who were allegedly responsible for the violence be handed over to Kofi Annan for submission to the ICC for investigation and prosecution (International Crisis Group, 2012; Wanyeki, 2012). Therefore, upon failure by the Grand Coalition Government to establish the special tribunal despite two attempts by the national assembly that flopped, the list was handed over to the ICC. The Grand Coalition Government was the outcome of Koffi Annan lead team of negotiation. It was formed through negotiations between Raila Odinga and Mwai Kibaki following the 2007/2008 political crisis (Amadi, 2009). The failure to establish a local tribunal was presumably driven by the assumption that the process would take longer and more drawn out (International Crisis Group, 2012). The inclination for the court could also have been underscored by the inept nature of local judicial system; therefore, no special tribunal could be trusted to deal independently and impartially with the post-elections violence (Wanyeki, 2012). Therefore, any prospect of local tribunal was destroyed under the slogan "don't be vague, go to Hague" (Wanyeki, 2012).

However, upon revelations of the six names of the suspects by the then ICC prosecutor Louis Moreno-Ocampo on 15 December 2010, the same legislators who had derailed attempts to establish local tribunal accused the court of selective trial (International Crisis Group, 2012). This adulterated the fetish argument of the Hague process taking long and drawn out. The six suspects that were indicted by the court were Uhuru Kenyatta (later president) William Samoei Ruto (his deputy president), Mohamed Hussein Ali, Henry Kiprono Kosgey, Joshua Arap Sang, and Francis Kirimi Muthaura (Bjork & Goebertus, 2011). At the time of their indictment, they (except Sang) held prominent positions in public and private sectors. For example, Uhuru, Ruto and Kosgey were government ministers; Ali was the Commissioner for the Kenya Police, Sang' was a radio journalist, while Mathaura was the Chairman of the National Security Advisory Committee (ibid).

The swiftness with which the court acted was to have political implications, which impacted on nation-building. This helped redefine the Coalition Government of President Mwai Kibaki and Prime Minister Raila Odinga. The government engaged in shuttle diplomacy in an attempt to gain the African Union's (AU) support for its non-cooperation with the ICC (Wanyeki, 2012). Nonetheless, the government also tried to have the cases brought back and tried in the local courts following the enactment of the new constitutions in 2010 that codified most of the reforms. These only revealed government's obsession with securing freedom of the suspects and not securing justice for the victims thus, it eroded government credibility. This was also carried out in the pretext to promote nation-building and prevent any prospect of violence during the 2013 election.

Therefore, in the run up to 2013 General Elections, the ICC cases helped define political alliances. Uhuru Kenyatta and his co-accused formed the Jubilee Alliance. It is worthwhile noting that in 2007 election the two were in opposing camps. Kenyatta was in KANU but supported Mwai Kibaki of Party of National Unity (PNU) and Ruto was a member of the Orange Democratic Movement (ODM). Therefore, in the run up to the 2013 elections, they "came together in the name of bringing peace between their Kikuyu and Kalenjin communities following the ICC's confirmation of charges against them" (Lynch & Zgonec-Rozej, 2013: 9). However, was this fostering nation-building, where were the other tribes? Does it mean that during the post-election violence, it was the only Kikuyus and Kalenjins who were affected? Nonetheless, the alliance helped bring the two communities together politically, even though this has not changed the inter-communal narratives of injustice, mistrust, and stereotypes at the local levels, which remain a great challenge to nation-building (Lynch & Zgonec-Rozej, 2013).

The ICC cases engendered the 2013 elections to a perceived plebiscite on the ICC. Those who wanted to vote for the Coalition for Reforms and Democracy (CORD) led by Raila Odinga were perceived by their critics to be in support of the ICC, while those who voted for The National Alliance were perceived to be against the court. This was partly shaped by fetish and unfounded claim that the court's intervention was a political gambit by Odinga and his purported 'Western allies' to ensure the electoral victory of CORD (Lynch & Zgonec-Rozej, 2013).

This engendered tension between Odinga's ethnic community, the Luo, on the one hand, and Uhuru's the Kikuyu and Ruto's Kalenjin communities, respectively. As a result, the members of The

National Alliance (predominantly Kikuyu and Kalenjin communities) perceived the ICC to be ethnically biased for not having indicted Odinga (Luo). This, according to Hodgins (2015), lent dubious credence to claims that Odinga was ostensibly supporting the ICC process as a political means to win the election. To this end, a popular song dubbed 'Hague Bound' depicted Kenyatta as being forcefully pushed to The Hague by an uncircumcised man (presumably Odinga) (Branch, 2012 as quoted in Hodgins, 2015). This song was eventually banned from being played on the radio on the grounds that it promoted negative ethnicity and could instigate violence. However, it did not dispel the popular belief among the Kikuyu and the Kalenjins that Odinga was using the court to stop the Kikuyu and Kalenjins from ascending to power (Hodgins, 2015). According to Mueller (2014: 35), demonizing the opponents and the ICC became a way of solidifying ethnic polarization, which turned the 2013 election into another zero sum ethnic contests. Through this, the cases against Kenyatta, Ruto, and Sang were seen as indictment against the two communities, which typifies personalization of the community rather than individual legal and political accountability. Therefore, the election was a manifestation of "'exclusionary ethnicity': voting against the other, in part out of fear, more than for one's own" (Mueller, 2014). This was even reflected following the 2013.

Therefore, following the 2013 election that brought to power President Kenyatta and his deputy, Ruto, personalisation of the state became even more entrenched. This created a situation, which the objectives of the state and those of the leadership became indistinguishable in regards to the ICC. The president and his deputy, rather than facing the ICC trial as individuals, dragged the state and communities with them. To the presidency nation-building is supposed to be forged around them and the two communities that they hailed from. Beyond this, nation-building does not exist and that which exists is negative ethnicity. Therefore, how can nation-building be promoted in the guise of political alliance between two ethnic communities? Where are the other ethnic groups? Despite these shortfalls, the importance of the court in deterring possible election violence in 2013 cannot be underestimated.

As stated in the Rome Statute, one objective of the court is to deter future war crimes. The court is considered as deterrence for commission of genocide, crimes against humanity, and war crimes in the future. Punishment of convicted individuals with criminal responsibility at the court is considered as an effective deterrence against future acts of war crimes, genocide, and crimes against humanity and potential offenders (Schabas, 2004). One could possibly argue that the ICC acted as deterrence to election violence in 2013 elections in Kenya. However, this should not be exclusively applied to other countries. Nonetheless, in Kenya it increased the powers and prominence of the accused (Block, 2014). As a result, the president and his deputy used their political victory to gain more delays and other concessions from the court (Mueller, 2014). The court, however, failed to handle the Kenyan case following the acquittal of President Uhuru Kenyatta, his deputy William Ruto, and radio journalist Sang in 2016. The three were acquitted due to alleged lack of sufficient evidence. Despite this, there were allegations of witness tampering, intimidation, bribing, and even killing of by the suspects (Mueller, 2014). Therefore, this begs the question whether the court should have detained the suspects during the trial to avoid evidence tampering. In retrospect, the call by African leadership for mass withdrawal of African states from the Rome Statute is uncalled for. However, the recent sentencing of former Chadian President Hisene Habre has shown that African solution can work. African Union backed court sentenced the former Chadian president to life imprisonment for crimes against humanity during his leadership (1982-1990). Despite this success, there is need for political will among the African leaders to prosecute perpetrators of crimes against human rights.

Conclusion

The institution of the ICC could have been a good course to deal with crimes committed against humanity, but it has failed in its mandate due to selective justice, which is specifically perceived to be targeting the third world countries. Despite the fact some of the leaders in developed countries have committed more heinous crimes, no charges have been brought against them even if they are not party the Rome statute. For example, the 2003, intervention of the United States President George Bush in Iraq which lead to heinous crimes against humanity. Nonetheless, there is growing dissent against the court among the third world leadership on what is perceived to be western interference with the courts' operations. However, the court was established as the last resort for trial of crimes against humanity, but this has not been the case for some cases such as that of Gbagbo. The prospect of the ICC addressing crimes against humanity in Africa is very little due to lack of credibility. However, the solution for addressing the crimes against humanity is embedded in "African problems, African solutions" and not much publicized predatory imperialist driven solutions. The concept of "African problems, African solutions" should be driven by African Union, which at the same time should promote good governance, which is key to nation-building.

Chapter 8

The Marginalized, Forgotten and Revived Political Actors in Kenya's Nation-building

Zarina Patel and Gordon Omenya

Introduction

Over time, (formerly) colonised people struggled, and the Kenyan masses continue to struggle, valiantly and courageously with self-sacrifice and determination; to attain social justice and a democracy that works for all, as opposed to one that works only for the minority elite. However, historical revisionism is equally appealing to state and non-state actors during periods of intense socio-political change, especially following civil conflict, when the need for unification is paramount. There has been an upsurge in public memorialisation and debate about the liberation movement in Kenya. This has been accompanied by increasing calls for 'true' history to be written. Former freedom fighters including Gitu wa Kahengeri have persuaded the state to support a project on rewriting Kenya history, which links to efforts to commemorate heroes and broaden official definitions of heroism to include a wide range of ethnic communities and African leaders from different periods of anti-colonial resistance. These themes are reflected in two new history exhibitions developed by National Museums of Kenya (NMK), and in the local media, which has done more to popularise these histories and commemorative initiatives than any scholarly texts (Hughes, 2011). As far as memorialization and recognition of Kenyans who struggled for independence is concerned, there has been a concerted effort by the state to produce and reproduce certain personalities as the main heroes and liberators of the state at the expense of others who equally sacrificed their life for the state (Fouere and Hughes, 2015). This could be attributed to the fact that the state is the main agent in the memorialisation of political heroes and, as committed as ever to the same nation-building strategy since independence, favours centrality rather than plurality (Fouere & Hughes, 2015). Kenya's South Asian community has been a victim of this skewed history of heroes and heroines in Kenya either by default or by design.

The state, memorialization and recognition of heroes and heroines

In Kenya, the state has also dominated the monumental landscape of commemoration of political heroes, but not without a struggle. Some monuments have become, as Coombes argues for the statue of *Mau Mau* leader Dedan Kimathi in Nairobi city centre, "susceptible to multiple symbolic stagings by competing constituencies" (Coombes, 2011; Larsen, 2011). The Kenya Human Rights Commission (KHRC) has played a leading role in pushing for the commemoration of heroes. The KHRC also promoted the idea that earlier anti-colonial resisters had equally helped to bring about independence and ought to be hailed as liberation heroes alongside *Mau Mau* (Hughes, 2011). It is always the mission of the dominant group to do everything in their power to promote their 'heroes' and to obliterate as far as possible the people's heroes. We, in this chapter, prefer not to have a separate category of 'heroines' for women because that would introduce perceptions of hierarchy and competition. This is because in spite of all the resources and power in the women's' domain, they are fighting a losing battle. The people through their songs and art, their rich oral traditions, and their story telling, have kept alive the memory of their heroes from generation to generation (Vansina, 1961). That is why it is so important for us, the ruled, to research and write our own history, to learn from it and to disseminate it.

Fortunately, Kenya's and Africa's histories are being rewritten from a patriotic perspective. We may not agree with all the debates put forth by scholars on the issue of Kenyan history. Nevertheless, it is important to note that history is not cast on stone and people have their reservations, contestations, and contradictions on what has been put down as part of our history. However, in our opinion, it is only valid when it encompasses the experiences of the majority and confronts the discourse which subjugates and exploits our world today. Suppression, marginalization, and outright distortion of the social context of Kenya's South Asian community was contiguous with the advent of colonial rule. In Kenya, for instance, Indians were demographically populous as compared to the Europeans. This is supported both by the 1948 and 1962 population census as documented by Ominde (1971, see also Ochieng and Maxon 1992). From an administrative point of view, the British East Africa Protectorate was at its beginning a mere extension of the empire of India, which notably imposed the use of the Indian rupee in the new colony of Kenya. An important part of the subordinate civil service in Kenya was therefore made up of staff from India, in particular many Catholic Goans. The British army of occupation was equally constituted of Indian recruits, mostly Sikhs and Muslims from the Punjab (Omenya, 2016). The Indian rupee and Indian laws thus governed the Kenyan society.

The Indian *babu* may have come to East Africa penniless, but his communal networks gave him access to capital. Additionally the Asian, known for thrift and hard work – clearly the Happy Valley set did not stand a chance. It was not only thrift but industry and a shrewd business practice that determined the Asians' success. Whether the item had to be sold at cost or occasionally even below cost was not so important as retaining a satisfied customer (Gregory, 1993). But the major factor which informed their drive for equality and freedom was the colonial experience that the Indians and Africans shared – a unity of purpose which made them a formidable opponent of colonial injustice; and which therefore, became a major target of Britain's divide and rule policy. Class-consciousness became mixed with race consciousness, and labour protests became linked with African nationalism, which cemented Afro-Asian relations towards the struggle for African Independence (Omenya, 2016).

Lamentably, these colonially inspired divisions and categorisations either based on class or race still persist, fifty years after Kenya's independence. This is evident by the fact that it has taken many years for the Kenya government to recognise and honour real Kenya's *wazalendo*[1], not only of South Asian origin but also of other African origin. This has been truly an uphill task, more so for Kenyans of South Asian origin. Although many Kenyan Asians who struggled for our liberation have been forgotten, a road was named

---

[1] *Wazalendo* is a Kiswahili word for patriots, with the singular form, *Mzalendo*

in honour of Pio Gama Pinto who was one of Kenya's most acclaimed patriots through the efforts of the Asian African Heritage Trust. But apart from Desai Road and Pio Gama Pinto Road, no other major roads have been named after a nationally acclaimed South Asian leader. In fact, after independence, most of the roads with Asian names were Africanised. For instance Bazaar Street became known as the Biashara Street, Jeevanjee Avenue was renamed Mfangano Street (*East African Standard*, 3/4/2014). Statues, commemorative plaques, mentions on national days, inclusion in the school curriculum and official history are dreams for another generation.

It took Kenyans fifty years to begin to politically and economically recognise the *Mau Mau* Movement and its armed wing, the Land and Freedom Army, and to address the gross injustices and human rights violations perpetrated against the *Mau Mau* heroes. Almost more than fifty years down the line, the task remains a civil society initiative, with government making token gestures. It was up to very recent that the government decided to put up a task force to come up with a criterion of recognizing our heroes. This task force, in its own discretion also thought it wise to recognise heroines having realized that women also contributed immensely to the liberation struggle. For instance, the family of Dedan Kimathi was only recognised so recently after several eras of living in poverty after the execution of Kimathi himself. Needless to say, the South Asian component is never featured. And yet, while there were those South Asians who fought alongside the British army and many more who sat on the fence, there were those who equally and actively supported the Land and Freedom Army and the struggle for independence. To name just a few: Pio Gama Pinto who sourced for funds from India, ferried arms to the forest fighters and fed the communication channels nationally and internationally. Jaswant Bharaj imparted the skill of making home-made guns to Africans while Amba Patel ran the printing press in Mathare Valley and published the documents of the *Mau Mau* Central Command. Similarly, Yacoob Deen of Karatina supplied food, weapons and medicines to the forest fighters, among Asian players in the struggle.

Mbembe (2001:31) postulates that beginning with the high age of colonialism, "power and authority" were founded on illiberal grounds that systematically shunned decent notions of rights. In the colony, the dominated "had no rights against the state. He/she was bound to the power structure like a slave to the master". The colonial government restricted African political activities to the district level. This restriction, however, laid a better foundation for Afro-Asian political alliance. Asian political activities were conditioned by the consolidation of the new African nationalist interests, including the development of the Kenya African Union. But more important was the fact that the Asian press, centred on the Colonial Printing Works, became the Asians official news agency as well as a focus of African political expression. Indeed, the *Colonial Times* probably played a bigger part than any other newspaper in championing the cause of African independence (Seidenberg, 1996). For instance, among the Asian trade unionists, it was not only Makhan Singh and Pinto who strove for working class solidarity, but also Pranlel Sheth, who worked closely with Makhan Singh and was influential as a journalist as well as a trade unionist. Clearly, a number of Asians supported Africans even against the interest of their own community. The Afro-Asian political alliance and activities were therefore a subversive resistance to colonialism and a means of achieving political freedom (Omenya, 2016). It is, therefore, evident that there was a stark relief of the hybrid and dual characteristics that were most often associated with postcolonial discourses (Jaspal, 2011).

However, the gaping ideological divide in the post-colonial, or more correctly the neo-colonial, government policy, between a people-centred approach and the rule of an elite minority with vested interests, continues to stymie efforts to build a functioning democracy and an all-inclusive history which would generate a Kenyan identity. The South Asian community, being less than 1% of the population and easily identified, is prone to marginalization and discrimination as happened during the 1960s when the government decided not to renew trade licenses for members of the South Asian community. Members of this community were also barred from doing business in certain localities in favour of Africans as a way of enforcing the Africanisation policy. This policy became a source of conflict and tension among Africans and Asians, which it intended to integrate, leading to a situation where Asians became a source of resentment. The more they were resented, the more they became isolated and the more they became isolated the more they were resented (Omenya 2016). Nevertheless, in the rewriting of both the colonial and postcolonial histories, Kenyans are discovering what this minority Asian community has politically and economically contributed to the Kenyan history. This is evident in the life history of Allidina Visram as one of the many forgotten and marginalized South Asian heroes in Kenya.

Celebrating the unsung Kenyan Asian Heroes

Granted, the colonial history recognized Allidina Visram as a highly successful trader and as a compliant partner. However, a much lesser known fact is that Allidina Visram had teamed up with Alibhai Mulla Jeevanjee and others to confront Lord Delamere, Grogan, and the settler crowd, and was the first president of the Nairobi Indian Association founded in 1907, and was committed to the fight for equality of all the people (Patel, 1997). Alibhai Mulla Jeevanjee, maternal grandfather to one of the current co-authors (Zarina Patel), came to East Africa to expand his business, but provoked by settler racism, took on the colonial authorities, turned to politics and demanded equal rights (Patel, 1997). In that struggle, he lost his business empire and vast fortune and died bankrupt in Nairobi in 1935. In 1972, almost a decade after independence, Zarina Patel was appointed by the National Christian Council of Kenya (NCCK) to head a Community and Race Relations Project whose mandate was to try and eradicate racial discrimination seen as a hindrance to development (Gona, 2014). In this project, Zarina Patel argued that discrimination of a group of people in the denial of equal opportunities to that group in some or all spheres of the nation's life was counterproductive because it led inevitably to the inability of that group to make the maximum possible contribution to the process of nation-building (Gona, 2014). The Secretary General of the NCCK then, John Kamau, advised Patel not to refer to her ancestry as Jeevanjee because the latter had the reputation of being a hustler. It was only when Kenya's much revered patriot Jaramogi Oginga Odinga introduced her as Jeevanjee's descendant, that she realised that there was a serious disconnect in our understanding of history.

Jeevanjee was not only the father of South Asian politics in Kenya. By founding the East Africa Indian National Congress (EAINC) in 1914, he brought Kenya's anti-colonial struggle onto the national stage and internationalised it. He, and later the EAINC, raised awareness in London and Bombay, about the colonial injustices being perpetrated in Kenya. All African political organisations, in accordance with colonial law at that time, were ethnically based; but the EAINC was not only nation-wide, but also regional (Patel, 1996). In her biographies of Makhan Singh and Alibhai Mullah Jeevanjee, Patel (1997; 2006) and the biography of Manilal Ambalal Desai (2010), painstakingly chronicles the intriguing history and struggles of the three anti-colonial freedom fighters whose lives and times epitomized the crucial and central role the Asians have played in the political development and multiracialism in Kenya. She traces the post-independence political consolidation of power by the Kenyatta regime, marginalization and political assassinations based on ideological confrontation between capitalism and socialism as a framework of further understanding the genesis of marginalization of Asians and their contribution to the Kenyan state. Asians asserted themselves in the struggle for Kenya's independence through many ways, including participating in trade union activities as unionists, journalist and editors of magazines as well as politicians taking on political issues head on.

One of Jeevanjee's protégés was Manilal Desai, a young law clerk from India who took up the leadership of the East Africa Indian National Congress, and published the *East African Chronicle,* politicised and mobilised Indians and gave voice to their demands for justice and equality. Desai was a close friend of Harry Thuku and printed his broadsheet *Tangazo (Announcement/News)*. It can argued that due to his activities and passion for equality, Desai must have influenced Thuku in the latter's formation of Kenya's first multi-ethnic African political organisation, the East Africa Association in 1921. Desai was an outstanding fighter in his own right, yet the demolition in 1993 of the historical Desai Memorial Hall and Library built to commemorate him, and which had been a meeting place for African nationalists, Asian and African trade unionists in the colonial times, went completely unnoticed by the government (Patel, 2010; Salvadori, 1983). Following the unexpected demise of Desai in 1926,

Jeevanjee brought in Isher Dass whom he had met in London, to fill the vacuum. Dass was a fiery Marxist who accompanied Jomo Kenyatta on his first trip to Europe in 1928, and was a strident voice for African rights in the Legislative Council. It was he who organised the sit-in led by Muindi Mbingu to protest against the decimation of Kamba cattle by the colonial government (Tignor, 1976). Today we have a Muindi Mbingu Street in Nairobi but there is no mention of Dass anywhere. The Asian owned press which printed Sitaram Achariar's *Democrat* paper also printed Kenyatta's *Muigwithania*.[2] The fundamental question that this chapter raises is: why was the EAINC and its patriotic leadership so forgotten?

Hardly any Kenyans have heard about the Ghadr Party or know the names of any Ghadarites who lived in Kenya. *Ghadr* means revolution in the Hindu language – it was a political party formed in 1910 by workers and peasants of the Punjab, with its headquarters in San Francisco, USA. Based on the tenets of the Russian Revolution, Ghadr Party sought to both vanquish colonialism and unshackle the workers. The Ghadr Party had branches all over the world, including East Africa and Ghadarites were active members of the East Africa Indian National Congress and Trade Union Movement. Mombasa was a transit point for Ghadarites travelling to and from India and Moscow. At the start of the 1st World War, the colonial government deported some of the Ghadarites back to India, imprisoned several in Fort Jesus and three Indian fuel contractors in Voi were summarily executed on trumped up charges of collaborating with the German enemy. The Ghadarites are the forerunners of the progressive and left tendencies in East Africa, yet they remain virtually unknown.

Makhan Singh was a Ghadarite. He founded the Trade Union Movement in Kenya and, with Chege Kibachia, Fred Kubai and others, propelled it to become the engine of the *Mau Mau* Movement (Patel, 2006). Makhan Singh, together with Papa Pant and Pio Gama Pinto, had taken the *Mau Mau* oath. In a conversation between Zarina Patel and Achieng Oneko[3], the former freedom fighter told her that Makhan Singh was a *Mau Mau*. For his resolute struggle to uplift the workers and oust the colonialists, he was detained for over eleven

---

[2] Gikuyu term for the reconciler or unifier.
[3] Achieng Oneko is one of the Kenya's Kapenguria six who were detained alongside Jomo Kenyatt on charges that they were *Mau Mau*.

years in the Kenya's North Frontier District (NFD). This was preceded by a four year jail term in India. The experiences with which Makhan Singh came to Kenya enriched and developed the anti-colonial and anti-imperialist struggle in Kenya. He took a principled stand in the struggle for liberation of Kenya. It was this that made the colonial administration determined to take him and his ideas out of circulation by detaining and restricting him for the longest period that anyone in Kenya had suffered at the hands of colonialism. He was highly feared by the colonialists that they detained him before Kenyatta, and released him only after they had arrested Jomo Kenyatta. The aim was to isolate him from his base support – the working class, the trade union, and the national liberation movement (Durrani, 2015).

All these afore-mentioned Kenyans had been close comrades in the anti-colonial struggle, yet at independence in 1963, the relationship began to change drastically. Jomo Kenyatta, the then president of Kenya, turned on his one-time comrades. While the African radicals such as Fred Kubai, Achieng Oneko, Joseph Murumbi, and even Jaramogi Odinga were absorbed into the government, South Asians like Makhan Singh, Pranlal Sheth and Ambu and Lila Patel were excluded and consequently written out of history. The postcolonial Kenya was characterized by intimidation of vocal Asian politicians without any regard to their contribution for the independence of Kenya. Intimidation was a feature of the postcolony in its formal disposition. It is still the practice of the postcolony in its informal dispensation. Africans were simply replicating what whites had done (Omenya, 2015). For instance, on 24th February 1965, Pio Gama Pinto was shot dead in the driveway of his home (Zarina, 2004:22). In August 1966, President Kenyatta himself took up the theme when addressing the KANU branch at Nyali Beach Hotel in Mombasa, by sternly urging the "immigrant communities" to either identify themselves with the aspirations of the people of Kenya, or pack up and leave. Within the same year, Pranlel Sheth alongside other Asians were deported to India (Rattansi, 2004).

In *Unquiet: the Life and Times of Makhan Singh*, Patel (2006) argues that in her visit to the offices of the Central Organisation of Trade Unions (COTU) she saw no sign of the movement's founder,

Makhan Singh. On the contrary, its top officials asserted that it was Tom Mboya who founded the trade union movement which is a distortion of the history of trade unionism in Kenya. It was thus evident that COTU members knew nothing about Makhan Singh and they were not in the least interested in his memorialization as a hero and as a crusader for the rights of the workers. On many occasions, Zarina has been trying to have Park Road in Ngara where Singh lived and where Makhan's house has been gazetted as a national monument by the National Museums of Kenya, renamed in his honour but with no success. This is an issue that brings to limelight the question of true heroes and the criteria that is used to identify Kenya's heroes. It also brings to the limelight the mandate of the taskforce put in place to come up with the criteria of identifying our national heroes.

Ironically, unlike nationalists from the Kenya Asian community, colonial collaborators like Lenana and Karen (Boahen, 1985), have been recognized by naming certain roads under their names. The contribution of Pio Gama Pinto cannot be compared to colonial sympathisers such as Lenana. Pinto, quite literally, gave his life to the citizens of Kenya. He was a socialist, a freedom fighter, a trade unionist and a journalist, fully committed to the liberation of Kenya for the benefit of its people. The country has yet to produce another such icon. Also, some Asian journalists were the national and international voices of the anti-colonial struggle. Manilal Desai, Sitaram Achariar, Dharam Kumar Sharda, Pranlal Sheth, Haroon Ahmed, and Girdhari Lal Vidyarthi – who was the first journalist to be jailed for sedition in Kenya. Vidyarthi's sons (Bhushan, Anil, and Sudhir) today continue to run the Colourprint Press and remain committed to its motto of 'Free, Frank and Fearless' (*The Monitor*, 1993). The press has been raided and firebombed several times (*The Monitor*, 1993). Similarly, their opposition-friendly publications have occasionally been banned or destroyed, with some of its owners such as Anil arrested and tried for sedition. D. K. Sharda's *Daily Chronicle* was incapacitated by the colonial authorities and he himself was hounded out of Kenya as happened to Pranlal Sheth, who was Jaramogi Odinga's right hand man. Sheth would later settle in the United Kingdom where his exemplary contribution to British society was recognised by the Queen, who conferred a Commander of the

Most Excellent Order of the British Empire (CBE) on him. He later died in London in 2003.

There were also Asian lawyers who gave all their best by providing legal services to Africans in the face of much colonial hostility, to defend the *Mau Mau* fighters and the Kapenguria Six (Jomo Kenyatta, Kung'u Karumba, Achieng Oneko, Paul Ngei, Bildad Kaggia, and Fred Kubai) at a time when Argwings Kodhek was Kenya's only African lawyer. Chanan Singh, Saeed Cockar, Achhroo Kapila, Chunilal Madan, Jaswant Singh, and several others did a sterling job (Gona, 2015). To date, Justice Madan remains Kenya's most venerated lawyer for his honesty, his commitment to justice, his incorruptibility and his legal talent. To its credit, the Law Society of Kenya has him on their roll of honour. Although Justice Madan selflessly served this country especially during the reign of Moi when Kenya was under authoritarian one party rule, he too deserves some recognition, which has not been forthcoming. That would be same fate which befell Chanan Singh who was a fearless advocate, a prolific writer, an outstanding journalist and an incorruptible fighter for the independence of Kenya and for justice. He served his country selflessly for over fifty years. He was elected to parliament and was appointed as the Parliamentary Secretary to the Prime Minister, Jomo Kenyatta. Yet he never rose beyond the position of Assistant Minister in Kenya's independent government.

Conclusion

Forgetting our heroes, African, South Asian or European, is not just a historical omission – it leaves the population and succeeding generations without role models to emulate and to give hope. Right now, in our opinion, Kenya is a nation polarised and in despair – we badly need to remember our heroes, follow in their footsteps and mould a better future for our children. Remembering our heroes is a way of learning and appreciating each other and building nationhood. Most importantly, their histories affirm to us that 'there is another way'. In spite of all the negativity, there is hope that the state as a

137

major actor in recognizing her heroes and heroines will deem it fit to change the narrative and identify other Asian personalities such as Makhan Singh, Dr Shabbir, and Kalpana Rawal, who have diligently served this nation in various capacities. This would go along well with the few Asian personalities such as Pio Gama Pinto, Desai, and Makhan Singh whose effort in the liberation struggle have not gone in vain. The WaSwahili say: *Ukweli hauzami, unaelea* (the truth never drowns, it floats). It is for us to rescue it, revive it and share it. In a small way, this chapter tries to do just that.

Chapter 9

The Neglected Terrain in Post-Independence Kenya: Women's Struggle against Political Marginalisation Luo Nyanza

Dorothy Nyakwaka and Mildred Ndeda

Introduction

Women in Kenya constitute a vital national resource whose ideas, creativity and concern for social cohesion can help bring about positive change in society. However, this potential has not been fully exploited anywhere in Kenya and among the Luo community in particular. The marginalisation of women in Kenya and in politics in Luo land cannot be resolved without a clear understanding of its genesis. This chapter examines the vulnerability of Luo women in politics from late colonial times to the present, and demonstrates that a few women went against the culture of marginalisation and actively engaged in politics and decision making. The life histories of two women, Grace Onyango and Grace Ogot, are used as case studies to illustrate women's struggle for inclusion in politics. Significant mention is made regarding the question of the masculinity of husbands of the successful women. These two Luo women struggled against political marginalization. It examines their life histories and experiences as they went against the grain and captured political seats in a locality that is predominantly patriarchal.

Women in Kenya comprise more than half of the population and are actively involved in the economic and social life of the nation. In the traditional society, women's rights were closely matched to their responsibilities in the social, economic and political spheres (Ayot, 1990). Women wielded power in areas regarded as exclusively feminine which also guaranteed them some leverage in the political space. Apart from the feminine domain, there were instances where women became chiefs wielding power over the whole community, for example Chief Mang'ana of Kadem in Migori (Ayot 1990) and

139

Chief Wangu wa Makeri in Murang'a (Mwangi 2004). As Ayot (1990) posits during the colonial period women's power and spheres of influence largely diminish because the colonial administration undermined their traditional base of power. The administrators, who were exclusively male, also governed through the indigenous male institutions, thereby formalising them at the expense of the female equivalents. This marginalization of women's political institutions continued into independent Kenya, despite the fact that women were active participants in the nationalists' movements which led to independence (Ndeda2002). African women did not accept their loss of status passively, as a number of scholars have documented. These authors focus on women's protests against colonial tax, land, agriculture, education and labour policies [Ndeda, 1994; Hay, 2005; Nyakwaka, 1999]. In Kenya the women played an active role in the struggle for independence [Zeleza, 1989; Kanogo, 1987]. The women, like their men, had realised that their problems had to be articulated within the context of colonial domination and the only way to solve these problems once and for all was by fighting for independence.

Women's struggle against political marginalisation in independent Kenya

In most independent African countries, the marginalization of women that began during colonialism continues. Some works have shown that the post-independence state acted primarily as a vehicle for elite male interests, enhancing and extending men's power over women (Parpart & Staudt, 1989; Odim & Strobel, 1999; Kabira *et. al.*, 1993). Nationalism and independence left women unrewarded for participating in the struggle. At independence, women in Kenya were hopeful to join parliament and the cabinet in equal numbers as men, if not more [Gituto & Kabira, 1998]. Unfortunately, this was not to be as the marginalization of women continued in post-independence Kenya. Some authors have analysed women's roles in the state [Tsikata, 1989; Mama, 1995a]. These studies examine the important roles that the few women politicians and their organisations have played in national politics.

Kenya attained self-government from Britain in 1963. The year also witnessed the surfacing of long-simmering issues about ethnicity and gender. In the latter issue the key question was what was and should be the role of women in the new political dispensation. During the second Lancaster House Conference of 1962, Priscilla Abwao, the sole African female delegate, stated that Kenyan women were "not asking for a special position for ourselves" (Abwao, 2002). Their desire was that at independence and after they should "be treated as equal partners in the new society...." (Abwao, 2002). At the 1962 conference, Abwao was representing women who had marginalised in representative politics. Phoebe Asiyo, one of Kenya's outstanding women at independence, also expressed similar sentiments. The inclusion of Abwao and, earlier, Jemimah Gecaga (1958 nomination) were mere political acts of tokenism hardly expected to effectively represent women's gender concerns at that historical moment". (Nzomo. 2003) On attaining independence, Kenya did not change the status of women. (Nasong' & Ayot, 2007)

At independence Women's issues were not integrated into the national agenda. Violence, intimidation, detention, and police harassment constituted the political culture that characterised Kenya's politics during the 1960s and 1970s. Because of this harsh environment, many women kept off elective politics. Relationships of political domination and control developed quickly as men dominated Kenya's political scene and women retreated to the domestic sphere (Nasong'o & Ayot, 2007). They generally did not hold public office, and even the few like Margaret Kenyatta and Jane Kiano who were appointed to head institutions owed their allegiance to the president or his close allies. This is what we call here the feminisation of neo-patrimonial politics. The women remained relegated to the periphery, especially in the realm of politics. The majority only participated as voters, preparation and distribution of food in meetings, leafleting, dancers, and mobilizers during elections (Kabira &Wasamba, 1998). Thus, between 1964 and 1969, there was not a single woman member of parliament in Kenya. In 1964, Ruth Habwe was the first woman in the post-colonial Kenya to challenge a male only parliamentarian system, when she contested one of the three special parliamentary seats vacant at the time. For this act she was suspended. She was ridiculed by party membership for daring to contest the seat and ordered "to go back to the Kitchen and cook for Habwe's children". In November 1969, the first woman Grace Onyango was elected into the National Assembly and one more nominated (name her, because that highlights your argument) to sit in the legislative body along with eleven male nominated members (Waiyego, 2004).

Apart from the exclusion of women in politics, Kenya made no specific reference to women as a target group for development in all her national development plans and other official documents, until in the 1974-1978 Development Plan. It set a new trend in Kenya's development planning by having a bias towards activities which promoted women's integration in development. Women were referred to directly in the plan and subsequent development plans merely repeated and re-emphasized the trend set by it. This plan was influenced the rise in the public awareness of the importance of women's issues in the 1970s. This was partly fostered by the International Women's Decade (1975 – 1985) and the International Women's Conferences (Mexico, Copenhagen, and Nairobi Women's Conferences). Among the most significant issues articulated during the Mexico conference was the concept of women's development that emphasize equality, peace, and development of women (Staudt, 1990). This approach advocated for women's development in education, employment, and empowerment. Education was understood as a prerequisite for improvement in women's status. Access of girls and women to quality formal education was encouraged.

During this period women's representation generally improved slightly. The number of women members of parliament slightly increased. Julia Ojiambo was appointed Assistant Minister for Culture and Social Services 1974-1979. This was the highest office in the government ever held by a woman since independence. Other women members of parliament were Phoebe Asiyo, Winfred Nyiva Mwendwa, Grace Onyango, Eddah Gachukia, Jemima Gecaga, Philomena Chelagat Mutai, and Anarita Karimi. Women's' representation improved slightly between 1974 and 1979. However, the general trend during President Jomo Kenyatta's reign was one of women's marginalisation in political decision making at the local and national levels and, by implication, lack of inclusion of women's issues in the legislative agenda (Nzomo, 1991).

Despite the marginalisation of Kenyan women in general and Luo in particular in the political sphere, women used other vehicles to articulate their issues. Women groups evolved and grew as one of the instruments to fight against social, economic and political inequalities and marginalisation. The women's groups' movements traced their roots back to the traditional society (Ahlberg, 1992). The women were engaged in joint agricultural labour, social welfare activities, recreation and entertainment. In the 1950s, the colonial government initiated *Maendeleo Ya Wanawake Organisation* (MYWO) an organisation that was supposed to improve the lot of women by initiating development programmes that co-existed with the traditional based women groups. The MYWO was a colonial reflection of the view that women should contribute to improving the welfare and well-being of the family. Towards the end of the 1950s MYWO's Jael Mbogo and other pioneer African members began agitating for the "liberation" of MYWO from the minority leadership of British women. These women's efforts resulted in the organisation's first African President, Phoebe Asiyo (1960 – 1962) with Jael Mbogo as Secretary-General. The new leaders initiated an aggressive membership drive to create awareness about the organisation. It also broadened its agenda to include practical problem solving. At independence, MYW remained one of the major women organizations (Kiragu, 2006). However, it faced many challenges as the post-colonial state did not emphasize the development potential of women's self-help groups. Consequently, finances to these groups were cut down. Thus, most of the MYWO leaders joined the civil service as community development officers. They were involved in diverse community projects such as building of social halls and rural access roads (Ndeda, 2002).

In 1965, the government established the Kenya National Council of Women, a body which individual national women's organisations could affiliate to provide for co-ordination and co-operation (Ndeda, 2002). This was in recognition of the fact that women could and had played a very important role in development. That jointly, with their male counterparts, women had spearheaded the self-help movement and other endeavours. Indeed, experience had also shown that there

143

were more women involved in the projects than men. The government was began to realise that it was not possible to separate the role of women from men in the processes of development given that women's roles were vital to the nation as the welfare of the family depended on them. Therefore, to strengthen the family unit, the officers of the Department of Community Development worked with MYWO.

MYWO was the spring board for many women leaders in the public domain, in Kenya in general and in Luo Nyanza in particular. As Mathenge (2004) puts it, "few women would have made it to parliament and the cabinet without passing through M.Y.W.O". These include the first President of MYWO Phoebe Asiyo, who was elected as MP for Karachuonyo in 1974. MYWO's second President Jael Mbogo, contested as a candidate in 1969 but lost narrowly to Mwai Kibaki in Nairobi. Her narrow defeat made Kibaki to move to his native constituency, Othaya, in Central Province for the 1974 General Elections. The first women to be elected in Kenya in 1967 Grace Onyango had also worked closely with MYWO at the grassroots level before joining politics. The contribution of the MYWO in this respect is important since women need to be at strategic decision making tables where national economic policies are charted and allocation of budgets are made(Nzomo, n.d.). Thus because of their political significance, women groups under the umbrella of MYWO provide an important base for political support for women members of parliament.

Jane Kiano, the President of MYO after Phoebe Asiyo, is also credited for having mobilized women to contribute money that was used to construct the nine-floor Maendeleo House in Nairobi. The building became the MYWO's headquarters and a source of rental income for the organisation. MYWO was important as the sole vehicle for mobilizing Kenyan women nationally in the immediate post-independence period. The organisation encouraged and helped the members to organize development activities. It also provided women who aspired to leadership roles with a space to exercise those aspirations outside parliament. Apart from MYWO, other bodies that were involved in organising women include: Young Women Christian Association (YWCA), Anglican Mothers Union, Girl Guides, and Seventh Day Adventist Church.

Apart from political involvement and the women's movement, education also created increased awareness among women of their needs and the need to participate in various spheres of the political, economic, and social sectors of the state. With education, a few Luo women rose to prominence in the government offices, parastatals and in the private sector. For example, there were the Luo women politicians, Grace Onyango, Phoebe Asiyo and Grace Ogot. Other outstanding women included Asenath Odaga (writer and publisher), Damaris Ayodo) chairperson of the National Council of Women of Kenya and official of *Maendeleo ya Wanawake* Organisation) Joyce Aluoch (a Judge of the International Criminal Court in The Hague. lawyer and judge of the High Court of Kenya), First Chairperson of the Committee of African Union Experts on the Rights and Welfare of the Child and Vice-Chairperson of the United Nations Committee on the Rights of the Child from 2003 to 2009) Pamela Mboya (Diplomat), Pamela Kola (Respected author and educationist), Francesca Mboya Otete (Public Service Commissioner) and Achola Pala (Anthropologist and former U.N. executive scholar) to mention but just a few. The educated women also encouraged those who were illiterate to enrol in adult literacy classes so as to empower themselves. Education was seen as the tool women needed for their empowerment, through it they would increase their awareness regarding the running of the government, their rights in politics, and their rights as women. Education would provide the confidence and skills needed for women to participate actively in politics and in decision_making structures of the nation. In the late 1980s and early 1990s Kenyan women were also active participants in the struggles for pluralism, and the second liberation of their country (Gumboznsvanda, 2003). One of the few women who emerged as a strong activist for change was Jael Mbogo. She advocated for the reform of the electoral laws to deal with political violence against women (Wajibu, 2009). She captured the barriers and challenges that women politicians faced. Throughout the 1990s, political violence and gender discrimination constituted women's greatest hindrance to political engagement.

The restoration of the multi-party political system in Kenya in 1991, to an extent created some political space for civil society groups, including women's groups to participate actively in the democratic struggles for Kenya's second liberation. This period also saw the formation of new gender based lobby groups such as The National Commission on the Status of Women, the League of Kenya Women Voters, the Anti-Rape Organization, the Kenya Medical Women's Association, the Kenya Business and Professional Women's Club, the Coalition on Violence Against Women, The Kenya Women Finance Trust, Association of African Women for Research and Development, the Kenya Women Political Caucus, and the Forum for African Women Education(Choti, 2005) All these women's organizations were a testimony of the active engagement of Kenyan women and their desire to bring about democratic space within their society. Moreover, the new lobby groups were much more political in their orientation and more assertive, innovative, and willing to take political risks in the pursuit of women's agenda. They vigorously lobbied the political parties to integrate gender issues in their democratic agenda.

In the 1992 preparatory period for the multiparty elections in Kenya a high premium was placed on political empowerment as a means of achieving the goals associated with the advancement of the status of women (Nzomo, 1994). Thus from January 1992, women's lobby groups and organizations embarked on a mobilizing and strategizing campaign to ensure that the December 1992 general elections women candidates would win the maximum number of parliamentary and civic seats. They tried to sensitize and conscientise women about the fact that they were the majority of voters and the power and merit of voting for women. However, Kenya's multi-party politics was characterised by ethnicity making party affiliation tribal. Most of the parties were formed on tribal lines and many Kenyans approached voting as tribal solidarity groups, voting in blocks for the candidates of their party irrespective of their leadership abilities (Choti, 2005). This meant that each tribe voted for its candidates. Most of the women candidates had hoped that gender block voting would beat tribal block voting but the result was the reverse (Weru, 1995). However, multi-party elections in December 1992 reflected the enormous efforts of the women's movement to empower female votes and candidates. This election expounded the fact that state power was male power and women continued to be marginalized despite their effort. The few women in parliament were assertive.

Among the Luo, only Phoebe Asiyo made it as the MP for Karachuonyo, regaining the seat she had lost in 1988. Asiyo exhibited rare acumen and art in parliamentary business, the gender platform became one of her main reference points (Osaaji, 2006). Among the many motions she brought to the house, the most outstanding one was the Affirmative Action Motion, popularly called the Asiyo Motion of 1997. Even though the Motion was shot down by the male-dominated house, it left a major imprint on the Kenyan legislative landscape.

The second multi-party elections were held in 1997 and women were more prepared than they had been in 1992. During these elections, two women, Charity Ngilu and Wangari Maathai also joined the crowded field of fifteen presidential candidates. Their candidature challenged age old stereotypes against women. It was also a sign that women were targeting the highest seat in the country. Women were more visible during the 1997 elections. The women mostly belonged to KANU, the ruling party at the time. They also joined the opposition parties such as the National Democratic Party of Kenya (NDP), Ford Asili, Ford Kenya, the Social Democratic Party, and the Democratic Party. In the 1997 elections only four women were elected to the 200 member house. However, five more women were nominated to parliament to represent various interests, including of other women. This was only 4.0% representation, a far cry from the projected target of 30% (Choti, 2005). The majority of women voters at grassroots level were still susceptible to manipulation and this undermined their free choice in the electoral processes. The dismal performance of the women was blamed on party affiliation, culture, religion, education, and financial resources.

The 2002 elections in Kenya were significant in the sense that they were the first transitional elections. The women were not left out in the realignments, behind the scenes, women organisations were negotiating with parties to gain entry in to the campaign arena. Their main goal was to secure more parliamentary and civic seats for women. However, women's issues were given lip service by most of the parties; they did not link the fact that women constituted the majority of voters and their own policies. In 2002, although a total of 130 women had declared their interest in running for parliamentary seats, only forty-four, or four percent, were nominated to parliament after elections. No political party had an affirmative action policy on women candidates during the party nominations. Ida Odinga, then the chairperson of the League of Kenya Women Voters, points out that the reasons women failed badly in elective politics was due to their failure to penetrate the parties (Godia, 2007). The same sentiments were echoed by the then Chairperson of Kenya Women's Political Caucus, Phoebe Asiyo (Ombuor, 7). In the 2002 elections, the presidential succession debate further complicated matters for women. This is when women were sacrificed in the name of an elaborate succession battle. However, apart from nomination, women also faced other challenges, which included resources such as time and money, hostility, harassment, violence, bribery, and even rape (Oywa & Wangui, 2007).

The participation of women in politics and public affairs has been complicated by the long-standing cultural beliefs, held by men and women alike, that these roles are the men's preserve. The public and domestic sector divide that was preached by the colonialists has also been used in post-colonial times to frustrate the efforts of women aspiring to make a mark in politics (AWC, 2003) Thus, it was because of the challenges and barriers faced by women that led to their marginalization in the multi-party politics.

Although women's performance in parliamentary electoral politics in the first decade of independence was marginal, there has been a gradual increase in the number of women MPs. The only exception to this trend was in 1997 when the women's performance in electoral politics dropped despite the fielding of two women presidential candidates (Nzomo, 2003). The number of women in leadership positions has been on the rise. The number of women leaders has risen again during the multi-party era due to more women presenting themselves for elective positions, increased lobbying for the inclusion of women in decision-making (including advocacy for quotas and affirmative action), and the diminishing influence of oppressive cultural norms against women. More women are better educated and qualify for senior positions that were previously dominated by men. In addition, many women who are seeking leadership positions earn their own money and possess property, which has further reduced their dependence on men.

There has also been very low female representation in decision-making positions within government sectors / departments, (Njenga, 2007). In the Rainbow Coalition (NARC) government, the number of female MPs at least increased to eighteen out of the 222 members of parliament. However, this still fell short of the United Nations target of achieving 30% representation of women in politics and the Beijing Platform for Action (the Fourth World Conference for Women in 1995). The gender imbalance in Kenya's political playing field has widened so much, since the male political ideology continues to define the standards of evaluation of women's political performance and participation.

In the first General Election under the Constitution of Kenya (2010), it seemed that the space could be opened for an increased number of women to vie yet in the end, of the 290 MPs, only sixteen women were elected. Granted, the constitution provides for 47 women representatives from the counties. But even with nominations from the main political parties expected to add to their numbers, the anticipated sixty-eight women in the 349-member Lower House are still far short of the 117 needed to satisfy the constitutional requirement That said, women's performance in the recent polls cannot be discounted, given that it accounts for some 25% of the sixty-women women who have been elected to parliament since 1963 (Kweyu, 2013). The 11th parliament, therefore, brings on board the largest number of women to have ever sat in the house. The vast western region of the country elected just six of the sixteen women MPs — four of them from Rift Valley. It raises serious questions about why, almost thirty years after Kenya hosted the Third UN Conference on Women, and nearly two decades after the famed Beijing Conference, Kenya continues to perform so poorly in the all-important area of women in political leadership. Equally worrying is that no woman was elected to the high-profile positions of governor and senator. This chapter focuses on two Luo women who struggled against political marginalization. It examines their life histories and experiences as they went against the grain and captured political seats in a locality that is predominantly patriarchal.

Grace Onyango: the first Luo female mayor and Member of Parliament

Grace Onyango was born in 1927 at Gobei in the Sakwa in present day Siaya County. The second of nine children, she attended local primary schools in Sakwa before joining Ng'iya Girls Secondary School, and later training as a teacher at Vihiga Teachers Training College. Between 1951 and 1964 Onyango served as the Principal of Ng'iya Women's Teachers' Training College, a Girl Guide Assistant Commission in Kisumu District, and as the Chair of the Kisumu Branch of the Child Welfare Society. Grace Onyango was married to Onyango Baridi, a teacher who later joined the Kenya News Agency as a journalist, and they had six children. Though successful as a teacher, Onyango was constantly drawn to community service, and soon entered electoral politics. Onyango became the first East African woman to serve as a Councillor (1964), Mayor (1965), official of the Luo Union of East Africa (1969), Member of Parliament for Kisumu Town (1969) and temporary speaker of the House.

The political career of Onyango started her political career started in Kisumu, located on the shores of Lake Victoria. The Kisumu Municipal Council was charged with the management of the town's public services that entailed the management and provision of public housing, municipal roads and drainage systems, healthcare facilities, remand prisons, day-care facilities, educational institutions, the municipal dairy, entertainment facilities, and town cleanliness and hygiene, among other functions. These were the services Onyango was to manage as the Mayor of the Town. Long before her 1964 election to the Kisumu Municipal Council as a councillor, Onyango was aware of the gender imbalance in her environment. Thus, she and other local women formed the Gill Women Group under the leadership of a Mrs. Shabir. The group served as a meeting place and problem-solving arena for its members. At this time, Onyango recalls that "there was no woman in the Municipal Council, not even a sweeper!" (Baraka, 2002). Women found the *status quo* untenable and organised a demonstration in the streets of Kisumu to agitate for representation in the council. According to Onyango, "many men" opposed the women's nomination and argued that the council was no place for women. Onyango explained to journalist Karama Baraka that the opposition against their nomination was so intense that one of the women, Marsella Osir, opted to step down from the race, leaving Onyango to battle with the other nominees.

In 1964, Grace Onyango contested for a council seat alongside three male candidates and emerged the victor in Kaloleni Ward. By 1965, Onyango was not only a councillor, the first woman councillor in East Africa, but also the Chair of the Education Committee in the Municipal Council. Later, she became the Deputy Mayor of the town (DC/KSM/I/20/5, 1964). She was formally elected East African's first female mayor on April 1, 1965. One of Onyango's main achievements as Mayor of Kisumu was in solving the municipality's housing shortage (MCK, 1967). By 1966, the council's housing waiting list had grown to 1,500 and there was concern that 8,000 people living in the peri-urban areas of the municipality and working in the city would not get the houses that they badly needed. In the 1967 Annual Report, the municipality reported a lot of progress in the town and a fair deal of capital work carried out throughout the town. In the same year, the council had succeeded in utilizing a total of $123,412.885 for both low and high cost housing, a sum that was above the$64,954.15 in which the municipality had placed so much confidence in 1964.

The infrastructural is another sector in which Mayor Onyango made major achievements. Other capital works carried out in that year (1967) included roads (constructed on contract or council labour). The provision of adequate and affordable housing was to remain a major struggle not only for Kisumu Municipality, but for all other urban centres in independent Kenya. Thus because funding from the central government was not forthcoming, the municipality had to encourage private investment in real estate. Mayor Onyango furthermore had to deal with the politics that came with being at the helm of a municipal council, particularly in the second half of her term (1967-1968). During this era, Kenya's national political scene was focused on the heated Kenya African National Union (KANU) and Kenya Peoples Union (KPU) conflicts. The latter had a socialist political orientation, and was highly critical of the manner in which the KANU government was functioning in the years following independence. KPU was the only opposition party in existence then and therefore the government's only check and balance. Consequently, it found itself on the receiving end of repressive tactics deployed by both KANU and the government. These political conflicts at the national scene seeped into the local government structures. In her last years of service at the local government level, Onyango had to constantly mediate between KANU and KPU officials who brought their political battles into Kisumu Municipal Council Hall. During this period, there was a severe reduction in the democratic space, to the disadvantage of the opposition KPU party. The mayor increasingly encountered opposition from Tom Mboya, the then influential Minister for Economic Planning and Development as well as KANU's Secretary General.

Mboya was convinced that Onyango had become a KPU member and he accused her of having bought a KANU membership ticket and then refusing to admit that she had done so. Mboya wondered "Is she KPU or is she KANU?" He further demanded that Onyango should "tell us where she stands and we will know where we (the government party) stand" (Musandu, 2006). Because Onyango was the Mayor of Kisumu Municipality, a major town in the home of the opposition party KPU, the government was concerned about her party position. Yet, Onyango managed to stay on as Mayor to the end of her term in 1968 with a determination to further her political career. On August 26, 1968, she addressed the last Municipal Council Meeting of the year in a speech that both defended her record and left her with the ability to choose between either sides of the political divide. The Mayor said she was pleased with the co-operation shown by councillors and council officials. Therefore, Grace Onyango used her council performance record to take her political career to the national level, a move that saw her easily win a seat as Member of Parliament. It is possible that the mayor became popular not only because of her council duties but also her exemplary political skills that had enabled her to be elected as the mayor for four terms. Onyango was able to serve until the last year of her last term, in 1969, when she walked out of the council undefeated, ready for her next challenge over which she triumphed, winning the Kisumu Town parliamentary election.

In December 1969, Grace Onyango campaigned for and won the parliamentary seat for Kisumu Town with a comfortable majority of 5,500 votes against 2,020 for her nearest rival, Iganje Caleb Seveni. She was re-elected with an increased majority in 1974. Her career as the mayor of the town was the springboard from which she sprang to the next level of politics. By the time Onyango was elected MP, in 1969, women in Uganda and Tanzania had been serving in their national legislatures and governments for a decade. In West Africa, they had been wielding immense political power long before the independence movements of the postwar era. Consequently, it is difficult to escape the feeling that women in Kenya had been politically marginalised. Throughout her terms as MP, Onyango focused on issues that affected the country such as education, labour, industrial developments, health, security, and food security, corruption and nepotism (Republic of Kenya, 1972). At one time during her tenure, Onyango was the Acting Speaker of the National Assembly, showing her leadership capability.

During the 1979 elections, Kisumu Town Constituency attracted a number of aspirants to the seat. Onyango defeated a large field of male and female candidates to come through almost unscathed. The verdict of the voters was a clear mandate in support of Onyango. She garnered 7,793 votes while her closest rival, Mrs. Esther Odundo Owuor, managed 1,732 votes. The only man to register a four digit figure was Nicholas Otieno who polled 1,534. The rest could not manage more than a few hundred votes. The table below shows the results of the landslide victory for Mrs. Onyango.

Kisumu Town Constituency Election Results, 1979 Elections

Candidate	Votes
Onyango H. Akech Grace	7,793
Nicholas Otierio	1,534
Esther Odundo Owuor	942
Mark Makwata Saley	819
Slizaphan Onyancha Ongogi	243
Peter William Amukoa	214
Jackon B.L. Akumu	110

Source: 1979 General Elections Score Card (*The Weekly Review*, November 9, 1979).

With this landslide victory following on two successful terms, Onyango had become one of the longest-serving members of parliament in Luoland. Her victory also gave her a certain measure of seniority among Luo politicians and a vast amount of prestige. Few politicians of her era could claim to have achieved her record of electoral success. In the 1970s, of the sixteen Luo MPs, only a handful could be said to be household names among Kenya political observers. Yet Grace Onyango had made a mark for herself as the first woman elected MP in Kenya; she had become a household name in Kenya. After her career as a Member of Parliament for Kisumu Town, Onyango was appointed as a member of the KANU National Disciplinary Committee in 1983.

In conclusion, from her performance as a female, wife, teacher, principal of a teacher training college, councillor, mayor, and member of parliament, Grace Onyango proved that there is a great deal of scope for Luo women in particular and women in Kenya in general in the political life of their country. Throughout her political career, Onyango was able to overcome the tough challenges that she faced and to excel in her contributions in the parliament.

Grace Emily Akinyi Ogot: the first Luo female Assistant Minister

"I look at womanhood in a wider context. What has always been on my lips is equal opportunities for all" (Ogot, 2006).

Grace Emily Akinyi was born in 1930 in Asembo, Central Nyanza (present day Rarieda Sub-county). She is one of the Luo women's top achievers, having served as an assistant minister. Grace was the child of pioneering Christian parents in Asembo. Her father Joseph Nyandunga was an early convert to the Anglican Church and one of the first few in Asembo to receive colonial education. He later taught at the Church Missionary Society's Ng'iya School. Grace was educated at Maseno Junior School, Ngi'ya Girls School, and Butere Girls High School. She then went to the Mengo Nursing Training Hospital in Uganda in 1949, where she studied until 1953. After Mengo, she went to St. Thomas Hospital in London and the British Hospital for Mothers and Babies, where she qualified as a state midwife, after which she returned to Kenya and worked as a midwifery tutor at Maseno Hospital. Ogot (2012) asserts that the scholarship to Britain made her realize how chained the Kenyan women were. Her staying Britain contributed to her becoming a writer and female politician. Thus she was able to challenge the men in our male-dominated world. In 1959, she married Bethwell Ogot, who later became one of Kenya's best known historian.

Grace Ogot was a leading storywriter in East Africa and Africa. She first came to national prominence as an author. She gives credit for her writing talent to her father, who was a great storyteller and who also encouraged her to go to school, at a time when most girls did not go to school (Ogot, 2012). Her first book, *Year of Sacrifice*, was published in 1961, besides numerous short stories. Other titles include, *The Promised Land, Land without Thunder, A Call at Midnight, The Other Woman, The Island of Tears, The Graduate, The Strange Bride* and two books in Dholuo, *Miaha* and *Simbi Nyaima* (Ogot, 2012).

Grace Ogot points out that all her writings have different messages, but she shows particular concern for the family, which she considers as the nucleus of society and the basis of a stable community. It is on the theme of the family that she addresses a number of gender issues in her books. For example, she focuses on the struggles between women and men, highlighting male brutality towards women, rape, and domestic violence. In most of her works, she advocates for peaceful co-existence along the gender divide for the good of the family and the wider community at large. In *The Graduate,* she offers a comment on Kenyan women's inequality in the political process and intimates how successful they can be given the opportunity to participate. Hence, she believed in equal opportunities for all.

Because of her education and involvement in community service, Ogot found herself serving her people in the political realm. She asserts that it was only after joining politics that she came to realize how women were looked down upon by their counterparts. In 1961, she was a nominated Councillor in Kisumu Town. In 1983, Ogot was for the first time nominated as an MP by the then President, Daniel Arap Moi, thus bringing the number to two Luo-women members of parliament. This was quite an achievement for the Luo women, noting that the total number of women in parliament was a paltry three.

However, two years later, when Gem Member of Parliament, Horace Owiti died, Ogot resigned from her nominated seat to contest for Gem by-election. Ogot made history in Kenya as the first nominated MP to resign from parliament to seek an electoral mandate (Ogot, 2012). Ogot's decision to resign and get an electoral mandate from the people of Gem may have been informed by the limitations that came with being a nominated member of parliament. For instance, a nominated member of parliament could not be appointed to a cabinet post. Ogot had set her eyes on bigger things; she was not content to be just an MP. To some of her critics, Ogot was seen to have resigned because of personal ambition and the desire to be more than just an MP, rather than for better service to the people of Gem.

Her critics from Gem blamed her for denying the people of Gem the chance of having two serving MPs, one nominated and another elected. Ogot aggressively campaigned for two weeks before the actual polls. When the polls were held, Ogot won the elections with 4,198 votes against her nearest rival, Wycliffe Rading Omolo, who polled 3,403 votes (*Weekly Review*, 1985). As a result, there were two elected women MPs both from Luo Nyanza. This was an outstanding achievement for Luo women in the era of single party politics in Kenya. Their success was the success of all Kenyan women whom

156

they represented in parliament. Ogot asserts that she owes her success in politics to the strong support from Gem women who worked out her strategy, conducted a home-to-home campaign on foot, and never asked for any money (Ogot, 2012).

A few months after winning the parliamentary seat for Gem, Ogot was appointed an Assistant Minister for Culture and Social Services (Ogot, 2012), another first for her among Luo women, but the second woman to be appointed to the cabinet since independence. Julia Ojiambo, from Busia Central, had been an assistant minister, in the same ministry. Ogot was, therefore, the first Luo woman to occupy this highest level of decision-making in the country, representing the interests of all Kenyan women. She observes that as an assistant minister, she had the opportunity to deal with gender problems not merely at the problem solving level but also at the policy formulation and implementation (Ogot, 2012). As an assistant minister in the government from 1985 to 1993, Ogot was involved in women empowerment activities at national and international levels (Ogot, 2012).

Locally, Ogot formed a strong alliance with the other Siaya MPs who had supported her. This strong alliance came to wield considerable power in Siaya politics. Ogot was elected the Siaya Branch KANU Secretary. She traversed the constituency organizing many fundraising rallies and paying school fees for needy students. She also worked with women groups. For instance, she mobilized the women to form the Mabati Women Group (Ogot, 2012). They became the symbol of her efforts to mobilize the women in the constituency to work for social and economic self-sufficiency. This group was formed to provide better housing and living standards for the women. The concept was that the women were to help build *mabati* (iron sheet-roofed) houses for themselves, thus improve their living standards and move out of the grass-thatched houses that leaked during the rainy season. The women also acquired a plot at Yala Township on which they constructed their headquarters, consisting of workshops, exhibition halls, and a cafeteria. They also ventured into brick-laying, the making of roofing tiles and poultry farming. All these activities put the Mabati Women Group on the road to self-sufficiency (Ogot, 2012).

Ogot went back to her electorate seeking re-election in the 1988 General Elections. Because of the impressive development projects that Ogot had initiated and the alliances with the MPs in the larger Siaya District, she easily won. In spite of the queue (*Mlolongo*) vote model which was unpopular in Kenya, Ogot comfortably retained her seat by a landslide win over her competition at the KANU nomination stage. However, for Ogot this model seemed to have worked, mainly because of her development record that was appreciated by both men and women in her constituency. They wanted her given a second full term to complete her projects.

Candidate	Votes
Grace Emily Ogot	14, 118
O Achayo	917
Richard O. Owiti	678
J.B. Luke Akumu	128

Source: 1979 General Elections Score Card (*The Weekly Review*, November 9, 1979)

Consequently, as a result of the nominations, in which Ogot garnered nearly 90% of the votes, she was named the sole candidate for the Gem Constituency parliamentary seat. KANU's rule at the time was that if a candidate obtained over 70% of the votes at the nomination level, then she or he would be nominated to parliament unopposed. Thus, Ogot made it to parliament unopposed. She was to be joined in the sixth parliament by Agnes Mutindi Ndetei, MP for Kibwezi. Again there were only two elected women members of parliament, Asiyo having lost her Karachuonyo seat. Again the Luo women had won another landmark, at least having one of their own in the August House in spite of the competition and hurdles which the women faced. Just like her fellow Luo women politicians, Ogot left her mark as a sterling performer during her terms as Member of Parliament for her constituency, and as a major actor at the national and international level as a cabinet member.

After discussing the women's struggles against political marginalisation, it is important to note that the spouses of the successful women also face their own challenges and levels of marginalisation in the society. All the women acknowledged the support that they received from their families. However, since the Luo are a patriarchal society, there were a number of questions raised regarding the masculinity of their husbands. B. A. Ogot, Grace Ogot's husband, asserts that there are many challenges for families of women politicians. For example, he disliked the lack of privacy in the home. The constituents invaded the whole home at any time of day. He recalls that the family set aside a room in the house that was to be Grace's political office. In a day, between forty and fifty people would come to the home to see Grace. They overcrowded the home. The office restricted them to one room. This gave him peace and the freedom to continue with his professional work (O.I. Ogot, 2011). In an oral interview, Ogot states that the husbands of the women leaders are "treated as drivers". Accordingly, the Kenya government has no policy on protocol issues with regard to the male spouses of ministers and MPs. He observes that the wives of ministers and MPs are treated with respect and honour during official functions and dinners, but not the male spouses of the women leaders.

Ogot remembers one particular incident, when he was invited and accompanied his spouse, the Assistant Minister, to a fundraising meeting for Bunyore Girls High School. The former President Daniel Arap Moi was presiding. After the event, Grace was invited to sit at the high table and dine with the President and other Ministers. Ogot was not invited. He recalls,

> I decided to go home like the rest of the crowd. However, one of the state house officials went to the President and told him that he had seen me at the gate going away. The President ordered that I be called back to join the guests for lunch. I came back, but was not happy at all (O.I. Ogot, 2011).

It is clear that the government does not know what to do with the male spouses of the ministers. Ogot posits that the men must be treated with respect and honour, just like the female spouses of the ministers. There must be gender equality for all. He observes that the situation was better during the Moi era. In the post-KANU era, the government did not bother with the male spouses of the ministers at all.

Ogot also raises the issue of identity for the men. He recalls being addressed as the "husband of Grace" in the government functions, and yet he was a well-known academician. He asserts that he insisted on being addressed by his academic title 'Professor', which had always been used in official functions. However, the couple solved this protocol crisis amicably at home. Grace agreed to attend the functions that accommodated her spouse.

Ogot also had to deal with the attitudes of his own community. The Luo community is a patriarchal society where the man is the head of the home. According to their customs, a man is not supposed to follow his wife everywhere she goes. A man that followed his wife around was regarded as weak. However, Ogot posits, "[t]his attitude did not bother me. I accompanied Grace whenever I could. She did not have a problem with me being around her. Grace always invited me to greet the people before she addressed the gathering" (O.I. Ogot, 2011). Ogot fully supported Grace even when his own community considered it unmanly. This support is important for women politicians if they are to serve the community as leaders. Clearly, though, there are issues that must be addressed for men whose spouses are successful politicians. The state must treat the male spouses with dignity and respect just like they treat the female spouses.

Conclusion

Apart from the example of two female parliamentarians used in this chapter there are currently a number of other women who have participated in politics, and whose stories also ought to be told for scholars to achieve a comprehensive view of the experiences of all Kenyan female politicians. One Luo female politician who has also been extensively interviewed and studied by other scholars is Phoebe Asiyo Asiyo had a rich background that prepared her adequately for politics. She joined politics as a renowned social worker with long experience in working with prisons, child welfare groups and women's organisations. She had also been involved extensively in Luo political and social activities and was one of the most well-known women in Luoland (*The Weekly Review*, May 25, 1979). She joined politics because of her desire to help the people of

Karachuonyo in the same way she had served Kenyans in other capacities. She was also an eloquent public orator, whose patience and ability to explain complicated issue endeared her to her constituents. At the same time, her involvement with welfare organisations had given her an insight into the problems facing the least privileged members of society and the will to deal with them effectively and efficiently. She won the Karachuonyo Constituency elections in 1979. In 1983, President Moi called the first and only snap general election in Kenyan history in the midst of the crisis caused by the attempted coup in August, 1982. In the elections of 1983, the electorate handed Asiyo another term as their member of parliament in another hotly contested election. During the 1988 elections, Phoebe Asiyo stood to defend her seat but with the que voting model which lacked secrecy and privacy which were crucial for the women fold (OI, Catherine Akumu, 2010) she lost. In 1992 Asiyo was to be the first and only Luo woman to be elected in Nyanza in the era of multi-party politics. In parliament, she exhibited rare acumen and art in parliamentary business that she had mastered over time. This time round, the gender platform became her main point of reference.

From our discussion, it is evident that regardless of the women's background there is one common component, gender, which relegates them to a secondary status in politics. They all had to execute their political agendas within a historically entrenched patriarchal paradigm; not only was power and privilege held by men but it was also men who defined that power and its distribution. In fact, they adjusted very well to their double roles in the public and domestic spheres. Indeed, the female politicians carved a space for themselves within the dominant political institutions, thus introducing fresh perspectives to politics. Their experiences as women, mothers, wives and homemakers influenced the way they did politics in the public. They put emphasis on issues of reproductive health, maternity leave, child welfare, education, and jobs for women.

Generally, the profiles exemplified certain commonalities among the women. For instance, these women received western education; they came from the homes of Christian-converts who believed in educating girls. The education they obtained was vital in their political careers. They were supported by their various families. These women politicians put women's issues on Kenya's political agenda. However, it is not only women who struggle against marginalisation in politics. A number of the men face challenges regarding questions about their masculinity as their spouses become politicians. As more women join politics the issues raised by the men should be addressed.

Chapter 10

The President Who Never Was: Joseph Martin Shikuku 1933-2012

Washington Ndiiri and Albert Okinda

Introduction

Martin Shikuku, one politician whose sacrifice to the nation attracted and helped the liberation of people, never achieved much. Additionally, other leaders like Kenneth Matiba, Bildad Kaggia, Josiah Mwangi Kariuki, Tom Mboya, and Oginga Odinga, also stood for nation-building embroidered in political equality, social justice and the provision of equal economic opportunities. Martin Shikuku's contribution to nation-building has not been brought to the fore. He always believed in multiparty politics, as a gizmo of representing sundry interests and he never minced his words even if they would land him in trouble with the authorities. For this he was imprisoned a number of times, for example in 1975-1978 and 1985 (Omolo, 2002).

He served in parliament for long yet he never rose beyond an assistant minister despite representing the underprivileged people of Kenya. His works on earth were cynically inverted; for instance, the abbreviation D.D. was added to his name when he was an Assistant Minister for Home Affairs, which meant disgruntled and disloyal (Shikuku, 1972). His upbringing during the colonial period set his mind at that time, and the years that followed, towards the need for the struggle for one's rights. It is no wonder that for most of his time, he had the passion and determination to change politics of this country.

His famous declaration that "anyone who tries to lower the dignity of parliament is trying to kill parliament the way KANU has been killed" (Hornsby, 2012: 288), in reference to the excesses of the Jomo Kenyatta's regime, landed him into detention. Shikuku was considered one of Kenya's founding fathers of the Kenyan nation, just like Jomo Kenyatta. At 28 years of age, Shikuku was a member of the delegation to the 1962 Lancaster House Conference for talks to pave way for Kenya's independence.

Shikuku's early life

Martin Shikuku was born in 1933 near Lake Magadi in the then Rift Valley Province. He was the second-born child in a family of eight to Reuben Oyondi then working at Magadi Soda Mining Company. The ancestral home of the father was Western Kenya. This saw him attend Mumias Secondary School and St. Peters Seminary in Mukumu. He did not complete his studies in the Seminary School because of his independency of mind and interest in the country's politics. He was a committed Christian but not ready to go into fulltime ministering, as he believed he had another calling, 'the people's watchman' (Hornsby, 2012). He argued that the two, politics and Christianity were antagonistic spheres of life. However, it is ironical that he observes that Christian virtues could be used to propagate good governance, democracy, peaceful co-existence, and nationalism.

He was later expelled from St. Peters Seminary in Mukumu but remained an advocate of excellence in education. He believed education was the tool to emancipate the underprivileged from oppression and poverty. This fostered similarities to Julius Nyerere's education philosophy, which emphasised self-reliance (Kassam, 1994). Nyerere's philosophy and Shikuku's belief in education drew some parallels to Mahatma Gandhi's basic education plan, principally on self-reliance (Kassam, 1994). Shikuku believed that through education there would be equity in the distribution of resources from the family level. This dream, he believed, would come true through the construction of many independent schools, employment of adequate teachers, nurturing many writers and authors as a way of subjugating poverty and ignorance amongst the people of Kenya.

Shikuku left the seminary and took a job as laboratory assistant at Magadi, his first achievement on the labour market. The posting gave him material satisfaction but his biggest challenge was that Magadi was located in a remote area and he was an expressive individual who felt people mattered to him; this was not the ideal environment. Therefore, he quit the chemical firm and found work as a train guard at Nairobi Railways, apparently being the first African to hold that post (Abeingo Community Network, 2009). During his time at Nairobi Railways, he assisted the *Mau Mau* rebellion by hiding guns for the fighters (Kwayera, 2012). Shikuku's passion in politics can be traced to as early as 1939 when he was only six years old. He realized that there was a wide gap between the White man and his parents. This gave him the great determination to bring an end to the poor people's suffering. Joining politics became the only solution, but the pace of such action was slowed down by the declaration of the State of Emergency on the October 20, 1952. This was following the emergence of *Mau Mau* war in 1952, which demanded self-determination for the country (Hornsby, 2012). This declaration banned any form of political agitation.

The war strengthened political resolve for Kenya's self-determination, therefore forcing the colonial government to come up with constitutional proposals like the Lyttelton Constitution of 1954 and Lennox-Boyd Constitution of 1957 (Hornsby, 2012). These constitutional reforms increased political participation of the Africans. For example, the Lyttelton Constitution doubled the number of Africans appointed to the Legislative Council from four to eight, while Lennox-Boyd Constitution increased the numbers from eight to fourteen (Hornsby, 2012). Therefore, by 1959, the ban had eased and Martin Shikuku was elected as a national youth leader, and later that same year, the secretary general.

Working at the railways strategically placed him to successfully engage in politics. It is this determination to play a greater role in politics that saw him resign as a youth leader for the same position in Kenya African Democratic Union (KADU), where he joined other leaders like the former President Daniel Arap Moi and Ronald Ngala. KADU was formed as a counterpoise for KANU (Oyugi, 1997). Therefore, KADU was majorly composed of allegedly minority tribes such as Kalenjin, Mijikenda, among others. KADU leadership favoured federal system of government because through such system the interest of minority communities would not be overshadowed by majority tribes like the Kikuyu and Luo (Makinda, 1992; Murunga, 1999). In their visage, federalism would make the regional assemblies responsible for policies such as housing, education, and social

165

services among others, leaving responsibility for defence, foreign affairs, and central finances to the national government (Throup, 1993).

In 1963, Shikuku was elected on a KADU ticket as Member of Parliament for Butere Constituency, which he served until 1974. KADU later dissolved itself voluntarily in 1964 and joined KANU (Throup, 1993). This was based on the premise that the ideals of democracy were alien to African political organization and many political parties would result into divisions along ethnic lines. So persistent was his loyalty to KADU that he was the last person to cross the floor of the house to join one party government after the merger of KANU and KADU. The voluntary disbandment of KADU, according to Throup (1993), gave Kenyatta a tight grip on power to deal with dissidents within KANU, led by Oginga Odinga and Bildad Kaggia.

When Shikuku won the 1969 elections as an MP, the then President Jomo Kenyatta appointed him an Assistant Minister in the Office of the Vice President and Home Affairs. This was seen as a move to buy his silence on his critique of issues on the conduct of corruption and the handling of the common person's plight in the country. On several occasions, he was reminded that once in government all read from the same script, because of collective responsibility. This is an idea that he never bought into, as he continued to check the government that he was part of.

Shikuku had his reservations about the Kenyatta government, and he at one time referred to it as a dead government. When the then speaker of the national assembly Jean Marie Seroney was asked some members of parliament to impel Shikuku to substantiate what he had said, he answered: "there is no need to substantiate what is obvious" (Hornsby, 2012: 288). This ruling was admired by many Kenyans, a daring ruling not expected at a time when KANU was synonymous with the executive. The admiration evaporated as soon as it came as Shikuku was relieved of his ministerial position and detained alongside Seroney. Their detention was an absurdity because it was in violation of members' immunity from prosecution for their speeches in the Assembly contravention of the Parliamentary Powers and Privileges Act (ibid). There is little that could have been done, especially when the then one-party rule had a stranglehold on politics

166

and everything that went with it. Then, KANU was a moribund organisation owing to lack of formal elections at sub-branch, branch and national levels for close to a decade (Throup, 1993). When the former President Moi, a former KADU colleague, came to power in 1978 following the death of Kenyatta, he released Shikuku from detention and allowed him to proceed to Sweden for specialized treatment. On his return to Kenya, he bounced back into politics and subsequently recaptured the Butere parliamentary seat. Moi then appointed him an Assistant Minister for Livestock Development.

In the early 1990s when the impact of a one-party state was at its highest, the glamour of a multi-party system took root and the Forum for Restoration of Democracy (FORD) was founded by a team of reformists including Shikuku, Jaramogi Oginga Odinga, Kenneth Matiba, Charles Rubia, Mohammed Ahmed Bamahriz, George Nthenge, Masinde Muliro, Phillip Gachoka, and Salim Ndamwe. FORD later split, giving rise to FORD Kenya under the leadership of Jaramogi Oginga Odinga and FORD-Asili under Kenneth Matiba. Shikuku teamed up with Matiba in in FORD Asili as the secretary general.

In 1992, the first multi-party elections were held with several presidential aspirants, namely former President Daniel Arap Moi of KANU, Jaramogi Odinga of FORD Kenya, Kenneth Matiba of FORD Asili, and Mwai Kibaki of the Democratic Party (DP). Shikuku ran for parliament on a FORD Asili ticket and recaptured the Butere seat. During the 1992 election, Shikuku and Matiba's FORD Asili put up a remarkable performance against KANU, coming close to dislodging KANU from power. This was partly due to Shikuku's campaign carrying the majority of the votes from the populous former Western Province.

However, in FORD Asili there was great suspicion of loyalty. It emerged that Shikuku was secretly working with KANU to destroy the opposition. The then President Daniel Arap Moi was known for such political manipulations; defections were a familiar weapon for weakening the emerging opposition. Martin Shikuku and Kenneth Matiba broke ranks. The marriage between Shikuku and Matiba had been seen as one of convenience. The ideological differences between them could not be subsumed by their merger. Before

Shikuku died in 2012, both he and Matiba had been relegated to political margins.

The people's watchman

The self-declared 'People's Watchman' of Kenyan politics had a long, turbulent political career. He was referred to as the people's watchman because throughout his career he fought for the poor. He was popular among ordinary Kenyans, especially the poor who embraced his populist ideas that attacked Kenya's wealthy elites; elites Shikuku claimed were insensitive to ordinary Kenyan's demands. On several occasions, he astonished his often well-off colleagues in parliament by appealing to the government to lower the prices of maize meal (*Unga*) and other items that comprise Kenya's staple diet. Ever since his debut in Kenya's parliament in 1963, Shikuku was a star figure on the parliamentary floor, for his mastery of parliamentary rules and procedures. A free-talking hardliner, Shikuku would engage all and sundry even on the streets, and take to task journalists for thriving on Shikuku matters in order to earn a living.

As the people's watchman he ostracized the Asians, and was against their exploitation of Africans by underpaying them (Omenya, 2015). As a result, he pointed out that the Asians dominated trade and commerce in the country; however, he was doubtful if Africans did the same in India (ibid). The relation of Asian and Africans has been unequal with accusations of Asians of exploiting Africans by either paying Africans low wages of inflation of commodity prices (Omenya, 2015). For example, in Uganda because of the unequal relations, the South Asians were expelled by Idi Amin in 1970s. Therefore, Shikuku also advocated for the expulsion of South Asians from the Kenya. This according to Omenya (2015) was due to the South Asians dominance in the distribution sector of the economy. Nonetheless, during a debate on Trade and Licensing Bill in 1966, he ridiculed the meaning of fair competition between unequals by maintaining that:

So it is useless, although we are all citizens, to talk in terms of fair competition against the people who have been established for a time and who have the money and the know-how, just because they happen to be citizens. I reject this. We must discriminate, Mr. Speaker (House of Representatives Debates, x, 1966 as quoted in Rothchild, 1969).

Shikuku supported government ethnic quotas redressing racial imbalances by giving Africans first priorities since they had been marginalized during the colonial period. The colonial state was racial; therefore, the Africans were denied opportunities and enterprises as compared to their European and Asian counterparts (Rothchild, 1969). Therefore, there was no way that the imbalances would be addressed without applying discrimination in provision of opportunities.

His debut as people's watchman could possibly explain why FORD-Asili attracted ordinary individuals such as touts. Amutabi (2009) in explaining why FORD-Asili failed to attract support of Kikuyu conservative he underscores that this was because the party was under "Mr. Cleans" (Shikuku and George Nthenge). Nonetheless, due to ideological differences between Shikuku and Kenneth Matiba led to disintegration of FORD-Asili. It is alleged that he was given KShs 300 million by Moi to finance his bid for FORD presidential nomination, which was ostensibly to weaken the opposition and kept them divided (Hornsby, 2012; Throup & Hornsby, 1998). To this end, Shikuku was criticised for not maintaining his reputation for detest of the corrupt and denouncing the dubiously gained wealth of his adversaries, which he had used as a political springboard to gain reputation as incorruptible (Throup et. al., 1998). This instance cast Shikuku as a traitor.

The president that never was

Shikuku lived in his own world, many years ahead of his peers and other Kenyans. He aspired and lived a transparent, modest life. He set up an anti-corruption committee in parliament in 1975, long before the government's anti-graft editions. The government of the day scattered the committee as soon as they began their sittings (Hornsby, 2012). He was among the few post-independence leaders who supported the declaration of wealth and how it was acquired (ibid). He led by example by declaring his wealth. He declared 100 acres of land in Bungoma County, a piece of land in Mombasa, and justified the acquisition of his wealth (Omari, 2012). He never participated in public fundraisings (*Harambees*) as he saw these as a conduit of corruption. His philosophy was that he was employed to be the people's watchman and the people paid taxes for the government to provide services and employment.

He lived to fight for the second liberation after three decades of KANU misrule. He had peers who fought for independence and the second liberation, but none was in his world of transparency. A brilliant man, he used to brag, "I have never been to university, but no university in the world has a department called the Faculty of Experience" (Omari, 2012), which he would often repeat to the same to newcomer MPs in parliament. He memorized every quote from Erskine May's Parliamentary Practice in the Commonwealth (the document that contains centuries of old parliamentary standards in the world) (Omari, 2012). In retrospect, the best person to be the President of Kenya in a transition from the old to new era would have been Martin Shikuku because what Kenya needed was a true patriot who would only have one agenda, to put an abrupt stop to corruption. New ideas and initiatives would come later because this single mission, if executed successfully, would transform the country immensely. This spoke volumes about the manner in which Kenyans viewed this courageous politician.

Standing up to the vices in the Jomo Kenyatta era was brave; no wonder he took a thorough beating in detention (Hornsby, 2012). His spirit was unbroken and at 76 years he was still eloquent, his political fire unrestrained. His woes did not end with the death of Jomo Kenyatta. He quickly found himself in trouble with Moi too, in a weird twist of fate. He was dropped as an Assistant Minister for Home Affairs and became a backbencher in 1985 and was detained (Omolo, 2002). He was considered as 'the self-styled debater' and 'the president of the poor'. He would later team up with Matiba in an unexpected marriage of convenience in 1992 under FORD Asili (Hornby, 2002). The two fell short of the formation of what would have been the 'Government of the Poor'. As one of the critics of Kenyatta's nationalistic and Pan–Africanist contributions, Shikuku saw him as an opportunist and not nationalist (Kwayera, 2012). As the first President, Kenyatta ensured that members of the Kikuyu ethnic group and loyal members of his party dominated politics and economic realms for good political reasons at the expense of other communities. Through this, they would support him, by all means because Kenyatta loved power (Murunga, 2004; Murunga, 1999).

Shikuku died on 22 August 2012 the same date Jomo Kenyatta died in 1978. His journey ran right from the Lancaster House talks in London that designed Kenya's first constitution to the second liberation and search for a contemporary constitution. Though everybody amassed wealth during their political lives, he did none of it. In his initial days and to his last days he relied on the governments of the day for assistance to meet his medical bills. This explains what he stood for. Therefore, just like Julius Nyerere of Tanzania who during his tenure as the president did not amass wealth like most African political leaders, so was Shikuku.

Shikuku's vision on the future of Kenya

As he approached the last days of his political career, Shikuku became increasingly disillusioned that the reform agenda he fought for throughout his life, and for which he almost died during the KANU regime, had been hijacked. His hope for the Kenyan future lay in the former Prime Minister Raila Odinga (Kwayera, 2012; Abeingo Community Network, 2009). His remarks indicated a bitter man, for once he said: "What I fought for is not visible; I may die before I see it…. I regret that I fought the Whiteman; the people I fought for are worse" (Abeingo Community Network, 2009) He says this in a documentary that was recorded four months before he succumbed to prostate cancer.

On historical injustices and resource distribution Shikuku said:

What you saw happen during the post-election violence in 2007-8 will come to pass as a rehearsal to a bloodier working class revolution. The symptoms are everywhere. Anyone who cares deeply about our country can see where we are going. We must act now to forestall bloodletting. There seems to be a deliberate attempt by the ruling class to wish away agenda four of the National Accord 10. However, history shows that you cannot oppress all people all the time. I can see people saying enough is enough and what is their worth anyway. I mean the world is dotted with examples of people-driven revolutions" (Abeingo Community Network, 2009).

In an interview with Shad Bulimo of Abeingo Community Network in 2009, he maintained that

> [f]or twenty years we have been fighting to have a new constitution that will do away with imperial powers of the presidency. I am only one of two remaining individuals who attended the Lancaster House conference. The other was Ngala Mwendwa. I was there in the beginning and will push to be there in the end as long as I live" (Abeingo Community Network, 2009).

Shikuku will be remembered not only for his valiant lifestyle but also for his staunch belief in culture and traditions. He dug his grave in preparation for his death. Although a politician, he warned all who intended to attend his funeral against political speeches at his burial because Kenyan politicians had let him down.

Conclusion

Shikuku made his contribution to history. He fought for the common person. Through his oratory, he moved the masses to the extent that when he was against them they did not realize it. When the roads were impassable, he encouraged people to bear with the situation because that would be a source of employment for any vehicle that got stuck. Indeed this was the work of the government to provide services, but the approach to impel government to bring services lacked purposive coordination. This could be perceived that he wished for permanent poverty among the people for that was the fuel of his survival.

The public fundraiser or *Harambee* spirit introduced by President Jomo Kenyatta was a vibrant, progressive call, especially for young nations that were emerging from colonialism like Kenya. However, Shikuku simply did not take part. As people were propelled to build schools through this effort, Butere waited for it to be corruption-free before they could adapt it. Local authorities were very instrumental in the development of rural areas. "The roles and relevance that local government in Kenya had accumulated from its inception in 1924 until 1963 were undermined and rendered meaningless in a short span of just three years" (*The Standard Digital*, 2010). What was witnessed in 1965-1966 was the usurpation of the powers of the local government, part of an elaborate scheme by which Kenyatta arrogated to himself all power in the state. An examination of the Hansard record is a study in the ironies of Kenya's history of struggle for democracy. Martin Shikuku saw local councils as irritants and no longer fashionable and supported the parliamentary bill that desired to transfer to the central government the administration of health, education, and maintenance of secondary roads, which was previously under the county council administration. This was the antithesis of what his former party KADU stood for. He shocked his contemporaries like Jean Marie Seroney who were vigorously opposed to such a motion. This was the unpredictable character of Shikuku and it dogged his reputation even during the second liberation when he was accused of cohabiting with KANU when in FORD Asili with Matiba. Yet, Shikuku takes credit for his efforts to impel the authorities to address the reform agenda. Shikuku's impact was more felt at the national and at international levels than at the constituency level and that is partly why he was the president that never was.

During the advent of colonialism, the flag always followed the cross. The missionaries pacified Africa for colonialism. This is analogous to Martin Shikuku's journey towards the struggle for the decolonization and the creation of democratic space in Kenya. The seminary teaching instead of making him a submissive citizen conscienticised him to pave way to independence and even to the second liberation. Shikuku played an important role in the making of Kenya. His participation in the Lancaster House Conference and his efforts to fight for the return of multi-partyism saw him open up democratic space, yet his contributions have been scantly documented. This brief chapter has examined his early life and participation in politics. The outcome of the analysis is that here is a Kenyan who deserves a place as a hero in Kenya's history. Our remembrance of history is one of convenience. Memories get ethnicised and politicized. Universal memories would guarantee Shikuku a place at the heroes' corner. Memories should not be dictated by those who wield power but the record of one's lifetime achievements.

Chapter 11

The Power of Memory and Forgetting: Political Assassinations and Extra-Judicial Killings in Kenya, 1963-2007

Babere Chacha Kerata

"The colonialists designed the scenario for disaster, and the Africans seem to be trying their best to fulfil it" (Lamb, 1983).

Introduction

There has been extensive and disturbing history of politically motivated killings in Kenya. The Kenyatta, Moi, and even Kibaki regimes have presided over shocking and sometimes brutally effective record of inhumane laws, harassment, imprisonment, torture, and other forms of oppression to terrorize, silence or otherwise neutralize those in opposition to the system. The list of those who were assassinated during these periods, which is long, comes from a wide political spectrum. Sadly, while such state perpetrated atrocities have been committed against citizens, there has never been any form of official acknowledgement or even apology. Kenya has been ruled by regimes which have had scanty respect for human rights, the rule of law, social justice, transparency, accountability, and other trends of democracy. It is against this background that a Task Force on Truth, Justice and Reconciliation Commission (TJRC) was established in April 2003 in Kenya. The task of this commission was to uncover the colonial skeletons of land grabbing in Kenya and the *Mau Mau* massacres; the immediate post-independent assassinations of Pio Gama Pinto, Tom Mboya, and J. M. Kariuki; and later of Robert Ouko; the 'ethnic clashes' in the Rift Valley; and the Goldenberg Scandal. Once dealt with, the commission was supposed to put in place a reconciliation framework to deal firmly with these evils.

Nations throughout the world are coming to terms with their pasts; Europe with its colonial history, America with its dark past of slavery, South Africa with apartheid, and Germany with the scars left from the world war regimes. Within this evolving process of dealing with the past, the issue of compensating victims has often been at the forefront of the public discourse. Kenyans too, are increasingly becoming anxious to know 'what happened and why', 'who did what to whom', what constituted injustice and why. This means that by placing bare a report on historical injustices, TJRC would herald a new dispensation in Kenyan history (Stanton, 2010). Kenyans will not only know what constitute the truth in Kenya's dark history but also demand that such truth(s) be addressed through collective apology, compensation, reconciliation and / or repairing past injustices. This would further provide an opportunity to address broader social problems by setting out a factual record and making policy recommendations in a way that educates the public about the issues.

The first part of this chapter explores and problematizes the concept of history and memory in Kenya's history, and then examines the meaning of remembering and forgetting. It attempts to examine and locate points or areas of scars in Kenya's history and tries to evaluate the levels of justice that can be used to repair such scars. This section also analyses of the significance of assassinations and extra judicial killings in history and how this has altered the patterns of Kenya's cultural and political history. The second part attempts to provide an overview of the historical background of the three former Kenyan presidents and the scars of assassinations and extrajudicial killings that each inscribed in the history of Kenya. Generally, in this chapter, the actual story of particular individual victims of assassinations have been framed, and consequently, narratives of memory and pains of the same, have been appended, using the TJRC reports on oral submissions and reports of investigations and commissions of inquiries.

Scars of memory and scales of justice

While speaking to a gathered group of scholars at the Taylor Institute of Oxford University, on a topic he titled: *Scars of Memory and the Scales of Justice*, Wole Soyinka (2000) struggled to engage in a rather controversial subject of memory and forgiveness. He wondered how modern societies should respond to the commission of despicable acts in public life occurring on a systemic level; commissions of acts such as slavery in the US, apartheid in South Africa, or even tyranny through the hands of individual tyrants in Africa. Soyinka (2000) concluded that forgiveness as "a value is far more humanly exacting than vengeance … yet cannot swallow the proposition that it will, by itself, suffice." Most importantly though, in this juxtaposition, E. P. Thompson, admonished historians who rescue the "casualties of history […] from enormous condensation of posterity…by reconstituting the vanished components of the world we have lost…." (Thompson, 1975). These casualties are the heroes who suffered or were wounded or even killed either as individuals or as groups while states and governments made efforts to erase their memories from the public sphere. Consequently, to help societies to heal and bring to justice past atrocities committed by those in such autocratic regimes, historians would engage in tenuous exercises of indulgence by evoking those memories and bringing them to people's attention.

In a similar controversy over the subject, Americans too were caught by the *fin-de-siècle* disposition of past centuries memories. This was revealed at a conference organized by the Omuhondro Institute at Elimina Beach, Cape Coast Ghana in 2007. One of the participants reported that he had made a request to the then American President, George Bush II, to grant permission to set up a museum of memory to commemorate slave trade and slavery. The reluctant Bush is said to have replied that the "strength of Americans lies in what they forget and not necessarily what they can remember […] why then bring bad memory to them again?" This was a very controversial answer concerning the use of memory and quite significantly, history.

Indeed, Kammen's *Mystic Chords of Memory* adequately hooks us onto argument; he notes that Americans are devoted to memory. Kammen proves this character by chronicling the growth and development of historical societies, erections of historical monuments, government funding for preservation, and academic and popular sentiments through documented testimonies, public lectures, and private letters. He demonstrates America's pragmatic approach to memory; the things they choose to remember and the things they choose to forget. A seeming pattern of cultural amnesia and cultural re-remembering takes shape of the material that Kammen refers to. A major theme in his exposition is the ways in which nations have utilized the past in order to reconstruct an adequate national identity (Thelen, 1989). Collective memories work much the same way; they foster and define group identities, telling a group of people where they have come from, who they are, and how they should act in the present and future (Gillis, 1994). Kenya has never mended its past; it has an uncertain past haunted by a series of mysterious murders and state sponsored killings. As a result of this, for many decades now, the country is faced with an uncertain future that is characterized by ethnic mistrust and fear. This was the ultimate reason why TJRC was formed, not only to help Kenyans to narrate their past and come to terms with it, but to also account for the ills that have shaped their history.

Nevertheless, alongside such understanding of Soyinka and George Bush II on official national memory, as concretised in remembering or forgetting, we know that numerous sub-national memories are often maintained and transmitted on a more informal basis. For instance, while official memory of political *Mau Mau* assassinations and extra-judicial murders was suppressed through decades of state-endorsed amnesia, published memoirs of former fighters and detainees of the war allowed *Mau Mau* to stay alive in the public memory.

In the wider African context, orality as captured in historical narratives play a large role in maintaining and transmitting sub-national memories. The key role of orality, and in this case; the narratives of the established commissions of inquires play a vital role and primary foci of memory (*Sunday Nation*, 27 March 2007; Gathara, 2007). Further, the duty to remember and address the past is essential in helping ensure that future generations 'Never Again' repeat such violations, and the ability of memorials to preserve and communicate memory and history is invaluable in the process. Pierre Nora has argued that material sites of memory can become more about the production of history than the preservation of memory; distinguishing between the two where memory remains in permanent evolution, open to the dialectic of remembering and forgetting while history is the reconstruction, always problematic and incomplete, of what is no longer (Nora, 1989; Goldworthy,1982). The construction of memorials may allow forgetting with the reliance on the memorial to do the memory work. Memorials can only fulfil their role if they have some meaning to society, allowing the transfer of memory through active processes of remembrance such as intended visits to, and engagement with them.

Historical review of political assassinations and extra-judicial killings in Kenya will ameliorate social and political dilemmas that have shrouded and become part of the country's institutional architecture. However, the path from public history-telling in this country to national political transformation is often elusive and biased. This is so, mainly because Kenya is in a state of denial. It is denying its past; it is denying its present, and it is denying its future. The Kenyan state is suffering from what Onyango-Oloka calls a 'calculated' historical amnesia' or what has been referred to as selective amnesia. Kenyans tend to choose what to remember and what to forget. Thus data and individual testimonies in public hearings that have been collected and collated by TJRC will be useful since these experiences will be inserted into the national historiography of injustices in Kenya. In fact, in matters of theorisation of transitional justice, contributions from historians have always been conspicuous in their absence as Hannah Franzki (2012) argues, "…if anything, the 'turn to history' of societies wishing to come to terms with their violent past is perceived as an encroachment on or a distortion of academic historiography". However, in reviewing Berber Bevernage's book *History, Memory, and State-Sponsored Violence*, Franzki thinks argues that such an engagement is pertinent to both the field of transitional justice and history in itself as a discipline. An analysis of truth commissions and their practical use of history sheds light on the 'politics of time' that are at work in transitional justice practices.

Memory is often seen as a prerequisite for healing the wounds of the past, and therefore a necessary condition for reconciliation, both on an individual level as well as in politics and society. For only those who remember the past will be able to prevent the recurrence of evils from the past. It would be therefore, morally callous and possibly unjust to simply dismiss every historical injustice as superseded by the passage of time. Unfortunately, all former heads of state in Kenya have dismissed the past and admonished citizens to forge ahead and forget the past in popular aphorism: *tusahau yaliyopita tuanze upya* meaning, 'let's forget the past and begin afresh'. As a general issue, the challenge of dealing with any historical injustice touches on a wide range of deeply contested yet essential concepts in contemporary political philosophy, among them; nature of justice, rights and responsibility.

It is, however, ultimately true that TJRC in no way gave definite answers to those yearning for the actual things as they happened, but was able to identify those that are considered historical injustices, and tried as much as possible to deal with the subject of truth and answer the following questions; How much normative weight should it be given to the past? Which historical injustice mattered and why? To whom were reparations owed (if any)? Understanding and dealing with moral consequences of the past is one of the most important political issue of our time, and yet also the most intractable.

A theoretical perspective political assassinations, the state and the scare of nationhood in Kenya

Like war, political assassinations have produced insecurity at unprecedented proportions in many concerned countries around the world. The assassination's historical importance lies in a horde of factors; the most pertinent being the global context in which it took place, its impact on politics since then and the assassinated's overall legacy as national or political leaders. Rightly, assassinations are amongst the highest profile acts of political violence, and conventional wisdom holds that such events often have substantial political, social, and economic effects on states.

Assassinations in Africa have been employed as a political tool since independence, marking, altering, or determining the course of events through modern African history. It has been said that terror and assassinations are the mainspring of despotic governments. Even in contemporary times, the sins of assassination and its forms continue to plague most countries. In addition, acts of violence, such as ethnic tensions and *coup de tats*, executions, and civil wars, have continued to frequent societies and political systems in the 21st Century Africa. Apart from affecting or killing the victim, assassinations have direct consequences upon critical social-economic and political institutions and the targeted individual nation as a whole (Anderson, 1992). As studied and expounded by political theory and history, assassinations and assassination attempts of critical political personalities have far-reaching political and societal consequences and repercussions. For instance, the sudden and unexpected murder of a head of state or high-ranking official would not only interfere with a nation's political effectiveness, but also promulgates terror and unrest within a government (Beres, 1991). Most significantly, assassinations and attempts to assassinate often disturb or change the focus of domestic and foreign policy within a nation.

Today, international law differentiates between state-sponsored assassination and assassination that is not state-sponsored (Heaps, 1969). When an assassination is committed by a group that is not linked with a government or by an individual acting alone, it is not state-sponsored. There have been many well-known assassinations of this type throughout history. Assassinations that are not backed by states are usually treated as murders in the nations where they occur. Because no state is answerable, they usually do not infringe upon the international law (Wiebe, 2003). Except in the case of international criminal law, only states can be held accountable for violating international law. Assassination generally reflects a violation of the international law against treachery in war or aggression in times of peace (Wiebe, 2003). Further, it is possible, although less likely, that individuals or groups of individuals accused of assassination could be held responsible for committing genocide or crimes against humanity. Assassination could therefore rise to the level of a crime against humanity only if it was part of a systematic or prevalent pattern of attacks against a civilian population.

In Kenya, Tom Mboya's assassination is rightly viewed as the country's original sin. Coming six years after independence, it became a stumbling block to the ideals of national unity, economic independence, and pan-African solidarity that Mboya had championed, as well as a shattering blow to the hopes of millions of Kenyans for freedom and material prosperity. No matter how we look at it, the mere threat of assassination has always played a pivotal role in the history of human politics. It has also had a profound socio-economic impact upon all nations. Today, political leaders all over the world are routinely protected from motivated and opportunistic assassins. Nations adapt to this threat by implementing defensive strategies, which require the expenditure of time, effort, and resources (White, 2007). In sum, political assassinations in Africa have punctuated most political regimes; Egypt, historically, has had the most assassinations at sixteen, followed by South Africa (twelve), Algeria (eleven) and Nigeria at ten.[1]

Exemplified below are some of the most prominent assassinations in Africa since attainment of independence of states more than fifty years ago. Congolese Prime Minister Patrice Lumumba was assassinated in 1961, while Sylvanus Olympio, leader of Togo was killed in 1963. Hendrik Verwoed, the Prime Minister of South Africa was stabbed in parliament in 1966. In the same year, Johnson Aguiyi-Ironsi who was Nigeria's military head of state and the Prime Minister Sir Abubakar Tafawa Balewa were also were killed. In the 1970s, political murders continued with the assassinations of Ugandan Chief Justice Benedicto Kiwanuka in 1972 and that of the arch-bishop of Uganda, Janani Luwum in 1977 (U.S Department of State, 2012). Steve Biko, South Africa's anti-apartheid crusader was killed in police custody in 1974 while Francois Tombalbaye, the President of Chad, was killed a year later. In Nigeria, President Murtala Mohammed was assassinated in 1976. In the 1980s, Liberian President William Tolbert Jr was assassinated during the 1980 military coup. Egyptian President Anwar Sadat was shot during a military parade in 1981, while in 1987, Burkina Faso's Head of State Thomas Sankara, was assassinated. The 1990s saw the political murders of Rifaat al-Mahgoub, speaker of the Egyptian parliament in 1990. This is also the year Samuel Doe, the President of Liberia was killed. Chris Hani, the leader of South African

---

[1] Ali A. Mazru, "Thoughts on Assassination in Africa", *Political Science Quarterly*, Vol. 83, No. 1, 1968), p. 48.

Communist Party, was killed in 1993, while the plane carrying Rwandese President Juvenal Habyarimana was shot from the sky in 1994. Ibrahim Bare Mainassara, President of Niger, was assassinated in 1999. The 2000s saw the shooting of Congolese President Laurent Kabila in 2001. The list could go on.

In the wider East Africa, however, Kenya seems to be the most assassination-happy nation, with less than ten major political murders, followed by Burundi where three Prime Ministers were assassinated; Louis Rwangasore (1961), Pierre Ngendandumwe (1965) and Joseph Bamina (1965). Uganda has had two assassinations during the dictatorial regime of Idi Amin, while Tanzania has recorded only one assassination, the 1972 murder of the first President of Zanzibar and first Vice President of Tanzania, Sheikh Abeid Karume.

Kenya has had six major political assassinations, the most prominent being the murders of Pio Gama Pinto, Tom Mboya, J. M. Kariuki, Bruce MacKenzie, Robert Ouko, and Crispin Odhiambo-Mbai. The sequential cases of political assassination in Kenya and the mysterious circumstances in which they have occurred have put the country in a turbulent situation. The inconclusive state in which they have remained and the 'bloody' political war that loomed in some part of the country, heightening particularly the contest between the Luo and Kikuyu, have turned the Kenya political terrain into a boiling cauldron, where the nation is often but rudely awoken to the news of yet another conflict (Oucho, 2002; Ayodo, 1995; DuPré, 1968; Stewart, 2009).

Political assassinations and extra-judicial killings in Kenya: a historiographical review

Researching or writing on the subject of political assassinations and extra-judicial killings is the most seductive intellectual pleasures which can befall a historian, yet it has in many years constituted one of the most challenging and even frustrating enigmatic riddles in recent scholarship, especially in Africa. Both the African and Africanist literature give corroborating substantiation for the stabilizing interpretation of assassinations, which according to scholars, has been deliberately deployed by leaders to consolidate their regimes and intensify their power since independence (Bienen, 2015; Lemarchand, 1972; Rothchild, 1997; Van de Walle, 2007; Kitschelt, H., & Wilkinson, 2007). Leaders hold onto their positions and provide political stability in the process by eliminating those in competition with them or those that pose threats to their political dominance and, in the process, maintaining elite clientelist relationship.

However, the overwhelming majority of research on assassination appears in the global west, particularly America and Britain. These have been conducted majorly by journalists and amateur historians, who have largely addressed specific assassinations; most notably the Lincoln and Kennedy assassinations. So why are there so few scholars in Africa working on that subject of political assassinations? TJRC searched through the thesis and dissertation scholarly database in Kenya and there is scarcely any one that deals entirely on the subject. African academics who have attempted to immerse themselves into assassination scholarship, have either faced deportation, imprisonment and or even got killed. In the mid-1980s, scholars who had membership in *Mwakenya* – a social movement – faced similar experiences (*Mzalendo Mwakenya*, 1994; United Movement For Democracy In Kenya, 1994; *Mwakenya*, 1987; Union Of Patriots For The Liberation Of Kenya, 1987; Widner, 1993). Being branded 'Marxist', most of them found themselves in problems with the state, particularly after the death of J. M. Kariuki.

In general, there is dissent within the literature on the best way to define an assassination. The theme itself presents a theoretical and conceptual problem. Mazrui for example, explains why many characterizations of an assassination are problematic (Mazrui, 1968). Accordingly, an assassination is "the killing of someone politically important by an agent other than himself/herself or the government, for reasons which are either political or unknown." However, there have been prominent cases of members of the government murdering their leaders. For example, Kim Jae Kyu, director of the KCIA, shot South Korean president, dictator Park Chun Hee; it would be strange not to count this incident as an assassination (Lee,

1980). Moreover, the "unknown reason" aspect of this definition is vague and therefore leaves its value up for debate (Kirkham, Levy & Crotty, 1970).

For the purposes of this chapter, an assassination is the murder of a prominent political leader in which the assassin does not intend to usurp the position of the head of state or political leader. Assassinations are often considered the most incisive political statements possible to perpetrate. Mazrui notes that as a leader becomes more dynamic and is known to constituents because of his personality traits, opposition to the leader's authority becomes more personal. In autocratic societies, legal institutions for opposing leadership are weak or non-existent. An assassination of a leader is the ultimate manifestation of opposition against the figurehead of the political institution of a state.

Though the effects of assassinations on political institutions have attracted much attention, very little empirical work has been done regarding these effects. Much of the current and past literature draws conclusions from specific case studies involving notorious assassinations. Indeed, a surge of literature regarding the political effects of assassinations which appeared in the late 1960s and early 1970s were spurred by the assassinations of John F. Kennedy, Robert Kennedy, and Martin Luther King, Jr. For instance, in his book *Assassination*, after examining eighteen selected murders, Hudson (2000) curiously concludes that assassinations do not substantially change institutions. He emphasizes that assassinations are attempts to turn a "tide" that is beyond human control. Much of the qualitative literature suggests that assassinations have little transformative power, but then counts several cases (such as the assassination of the Archduke Franz Ferdinand or Mahatma Gandhi) as random exceptions. Even literature that cites substantial effects of assassinations, such as increasing distrust within the political elite and amplified expectations on the successor, concludes that assassinations tend to restore equilibrium (Marvick & Marvick, 1971).

Despite their profound social, economic, and political significance, the social sciences have contributed little to our understanding of the general phenomenon of assassination. It is true that the 1970s and 1980s produced a modest flurry of psychological and sociological research on assassination behaviour in America

(Wilcox, 1980; Havens, Leiden & Schmitt, 1970; Hurwood, 1970; Novak, 1974; Rapoport, 1971; Wilson, 2015; Wilkinson, 1976). Much of that work, however, viewed assassination as a form of deviance, and therefore focused on the psychological pathology of individual assassins, and / or the sociological pathology of individual regimes. Throughout this era the prevailing consensus was that political assassination could be best explained as unnatural behaviour exhibited by psychotics, nihilists, and neurotics (Clarke, 1981). Even today, the historical analysis of assassinations tends to focus upon the mental capacity of the assassins (Rosenberg, 1995). Both of these explanations have however been used by majority of African states to cover up major assassinations. For instance, the Tom Mboya and J. M. Kariuki assassins were at one time considered mentally deranged.

Few works have been done on assassination in Kenya. What is available is little mention of the theme in many texts, but in a scattered way. We therefore turn to examine a few of the assassin cases, and account for the nature of coverage. Jay Robbert Nash for example, while writing only a paragraph in an *Encyclopedia of World Crime*, curiously lays it bear and reports that "…Tom Mboya was murdered in Nairobi by members of the Agikuyu tribe of Kenya (Nash, 1990). Arthur S. Banks emphasizes this fact elsewhere in his study (Banks, 1987). In fact, according to Kwame and L. E Henry in the *Encyclopaedia of African and African American Experience,* the late Tom Mboya was in July 1969 assassinated in Nairobi by a Kikuyu man. This consequently aggravated tensions between the Luo and the politically dominant Kikuyu. This led to Luo demonstrations in the western town of Kisumu; an act which gave the then President Kenyatta an excuse to ban the KPU and place the late Jaramogi Oginga Odinga under house arrest, without charges until 1971 (Kwame & Henry, 1999).

On the other hand, and in a more bold way, the firebrand historian and ardent critique of the Kenyatta state, William Ochieng (1989), argues that the assassination of Tom Mboya caused a tremendous growth of tribalism in Kenya between 1965 and 1978. This development was made worse by the ambition of the Agikuyu bourgeoisie to dominate and monopolize Kenya's political and economic life. Ochieng further explains that part of this dream was manifested in the expulsion of radicals from KANU in 1966, the killing of Mboya and the banning of KPU in 1969. Ochieng contends that the killing of Mboya, in particular, brought a big rift between the Luo and the Kikuyu, and spontaneous demonstration of the Luo in Nairobi against President Kenyatta at Mboya's requiem service. Further to this, the Luo and the Kikuyu leadership separately organized a tribal response to this. In October 1969 for example, Kenyatta's motorcade was pelted with stones by the Luo when he went to Kisumu to officially open the Russian built hospital. He died nine years later without stepping foot in Nyanza again. Kabaji (2000) contributes to this debate by observing the same sentiments that another great threat to the unity of the country occurred when Tom Mboya was shot down on a Nairobi street in 1969. The event set off street battles and mistrust between people all over the country. Kenyatta had to appeal to all citizens not to destroy all that they had achieved in building a strong unified nation. This argument on the consequences of Mboya's murder is also corroborated by Sibi-Okumu (2008).

It is argued that even African literary writers have also an enduring propensity for social and political commitment. The available texts mainly reflect and refract the socio-political events in their societies. This notwithstanding, African literature was originally a tool for celebrating the heroic grandeur of the African past; later it was used for anti-colonial struggle. Most of these texts include those of Ngugi wa Thiong'o, Francis Imbuga, and Meja Mwangi. The referent society of the text has been enmeshed since 1963 in the crucible of deaths and births, agony, poverty, dehumanisation and starving Africa. Meja Mwangi's, *Kill Me Quick,* for example like many other post-colonial African novels, reveals an atmosphere of fear, hate, humiliation and an aura of repression, in forms of arrest, exile and execution. It highlights the dictatorial and oppressive tendencies of the imperialist and comprador bourgeoisie in neo-colonial African countries.

According to Kubayanda (1990), this is the general visceral sentiment that forms the background of Mwangi's fiction, as well as most post-colonial African texts. Actually, common issues in postcolonial literary works include tyranny, corruption and other forms of oppression. Said declares: "domination and inequities of power and wealth are perennial facts of human society" (2012). There emerges from Mwangi's handling of disillusionment and pains in his text, a virulent critique of the African past and present, and a pessimistic view of future evolution. Presently, it is being employed as a veritable weapon for depicting the post-colonial disillusionment in African nations.

On the other hand, Marjorie Oludhe Macgoye discusses Mboya in her novel, *Coming to Birth* and describes him during one of his meetings in Kenya. She writes, that "Martin was present at that Adult Education rally at Bahati where Tom finished his speech, debonair and controlled as ever and then rushed into the meeting which had been organised to exclude him." On reading this, we realize that had the author captured Tom in a lively manner; Tom's image in action may have vivified this work tremendously. After all, Mboya's life had a marked effect on the major characters, Paulina and Martin. This minister was Martin's hero and when he died, Martin's life was deeply influenced. It is then that Martin, and the author question the real meaning of freedom. There is so much pain. There are no words. The characters speak in sorrow. Martin says in Dholuo.., *wawuok mondi* (let us go)… *woud minwa*, nyathiwa; which means `child of my mother, my sibling'. Macgoye further describes the situation in her poetry.

Macgoye asks pertinent questions about the death of Tom Mboya which led to so much distress in the land. She asks a question for freedom, for "the hunters go unchecked" after they have taken away the freedom to live, think and act from a leader who promised to be extremely helpful to the poor who needed him most and to the nation: "Who calls him rich in worldly things? / We knew him rich in peasant tongue, / Thought in each language newly sprung / and courtesy, the grace of kings" (Said, 2012). Macgoye narrates in *Coming to Birth* how the people never stopped to miss their elected but killed leaders. They mourned and commemorated them. She writes that: "J. M. Kariuki burst upon the scene as a martyr, and a paroxysm of grief ran through the city. The skies were laden that April and it grew colder and colder." Macgoye shows the negative impact of these mysterious deaths of leaders on the people and on the country as a whole. In so doing, Macgoye is questioning the fact that some individuals' political careers and by extension their freedom were thwarted.

And pop music makers of the day, Kamaru and others did not fear so they asked Kenyatta in songs in his mother tongue which they spoke on what happened to Kariuki. The song went... "People of our mother since Kariuki has died... and he has not stolen or killed anybody / He has died for being good... and you ask yourself what you will die for... a song I heard and which moves me still. *"Andu a maitu tondu Kariuk iniakua ... natikuiya kana kuragana. tundoarakuaarakwirewegawake. Eee nainyuimwiyuragieemugakuakiii oiiioiiiooiii ye... J M Kariukimwendwoniiri...."* Kenyatta banned the song.

A Tanzania musical band too commemorated J.M. only for the song to be banned by the then President Julius Nyerere, upon the request of the former president Kenyatta. The song *Kifo cha JM Kariuki* [The Death of J.M. Kariuki] goes: "Sisi watu wakenya tuna uchungu mwingi sana / Eeh kariuki enda salama sisi tuliobaki tuko taabuni / Sisi sote twajua sio kawaida, nasio cha halali / Tunajua na tunakungoja urudi" (Palicidia, 1976).

Conclusion

Political assassinations have been gruesomely employed by successive regimes in Kenya since independence. While motives have varied; from getting rid of political competition, weeding ambitious politicians, perceived "dissidents" of the government or those who posed as "threats" to power, state involvement and subsequent cover ups using decoys in a well-oiled and premeditated assassination machinery have been employed in the majority of political murders. Propaganda and Commissions of Enquiry are often used as smokescreens to get into "the bottom of the matter," but are nothing more than public relations exercises to mask the motives and faces behind the assassinations. Prominent figures in government are normally involved. Key witnesses into the assassinations disappear or die mysteriously. No real perpetrators, for that reason, have ever been brought to book and majority of those found guilty were only scapegoats of the regime and the security system which is extensively used in most of the political assassinations.

As such, Kenyan presidents have failed significantly since independence to provide viable security and protect its own citizens. As such, many hopes have been shattered leading to despondency and apathy. Post-independence Kenyan governments have not shied away from engaging youth wingers as vigilantes to serve their political ends and silence opposition from within and without their parties. Political violence linked to KANU youth wingers increased during nominations and campaign periods in the general elections in 1969, 1974, 1979, 1983 and 1988.

The failure of the state has collapsed almost all other institutions within it. Today, Kenyans talk of the failure of religion to solve fundamental problems of ordinary people. What remains now is that people, especially the youth, have tended to organise themselves to gain access to food, security and even resources where the government has failed. To them, independence has very little meaning over fifty years along the line.

Similar to many other African countries, Kenya faces the challenge of providing adequate security to its citizens due to many reasons. Hence, many people resort to making their own security arrangements. While the rich in the urban areas hire private security services, the poor are mostly under the mercy of vigilantes. Traditionally, the field of security has been associated with the state as the provider of protection, law, and order. The state-centric security focused on threats to national interests from within and without. However, this notion has been challenged and there has been a move to widen the scope of security to mean the well-being of individuals and protection from hunger, diseases, violence, oppression, fulfilment of human rights, and social justice (UNDP, 1994).

This shift from state-centred to human centred security has, however, revealed the limitations of the state in adequately providing security services. It has also exposed the state to a host of other challenges like multinationals that have become powerful and almost become governments on their own. Faced with increasing demands to protect its citizens from physical violence and at the same time ensure that their well-being is secure, the state has not managed to meet these demands. The weakness of the state has thus contributed to a gradual erosion of the idea of security as a public good and loss of faith in security institutions. This has led to proliferation of informal private security largely determined by wealth and poverty. In the informal settlements, this has seen the proliferation of vigilante groups who exercise control outside the formal institution of the state. In such areas, the state is normally not capable of providing basic services, including security and on the few times that it intervenes, it is normally in a reactive and disciplinary manner rather than protective (Abello & Pearce, 2009). Hence, the state is not the main institution for security provision and alternative actors, these vigilantes, normally conduct lucrative illegal and informal economic activities, replacing the state in not only providing protection, but also offering basic services at a fee. Vigilante groups are therefore mostly created in response to this security vacuum left by the inadequacy of the state and its security forces.

Hannah Arendt once remarked that "[w]e can no longer afford to take that which was good in the past and simply call it our heritage, to discard the bad and simply think of it as a dead load which by itself time will bury in oblivion…This is the reality in which something missing live" (Arendt, 1973). As Bethwell Kiplagat once said, we have both ugly and inspiring history" (Institute of Historical Justice and Reconciliation, 2009).

Redressing past wrongs is essential to establishing conditions of justice in a society scarred by the enduring and pervasive effects of those wrongs (Torpey, 2003). Similarly, while addressing the contemporary spread of movements seeking redress for past injustices, historian Charles Maier gave a world formula for doing this by proliferation of words like "reparation, remembering, recording, reconciliation." Canada, for instance, in campaigns for redress, elicited apologies and financial compensation for the 2nd World War internment of Japanese Canadians and the past policy of forcing Aboriginal children to attend residential schools. However, it is not only monetary compensation that they seek. Non-monetary forms of redress are equally important. They need "material" redress like programs, policies, and institutional reforms designed to correct inequalities in housing, healthcare, education, and job training. They also need "symbolic" redress like public acknowledgements, official apologies, memorials, commemorations, museums, and curricular reforms. As in many of the other reparations struggles mentioned above, the ultimate aim is to involve the national government in redressing, through legislation, the legacy of injustice in which it has been deeply implicated. Judicial recourse is a means to that end.

Chapter 12

General Conclusion
Reversals and Gains of Nation-building

Susan Waiyego Mwangi

The 1960s and 1970s represented a unique phase in Kenya's history, for like many other African states emerging from colonialism, she had to grapple with the contradictions of development generated by the colonial state. Some of the burning development questions revolved around political equality, social justice, freedom from want, and the provision of equal economic opportunities as laid out in Sessional Paper No. 10 of 1965 (Republic of Kenya, 1965). Ogot and Ochieng' (1995) point out that the achievement of independence was a blessing in disguise as it presented other problems which extended beyond political change, to include economic and social changes. Kenya, as any other African country after independence, wanted to shackle off the colonial legacy and promote the indigenous culture. This transformation was embellished under the notion nation-building.

Ogot *et. al.*, (1995) argue that the idea of nation-building in Kenya required the visionary women and men of public affairs to take the leading role in the drawing and drafting the desired ends of the nation-building and at the same time chattering the way forward to their achievements. It was on this that the late Jomo Kenyatta reiterated that his government would be building on a democratic African socialist state (Kenyatta's statement after electoral victory in May 1963, as quoted in Gertzel, Goldschmidt & Rothchild, 1972). This was to be founded on equality to social and economic developments with no reservations at all whether race or tribe. This remained an idea, as the subsequent years proved otherwise.

From the time of independence, Kenya lurched from one political assassination to another. Prominent political figures have been assassinated since independence, such as Pio Gama Pinto in 1965, Tom Mboya in 1969 and Josiah. M. Kariuki in 1975, and

Robert Ouko in 1990 (Hornsby, 2012). These assassinations have continued to disfigure the relationship between the state and the citizens. The assassinations also indicated the resolve by the various governments to deal with its critics, while at the same time entrenching the continued extrajudicial killings by security agencies.

At independence, Kenya was a multi-party state, but by 1969, it had become a *de facto* single party state. Through coercion and intimidation members of minority party, Kenya African Democratic Union (KADU), representing a coalition of small ethnic groups, in 1964 crossed the floor to join KANU. During this period civilian politicians who had inherited leadership from the colonial masters disbanded political parties in the name of nation building. This was not only unique to Kenya. In Ghana, Kwame Nkrumah banned all political parties declaring that "Ghana is the Convention People's Party (CPP) and the CPP is Ghana" (Bandyopadhyay & Green, 2013). This was misguided by the philosophy that the ideals of democracy were alien to African political organization and many political parties would result into division along ethnic lines, and that only single party system would trounce ethnicity. Single party state gave Kenyatta and Moi tight grips on power, and a conduit to deal with political dissidents (Hornsby, 2012).

To ensure tight control of power and to deal with political dissidents, the presidency has always engineered a wide array of constitutional amendments. For example, the 1963 amendments that led to the collapse of regionalised system of governance, and the 1966 Preservation of Public Security Act that introduced detention without trial (Hornsby, 2012: Ruteere, 2014). During this period, parliament's ability to check the executive was eroded and parliament was transformed into a mannequin of the executive (Horns, 2012). This was epitomized by the June 1982 constitutional amendment that made Kenya a *de jure* one-party state (Hornsby, 2012).

The constitutional amendments centralised power to the presidency. To this end, the presidency as an institution became a powerful organ that always acted like a Leviathan. Parliament was itself reduced to executive and presidency rubber stamp due to coercion by the state. The centralisation of power to the presidency was characterised by the presence of the president's portrait in public offices, private enterprises, and on the currency. Therefore, the presidency developed a penchant for authoritarianism for which ethnicity and elitism became entrenched.

The other challenge that Kenya has faced since independence is ethnicity, which has been used as tool for political power through rewarding members of one's own ethnic group for political support. The ensuing years of Jomo Kenyatta witnessed entrenchment of ethnicity as factor which determined who got the share of the national cake. This was embroidered in the Africanisation of government positions. The Africanisation was seen as 'Kikuyunisation' of the government professions as most appointees to different government position were predominantly Kikuyu (Hornsby, 2012). Therefore, in the pretext of promoting national unity, president Moi banned tribal unions such as Gikuyu, Embu, Meru Association (GEMA) and Luo Union. However, the absurdity was that Moi himself upheld tribalism and nepotism in the manner he appointed state officials (Miller, 1984: Hornsby, 2012). During his regime spanning 1978 to 2002, he only reversed the ethnic factor by replacing the Kikuyus with the Kalenjins (Amutabi, 2009). Therefore, just like Kenyatta and the Moi regimes, the Uhuru Kenyatta government has also developed a penchant of rewarding loyalists and members of community of the two principals; President Uhuru Kenyatta (Kikuyu) and his deputy William Ruto (Kalenjin).

In the 1980s, there was increased political demand for increased political freedom, following the constitutional amendment that banned all political parties. The sustained international and national pressure by churches and opposition leaders in particular eventually made the government to repeal Section 2A of the constitution in December 1991 which allowed for multi-party democracy. This somehow represented a rebirth of the Kenyan state as citizens increasing became vocal in criticising the KANU regime, a hitherto unknown idea during earlier years of President Moi's rule. The repeal also saw the emergence of a vibrant civil society which constantly petitioned the regime in case of political excesses.

Therefore, by early 1992, a number of new parties had been formed, such as Forum for Restoration of Democracy (FORD) and Democratic Party (DP) (Amutabi, 2009; Hornsby, 2012). Since ethnicity had permeated Kenya's politics, the opposition became divided on ethnic lines, thus leading to Moi's re-election in 1992 and

1997 elections. However, in October 2002, a coalition of opposition parties joined forces with a faction that broke away from KANU to form the National Rainbow Coalition (NARC). NARC was composed of National Alliance Party of Kenya (NAK) and Liberal Democratic Party (LDP) and other small parties (Amutabi, 2009: Hornsby, 2012). In December 2002, the NARC's candidate, Mwai Kibaki, was elected President. The triumph was on the platform that they would fight corruption, form government inclusive of all ethnic groups, provide free primary education, and change the constitution within 100 days of being elected, to limit the power of the executive (Makau, 2008 as quoted in Roberts, 2009). However, this disintegrated due inauguration of divisive politics and rewarding of old political elites from GEMA and Makerere 'godfathers' by President Kibaki (Amutabi, 2009). Therefore, for Amutabi (2009), Kibaki regime "confirmed that Kenya's political elite is largely self-centred, narcissistic and unrefined hodgepodge of ethnic barons with no national vision for the country" (p. 74).

After the election, the coalition government was engaged in altercations on the ownership of the Memorandum of Understanding (MOU) as four key positions that were supposed to be created, including prime minister, and two deputy prime minister positions, did not materialize (Gachigua, 2014). The aforementioned occasioned the rejection of the proposed constitution in 2005 that engendered a tense political environment. This ultimately resulted to the disputed presidential elections of 2007 and the resultant post-election violence crisis. The violence resulted to the death of over 1000 individuals and displacement of estimated 600,000 people (Pyne-Mercier, 2011). The crisis was resolved through a political settlement between the two leaders, Mwai Kibaki and Raila Odinga, resulting to a coalition government with Kibaki as the president and Raila as prime minister. This culminated to the assigning of the National Accord and Reconciliation Agreement on February 28th 2008 mediated by the African Union appointed Panel of Eminent Persons led by Kofi Annan, the former UN Secretary General. The National Accord and Reconciliation Agreement had four-point agenda: immediate action to stop the violence, immediate measures to address the humanitarian crisis, how to overcome the political crisis, and addressing long-term issues such as constitutional review.

Part of the components of the National Accord was the agreement for the reviving of constitutional review process. This finally culminated to the promulgation of the new constitution on August 2010. The new constitution has been hailed for its expansiveness on human rights, introducing devolved system of governance, promoting good governance under Article 6, empowering marginalized groups in the society such as youth and women, separating the power of the different arms of government, and establishing different commission to address reforms in different sectors such as in police reforms.

The reforms that were initiated by the National Accord were mostly codified in the 2010 constitution and some came about as national legislation. However, despite the constitution ushering in a wide range of reforms, the political context in which the constitution has to be implemented remains ambivalent. The constitution presents the aspirations of many Kenyans, but the political elite have acted in manner indicating unwillingness to implement the key tenets of the constitution. The political unwillingness by the political elite has been witnessed through enactment of legislations or carrying out actions that contravenes the constitution. For example, the government has been hesitant to restructure the Provincial Administration in line with the new constitutional requirement, instead; they have appointed county commissioners, an office that is not in the constitution (Osse, 2014).

The prospects of nation-building

The prospect of nation building is greatly hinged on the Constitution of Kenya (2010). However, Kenya is at a nascent stage of implementing the constitution it promises a lot in advancing nation-building. Through Article 6, the constitution promotes good governance by setting out the responsibilities of leadership or state officers by requiring that individuals occupying public offices should be selected on merit, not corrupt, be accountable to the public, and committed to serving the people. The constitution also establishes different commissions and independent offices to deal with different issues that have bedevilled Kenya's history, such as land, human rights, and constitutionalism. The constitution also introduced the devolved system of government. Through this, it decentralises political power and economic resources to the county levels. This broke away from the traditional concept that development could only be spurred by supporting the incumbency, a culture that the Jomo Kenyatta, Moi, and Kibaki regimes perfected. Further, the Constitution of Kenya (2010) reintroduced bicameral legislative system-national assembly and senate, therefore, enhancing on checks and balances against the different arms of government.

Even though the 2010 constitution introduced heroes day, commonly referred as *Mashujaa Day* (*Mashujaa* is a Swahili word meaning heroes) to honour all those who contributed towards the struggle for Kenya's self-determination and recognizing those who have positively contributed in the post-independence, some groups have been left out. Great attention has focused on only a small group of political movements, forgetting the youth, elderly women, academics, heroes and heroines and political detainees who have greatly contributed to nation-building. The *Mashujaa Day*, while having depersonalized celebrations, centred on politicians such as former presidents Jomo Kenyatta and Moi, who can barely fall in these categories, given they did not achieve much. The heroes day has only focused on those whose achievements are known, more specifically the political elite and recorded in the books of history. This has placed the contribution of the local population who, in their actions, helped promote nation-building at the periphery. Therefore, heroism should recognize the ordinary population whose contributions have been immense, thus to help spur supra-nationalism above ethnic sheaths. However, for the above to be achieved there should be political will among the political leadership to implement the constitution.

Afterword

Godfrey Muriuki

Since 1992 the historiography of Kenya has faced a critical re-examination. Firstly, this has been sparked off by the ethnic clashes that took place during the elections of 1992, 1997, and 2007/08. As Kenyans grappled with these calamities, they began to ponder on their causes and looked to the history of Kenya in search of answers and possible remedies. The second catalyst arose from the debates and struggle for the writing of a new constitution. In particular, the protagonists focused on the checkered career of the independence constitution that was thrust upon Kenya by the departing colonial power in 1963.

The main outline of the modern history of Kenya is fairly well known. Like other white settled colonies in Africa, Kenya witnessed a robust nationalist movement pitted against the colonial government, besides European settlers. Available literature indicates that the seeds of Kenya's nationalist movement are to be found in the armed pacification, alienation of land, demands for labour and taxation, to mention only a few. And besides individual defiance, this culminated in organized resistance as epitomized by the East African Association of Harry Thuku. This multi-ethnic endeavour alarmed the colonial government, which soon thereafter took measures to alter the political landscape by sponsoring regional / ethnic political organizations, the Kavirondo Taxpayers Welfare Association being the most prominent one. And so African political landscape was balkanized until the formation of the Kenya African Union in 1946, which was banned in 1952 during the State of the Emergency. But balkanization once again came into being from 1955 when the formation of district-cum- tribal political parties was permitted. In 1960, these formed the bedrock of Kenya African Union (KANU) and Kenya African Democratic Union (KADU), which were essentially tribal alliances.

Eventually, Kenya gained her independence in 1963 under KANU led by Jomo Kenyatta and Oginga Odinga, under a majimbo constitution. But the Kikuyu/Luo alliance did not last long; it disintegrated in 1966 due to ethnicity and Cold War machinations. The fallout led to constitutional amendments that created an imperial presidency, a *de facto* one-party state that deliberately marginalized some communities and brooked no opposition. That state of affairs was to continue in the Moi era until the end of the Cold War led to a shift on the international scene that ushered multi-party politics. But this did not solve Kenya's political problems. If anything, the so called Second Liberation witnessed the mobilization of political ethnicity, which has become Kenya's bane.

Under these circumstances, what is the state of the art as far as Kenya history is concerned? By focusing on the history of the main Kenyan communities, art has been accused of furthering ethnicity, ignoring the minorities, and miserably failing to produce a comprehensive history of Kenya due to ideological, ethnic, and political differences. A case in point is the death of the Kenya Historical Association. Worse still, some of their studies of the colonial and post-colonial periods have been judged to be pandering to political interests. In short, they have failed to positively contribute to the nation building agenda, so they are accused.

To others, they have been selective and neglected important themes or communities like the role of peasants and women. In this regard, it has been pointed out that the role of South East Asians, such as Desai and Apa Pant, has not received its due regard. And yet, their role in the economy and support for the nationalist struggle cannot be gainsaid. And how about European mavericks, such as Derek Erskine and Ernest Vasey, who went against the grain and chose to support the nationalist cause?

This brings me to the question of who decides what and who ought to be memorialized? Who are the heroes and heroines of this nation? What criteria shall we use to choose them? The *Mau Mau* saga vividly illustrates this. There are diverse groups and individuals claiming to be *Mau Mau* veterans. Secondly, a recent exercise to gather material for the history gallery at the National Museums of Kenya caused deep controversy.

Further, history as an academic discipline is an endangered species. For example, while Political Science and Sociology courses are oversubscribed, very few students want to specialize in history. Indeed, the Teachers Service Commission is facing a crisis because it is unable to get enough history teachers. This is the result of a deliberate government policy to downgrade history and emphasize the sciences. And so the question is – can we afford to keep our children ignorant of their history?

Looking at the future of Kenya's heritage, it will be important to take cognizance of a number of factors that will impact on this. To begin with, students both in schools and colleges do not wish to study history because they do not see its relevance to their lives. This, therefore, makes history an endangered species. Indeed, history is now a component under social studies. A campaign of sorts will need to be carried to reverse this trend.

Another area of concern is the role of women in peace making. Women studies have come of age. Unfortunately, in Kenya not much has been done. Yet the meagre studies available clearly show that women played a crucial role in making warriors go to war or persuading them to make peace. Peace museums have begun to appear on the Kenyan scene. But to date, not much is known regarding their role in society. There is a dire need to embark on educating Kenyans about them. In short, civic education must be given priority in order to show that peace museums do not exist simply as a method of extracting a few dollars from gullible foreign tourists. Finally, extant historical studies in Kenya have been regarded as having excluded a number of communities. Hence the problem of marginalization has to be addressed. This calls for the preparation of a research agenda that ought to cover all counties and communities.

References

Gikandi, B. (2008). "Monuments of slave labour and its shame: It was hell on Earth, says camp survivor." *The Standard*, 19th October, p. 25.

Gillis, J. R. (1994). "Memory and identity: The history of a relationship." *Commemorations: The politics of national identity, 3*.

Glasius, M. (2006). *The International Criminal Court: A Global Civil Society Achievement*. London: Routledge.

Godia, J. (2007). "Nyanza women all set to tear down male supremacy" In Focus, *The Sunday* Standard, April 29, Pg. 22 - 23

Goerg, O., Martineau, J. L., & Nativel, D. (2013). Les indépendances en Afrique: l'événement et ses mémoires: 1957/1960-2010.

Goldworthy, D. (1982). *Tom Mboya: the man Kenya wanted to forget*. East African Publishers.

Gona, G. (2014). *Zarina Patel: An Indomitable Spirit*, Nairobi: Zand Graphics Limited

Gould, W. (1995). "Migration and Recent economic and Environmental Change in East Africa," in Baker J. and T. Aina (eds). *The Migration Experience in Africa*. Sweden: Nordic Afrkainstitute.

Gregory, R. (1971). *India and East Africa – A History of Race Relations within the British Empire 1890-1939*, London: Oxford University Press.

Gregory, R. (1993). *Quest for Equality – Asian Politics in East Africa 1900-1967*, New Delhi: Orient Longman

Gumboznsvanda, N. *et. al.*, A. (2003). *Journey of Courage: Kenyan Women's Experiences of the 2002 General Elections*, Nairobi.

Havard, J. F. (2007). Histoire (s), mémoire (s) collective (s) et construction des identités nationales dans l'Afrique subsaharienne postcoloniale. *Cités*, (1), 71-79.

Havens, M. C., Leiden, C., & Schmitt, K. M. (1970). *The politics of assassination*. Prentice Hall.

Hay, J. (1976). "Luo Women and Economic Change during the Colonial Period". In Hafkin, N. and Bay, G. E. [eds.]. *Women in Africa: Studies in Social and Economic Change*. California Stanford University Press, Pp. 87-110.

Heaps, W. (1969). *Assassination: a special kind of murder.* Hawthorn Books.

Herbst, J. (2000). *States and Power in Africa: Comparative Lessons in Authority and Control.* Princeton: Princeton University Press.

Hickey, S. (2013). "African Union says ICC should not prosecute sitting leaders." *The Guardian.* Available at: https://www.theguardian.com/world/2013/oct/12/african-union-icc-kenyan-president (Accessed on 29/12/2016)

Hobsbawm, E. J. (2012). *Nations and nationalism since 1780: Programme, myth, reality.* Cambridge University Press.

Hobsbawm, E., & Ranger, T. (Eds.). (2012). *The invention of tradition.* Cambridge University Press.

Hodgins, S. (2015). "Uhuru Kenyatta vs. The International Criminal Court: Narratives of Injustice & Solidarity."

Hornsby, C. (2013). *Kenya: A history since independence.* New York: I.B Tauris.

Hudson, M. (2000). "Assassination."

Hughes, L. (2011). "Truth be told': some problems with historical revisionism in Kenya." *African Studies 70: 182–201.*

Hurwood, B. J. (1970). *Society and the assassin: a background book on political murder.* Parents' Magazine Press.

Institute of Historical Justice and Reconciliation, Meeting to Discuss a Kenya Project, Panafric Hotel, Nairobi, 8th & 9th January 2009

Interview with Hon. Martin Shikuku, former MP for Butere, 2011

Jamhuri Magazine, Kenyatta Government and Kenya 1974 2 3 Nov Feb 2012

Jaspal, K. (2011). "South African Indian Fiction: Transformations in Ahmed Essops Political Ethos" *Research in African Literatures Vol 42, (3) 46-55*

Kabaji, E. (2000). *Jomo Kenyatta: Father of Harambee.* Sasa Sema Publications.

Kabira, W. & Gituto, M. (1996). *Affirmative Action. The Promise of a New Dawn.* Nairobi: CCGD.

Kabira, W. & Wasamba, P. (1998). *Reclaiming Women's Space in Politics,* Nairobi, Centre for Gender and Development.

Kabira, W. *et. al.* (1993). *Democratic Change in Africa: Women's Perspective.* Nairobi: Acts.

Kagwanja, M. (2001). 'Politics of Marionettes' Extra-legal Violence and the 1997 Elections in Kenya. In Rutlen, M. *et. al.* (Eds.). *Democracy in Kenya.* Nairobi: Fountain Publishers.

Kagwanja, P. M. (2003). 'Power to Uhuru': Youth identity and generational politics in Kenya's 2002 Elections. *African affairs, 105*(418), 51-75.

Kahengeri, (2013). 'Personal experiences'. Conference paper presented at the International Conference on Liberation Movements, Karatina University.

Kakai, P. (2010). "Historicizing Negative Ethnicity in Kenya," in Wa-Mungai and Gona (Eds.) *Re-Membering Kenya,* Nairobi, Twaweza Communications.

Kanogo, T. (1989): "Kenya and the Depression, 1929-1939," in Ochieng' W.R. (Ed.), *A Modern History of Kenya, 1895-1980,* Nairobi, Evans Brothers LTD.

Kanyinga, K. (2010). "Contradictions of Transition to Democracy in Fragmented Societies: The Kenya 2007 General Elections in Perspective." In Kanyinga, K. and Okello, D. (Eds.). *Tensions and Reversals in Democratic Transitions: The Kenya 2007 General Elections.* Nairobi: Society for International Development (SID) and Institute for Development Studies (IDS).

Kassam, Y. (1994). Julius Kambarage Nyerere. *Prospects: The Quarterly Review of Comparative.* Vol. XXIV, no. 1/2, pp. 247-259.

KDM (Kenya Daily Mail) (18th November 1952). 'Mr. Kenyatta to be put on trial along with 5 other African detainees', p.1

KDM (Kenya Daily Mail) (21st May 1954). '*Mau Mau* convicts work at new airport', p.1

KDM (Kenya Daily Mail) (22nd January, 1954). '*Mau Mau* leader with £500 prize captured', p.10

Kedourie, E. (1985). *Nationalism.* London: Hutchinson and Company.

Kenney, A. (2006). "Multi-ethnicity and Democracy in Kenya: ethnicity as foundation of democratic institutionalization", thesis, Aalorg University, Denmark.

Kenya Committee, (1954). Press Extracts, Vol. 1 p.67.

Kersting, N. (2009). *New Nationalism and Xenophobia in Africa – A New Inclination?* In *Spectrum,* Volume 44, 1 pp. 7-18.

Khadiagala G. (2010). "Boundaries in Eastern Africa" in *JEAS Vol.4 No.2*. July. London: Routledge Taylor and Francis Group.

Kinyatti, M. (2008). *History of resistance in Kenya 1884-200*. Nairobi: *Mau Mau* Outreach Centre.

Kiragu, J. (2006). *Is there a Women's Movement?'* In Muteshi, Jacinta, Mapping Best Practices: Promoting Gender Equality and the advancement of Kenyan women. Nairobi, Heinrich Boll Foundation.

Kirkham, J. F., Levy, S. G., & Crotty, W. J. (1970). *Assassination and Political Violence: A Report*. Bantam Books.

Kiruthu, F. (2001). *Voices of Freedom: Great African Independence Speeches, Nairobi*. Bookprint Creative Services Ltd.

Kiruthu, F. (2014). "Masculinities, Femininities and Citizen Identities in a Global Era: Case Study of Kiambu District in Kenya, 1980-2007," in Laroussi Amri and Ramola Ramhotul (Eds.) *Gender and Citizenship in the Global* Age. Dakar, CODESRIA.

Kitschelt, H., & Wilkinson, S. I. (2007). *Patrons, clients and policies: Patterns of democratic accountability and political competition*. Cambridge University Press.

Klopp, J. (2001). Electoral despotism in Kenya: patronage and resistance in the multiparty context, thesis, McGill University.

Knoops, G. (2012, February). Prosecuting the Gaddafi's: Swift or political justice? In Amsterdam *Law Forum*. Vol. 4, No. 1, pp. 78-92.

Kopytoff, I. (1987). "The Internal African Frontier: The Making of African Political Culture", in I. Kopytoff (Ed.). *The African Frontier*. Bloomington: Indiana University Press

Kubayanda, J. B. (1990). "Introduction: Dictatorship, Oppression, and New Realism." *Research in African Literatures*, 5-11.

Kwame, A. and Henry, L. (1999). *Encyclopedia of African and African American Experience*, pp. 1087, 1279

Kwayera, J. (2012). "Shikuku: Kenyatta was an opportunist, not a nationalist." *The Standard*. Available at https://www.standardmedia.co.ke/article/2000064730/shikuku-kenyatta-was-an-opportunist-not-a-nationalist (Accessed on9/12/2016).

Kweyu, D. (2013). "Why Kenyan Women Perform Below Par in Elective Politics." *The Nation* Posted Saturday, March 23 2013 at 19:44

Kyle, K. (1999). *The Politics of the Independence of Kenya*. New York: Palgrave Macmillan.

Larsen, L. (2011). "Notions of nation in Nairobi's Nyayo-era monuments." *African Studies 70: 264–283*.

Lee, C. S. (1980). "South Korea 1979: Confrontation, assassination, and transition." *Asian Survey, 20*(1), 63-76.

Lee, R. (2000). *The International Criminal Court: The Making of the Rome Statute, Issues, Negotiations, Results*. The Hague: Kluwer Law International.

Lemarchand, R. (1972). "Political clientelism and ethnicity in tropical Africa: Competing solidarities in nation-building." *American political science review, 66*(01), 68-90.

Lonsdale, (1990). *Mau Mau*s of the mind. 'Making *Mau Mau* and remaking Kenya'. *Journal of African History*, 31(3) 393-421

Lonsdale, J., Odhiambo, A. (2003). *Mau Mau Nationhood*, James Currey, London.

Lonsdale, J. (2011). Le nationalisme, l'ethnicité et l'économie morale: parcours d'un pionnier de l'histoire africaine, entretien avec D. Conan » dans *Genèses*, 83.

Lynch, G. & Zgonec-Rozej, M. (2013). The ICC intervention in Kenya. *Chatham House Programme Paper AFP/ILP, 1*, 2013.

Maina, G. (2004). "Paths of the *Mau Mau* revolution: Victory and glory usurped." *Philippines Journal of Third World Studies,* Vol. 19, No. 1: pp. 92-112.

Makinda, S. (1992). Kenya: out of the straitjacket, slowly. *The World Today, 48*(10), 188-192.

Maloba, W. (1994). *Mau Mau and Kenya: An analysis of peasant revolt*. Indianapolis: Indianapolis University Press

Mama, A. (1995). *Women's Studies and Studies of Women in Africa during the 1990s*. Dakar: CODESRIA.

Marvick, D., and Marvick, E. W. (1971). The political consequences of assassination. In W. Crotty (Ed.), *Assassinations and the political order* (3-53). New York: Harper & Row.

Mathenge, G. (2008). 'Monuments of slave labour and its shame.' *The Standard*, October 19th pg. 24).

Matiba, S. (2000). *Aiming High: the Story of My Life*. Nairobi: People Ltd.

Mazrui, A. A. (1968). Thoughts on assassination in Africa. *Political Science Quarterly*, *83*(1), 40-58.

Mbembe, A. (1999). 'At the Edge of the World: Boundaries, Territoriality, and Sovereignty in Africa', in *CODESRIA BULLETIN* No. 3 and 4.

Mbembe, A. (2001). *On the Postcolony*, Berkeley: University of California Press.

McWilliams S., & Cowen M. (1996). *The Kenyan Capitalists*, Helsinki, Institute of Development Studies.

Miller, N. (1984). *Kenya: The Quest for Prosperity*. Boulder: West-view Press.

Mkutu, K. (2007). Small Arms and Light Weapons among Pastoral Groups in the Kenya-Uganda border area, in *African Affairs*. Vol. 106 No. 422.

Muchoki, F. (2012). The Changing Trends of Politics in Central Kenya and their Effects at the Local and National Levels C, 1960 – 2007, Unpublished PhD Thesis, Kenyatta University.

Mueller, S. (2014). Kenya and the International Criminal Court (ICC): politics, the election and the law. *Journal of Eastern African Studies*, *8*(1), 25-42.

Munene, M (2015). *Historical reflections on Kenya, intellectual's adventurism*, University Nairobi Press.

Muriithi K. and Ndoria P. (1981). *War in the forest: the autobiography of a Mau Mau leader*. Nairobi: EAPH.

Murunga G., (2014). "Elite compromises and the content of the 2010 constitution." In Sjögren, A., Murunga, G., & Okello, D. (Eds.). *Kenya: the struggle for a new constitutional order*. London: Zed Books Ltd, pp. 144-162.

Murunga, G. and Nasong'o, S. (2006). Bent on Self-Destruction: The Kibaki Regime in Kenya. *Journal of Contemporary African Studies*, 24, I. pp. 1-28

Murunga, R. (2004). The State, its Reform and the Question of Legitimacy in Kenya. *Identity, Culture and Politics*, Vol 5, No.'s 1 and 2 pp.179-206.

Murunga, G. (1999). Urban violence in Kenya's transition to pluralist politics, 1982-1992. *Africa Development*, *24*(1), 165-198.

Mwakenya, (1987). "The Draft Minimum Programme of *Mwakenya*." *Mwakenya*. 1 May 1994. Special Issue. "It Is Better To Die On Our Feet Than To Live On Our Knees!" Nairobi, P. 5

Mzalendo Mwakenya. (1994). Special Issue. "It Is Better to Die on Our Feet than to Live on Our Knees!";

Nash, J. (1990). *Encyclopedia of World Crime*: Vol. 4 S-Z Supplement, pp. 32-56.

Nasong'o, W. & Ayot, O. (2007). "Men in Kenya's Politics of Transition and

Democratisation." In Gordon, R.M. and Shadrack, W.N. (eds.) *Kenya: The Struggle for Democracy*, CODESRIA, Dakar, pp. 163 – 196.

National Assembly of Kenya Hansard Reports 1975-1992

National Museums and Heritage Act (NMHA) (2006). *Kenya Gazette Supplement*, No. 63 (Acts No. 6). Nairobi: Government Printer.

Ndeda, M. (2002). "Women and Development since Colonial Times" in W.R. Ochieng (Ed.). *Historical Studies and Social Change in Western Kenya*. EAEP, Nairobi, pp. 232-260.

Njama, K. and Barnett, D. (1966). *Mau Mau from Within*. London: Macgibbon and Kee, p. 335.

Njenga K. (2009). *Beyond Expectations: From Charcoal to Gold: An Autobiography*. Nairobi: East African Educational Publishers, pp. 205-206

Njenga, W. (2007). *Women in Kenyan Politics*. African Press International.

Nora, P. (1989). Between memory and history: Les lieux de mémoire. *Representations*, *26*, 7-24.

Novak, D. (1974). William J. Crotty, (ed.). *Assassinations and the Political Order*. New York: Harper and Row, 1972 [Toronto: Fitzhenry and Whiteside].

Nowrojee, B., & Manby, B. (1993). *Divide and rule: State-sponsored ethnic violence in Kenya* (Vol. 3169, No. 102). Human Rights Watch.

Nugent, P. (2002). *Smugglers, secessionists and Loyal Citizens on the Ghana-Togo Frontier*. Athens: Ohio University Press.

Nzomo, M. (1991). *Women in Politics*. Nairobi, AAWORD.

Nzomo, M. (1994). Empowerment of Women in the Process of Democratization: Experiences of Kenya, Uganda and Tanzania" A document of an International Conference held in Dar-es Salaam, Tanzania.

Nzomo, M. (2003). Taking stock – women's performance in Kenya's Parliamentary Politics in the 2002 General Elections, in M. Nzomo (ed.) *Perspectives on Gender Discourse: Women in Politics; Challenges of Democratic Transition in Kenya.* Heinrich Ball Foundation, Nairobi, Pg. 17 – 33.

Nzomo, M. "Engendering Governance through the Constitutional Review process", Constitution of Kenya Review Commission: Official Website;
http://www.KEnyaconstitution.org/docs/09cd.002.htm.

Ochieng, W. (1989). *A Modern History of Kenya*, 1895-1980. Geneva Printers, LTD Nairobi Kenya. p. 216.

Ochieng' W., & Maxon R. (1992). *An Economic History of Kenya, Nairobi*: East African Educational Publishers.

Ochwada, H. (2004). "Rethinking East African Integration: From economic to political and from State to civil society" *Africa Development,* Vol XXIX. No 2. Dakar: Codesria.

Odhiambo-Mbai, C. (2003). The rise and fall of the autocratic state in Kenya. *The politics of transition in Kenya: From KANU to NARC,* 51-95.

Odinga, O. (1967). *Not Yet Uhuru: An Autobiography of Odinga Oginga.* Nairobi: Heinemann.

Ogot B. (1978). "Three decades of historical studies in East Africa." *Kenya Historical Review,* Vol. 6, 1-2.

Ogot, B. (1995). "Transition from Single-Party to Multiparty Political System." In Ogot, B.A. and Ochieng, W.R. *Decolonization & [and] Independence in Kenya: 1940-93.* Nairobi: East African Publishers.

Ogot, B. (2003). *Mau Mau* and Nationhood: The Untold Story. In Atieno-Odhiambo, E. S. and Lonsdale, J. (Eds.). *Mau Mau and Nationhood.* Oxford: James Curry.

Ogot, B. A. (2012). "Kenyans, who are we: reflections on the meaning of national identity and nationalism."

Ogot, B. and Ochieng, W. (eds.). (1995). *Decolonization and independence in Kenya: 1940-1993.* Nairobi: East African Educational Publishers.

Okumu W. (2010). "Resources and Border Disputes in Eastern Africa" in *Journal of Eastern Africa Studies (JEAS)* Vol.4 No.2 July. London: Routledge Taylor and Francis Group

Omari, E. (2012). "The shrinking class of Uhuru heroes." *The Daily Nation*. Available at: http://www.nation.co.ke/news/politics/The-shrinking-class-of-Uhuru-heroes/1064-1486686-6cdevw/index.html (Accessed on9/12/2016).

Omenya, G. (2015). *The Relations between Asian and African Communities: A Comparative Study of Western and Nyanza Provinces of Kenya, 1900-2002*. PhD Thesis: L'université De Pau, et Pays de L'adour

Omolo, K. (2002). "Political ethnicity in the democratisation process in Kenya." *African Studies, 61*(2), 209-221.

Osse, A. (2014). "Police reform in Kenya: a process of 'Meddling Through'", *Policing and Society: An International Journal of Research and Policy*.

Oucho, J. O. (2002). *Undercurrents of ethnic conflicts in Kenya* (Vol. 3). Brill.

Oyugi, W. (1997). "Ethnicity in the electoral process: The 1992 general elections in Kenya." *African Journal of Political Science/ Revue Africaine de Science Politique*, 41-69.

Oywa, J. and Wangui B. (2007). *How Sexism locked women out*. Gender AGENDA Election Platform.

Paden, J. (1980). *Identities and National Integration: Empirical Research in Africa*. Evanston: North – Western University Press.

Patel, Z. (1997). *Challenge to Colonialism – The Struggle of Alibhai Mulla Jeevanjee for Equal Rights in Kenya*, Nairobi: Pre-Press Publication

Patel, P. (2004). 'I am A Kenyan South Asian' *Journal of Kenyan South Asian History Awaaz Issue 11*.

Patel, Z. (2006). *Unquiet – The Life & Times of Makhan Singh,* Nairobi: Zand Graphics Limited

Patel, Z. (2010). *Manilal Ambalal Desai – The Stormy Petrel,* Nairobi: Zand Graphics.

Pheroze, N. (2012-2013). *Vote for Kenya – The Election and the Constitution*. Nairobi: The Star Articles 2012 – 2013, p.8

Presley, C. (1988). "Kikuyu women, the *Mau Mau* war and social change." *Canadian Journal of African Studies*, 22:502-527.

Prunier, G. (1987). Mythes et histoire: les interprétations du mouvement *Mau Mau* de 1952 à 1986. *Revue française d'histoire d'outre-mer, 74*(277), 401-429.

Pyne-Mercier, L., John-Stewart, C., Richardson, A., Kagondu, L., Thiga, J., Noshy, H., & Chung, H. (2011). The consequences of post-election violence on antiretroviral HIV therapy in Kenya. *AIDS care*, 23(5), 562-568.

Ranger, T. (1971). "The 'New Historiography' in Dar es Salaam: An Answer." *African Affairs*, 70(278), 50-61.

Rapoport, D. C. (1971). *Assassination and terrorism* (p. 79). Toronto: Canadian Broadcasting Corporation.

Rattansi, P.M. (2004). "Rebel with a Cause" *Awaaz Issue 1*

Roberts, M. (2009). "Conflict analysis of the 2007 post-election violence in Kenya." *Managing Conflicts in Africa's Democratic Transitions*, 141-55.

Rosenberg, C. E. (1995). *The Trial of the Assassin Guiteau: Psychiatry and the Law in the Gilded Age*. University of Chicago Press.

Rothchild, D. (1969). "Ethnic Inequalities in Kenya." *The Journal of Modern African Studies*. Vol. 7, No. 4, pp. 689-711

Rothchild, D. S. (1997). *Managing ethnic conflict in Africa: Pressures and incentives for cooperation*. Brookings Institution Press.

Said, E. W. (2012). *Culture and imperialism*. Vintage.

Salvadori, C. (1983). *Through Open Doors: A view of Asian Cultures in Kenya*, Nairobi: Kenways Publishers.

Schabas, W. (2004). *International Criminal Court*. University Press.

Schiff, B. (2005). *Building the International Criminal Court*. Cambridge University Press.

Seaton, A. (1999). Guided by the dark: From Thenatopsis to Thenatourism. *International journal of heritage studies*, 2(4):234-244

Seidenberg, D. (1996). April; *The Mercantile Adventurers – The World of East African Asians 1750-1985*; 1996, New Delhi: New Age International (P) Limited Publishers

Shikuku, Martin, Kenya National Assembly Official Record (Hansard) 12 September-November 2013 1972, col. 1605

Sibi-Okumu, J. (2008). *Tom Mboya, Master of Mass Management*. Longhorn Publishers, Nairobi-Kenya. pp. 44-45.

SID (2011). "*Devolution in Kenya's New Constitution*," Working Paper No.4.Nairobi, Society for International Development.

Smith, A. (1981). *The Ethnic Revival in the Modern World*. Cambridge: Cambridge University Press. p. 133.

Smith, D. (2005). *Kenya, the Kikuyu and Mau Mau* East Sussex: Mawenzi Books

Smith, M. (2009). *Issues in cultural tourism studies* (2nd edition). London: Routledge.

Snyder, J., (2000). *From Voting to Violence: Democratisation and Nationalist Conflict.* W.W. Norton & Company, New York.

Song by Patrick Palicidia, Western Jazz Band, 1976

Soyinka, W. (2000). "The scars of memory and the scales of justice." *Olof Palme Memorial Lecture, Taylor Institution, University of Oxford,* 16.

Stanton, K. P. (2010). *Truth Commissions and Public Inquiries: Addressing Historical Injustices in Established Democracies* (Doctoral dissertation, University of Toronto).

Staudt. K. (1990). "Gender Politics in Bureaucracy: Theoretical issues in Comparative Perspective" in Staudt K. (ed.) *Women International Development and Politics, Philadelphia, The Bureaucratic Mire.*

Stewart, F. (2009). Horizontal inequalities as a cause of conflict. In *Bradford Development Lecture, November. Available at www. brad. ac. uk/acad/bcid/seminar/BDLStewart. pdf.* Accessed on 20/02/2013.

Strange C. and Kempa, M. (2009). "Shades of Dark Tourism: Alcatraz and Robben Island. Annals of Tourism research," 2(2):386-405.

Thelen, D. (1989). "Memory and American history." *The Journal of American History, 75*(4), 1117-1129.

The Standard Digital, (2010). "Intrigues behind devolution, and executive powers." *The Standard Digital.* Available at: https://www.standardmedia.co.ke/business/article/200000324 8/intrigues-behind-devolution-and-executive-powers-12288 (Accessed on9/12/2016).

Thompson, E. P. (1975). "The Making of the English Working Class (New York, 1963)" in Herbert Gutman (Ed.). *Work, Culture and Society in Industrializing America: Essays in American Working Class and Social History.*

Throup, D. (1993). Elections and political legitimacy in Kenya. *International African Institute, 63*(03), 371-396.

Throup, D., & Hornsby, C. (1998). Multi-party politics in Kenya: *The Kenyatta & Moi States & the triumph of the system in the 1992 election.* Ohio University Press.

Throup, D. (1985). The origins of *Mau Mau*, *African Affairs*, 84:399-433.

Tignor, R. (1976). *Colonial Transformation of Kenya: The Kamba, Kikuyu and Maasai from 1900-1939*, Princeton: Princeton University Press

Torpey, J. C. (2003). *Politics and the past: On repairing historical injustices.* Rowman & Littlefield.

Touval, S. (1969). 'The sources of Status quo and Irredentist Policies', in Widstrand C.G. (ed) *African Boundary Problems.* Uppsala: Scandinavian institute of African Studies.

UNDP, (1994). *Human Development Report,* New York, Oxford University Press.

UNESCO (2013). 'Mount Kenya national park/forest'. UNESCO World Heritage Centre'. http://whc.unesco.org/en/list/800. (Retrieved on 27th November, 2013).

Union Of Patriots For The Liberation Of Kenya, (1987).The Draft Minimum Programme of *Mwakenya*. Nairobi.

United Movement For Democracy In Kenya, (1994). "The Statement of *Mwakenya* at the 7th Pan-African Congress. 3rd-8th April 1994." Kampala, Uganda.

University of Arkansas, "British Kenya (1920-1963)." Available at:http://uca.edu/politicalscience/dadm-project/sub-saharan-africa-region/british-kenya-1920-1963/.

Van de Walle, N. (2006). Meet the new boss, same as the old boss? The evolution of political clientelism in Africa. *Patrons, clients and policies: Patterns of democratic accountability and political competition*, 50-67.

Vansina, J. (1961). *Oral Tradition as History*, Oxford: James Currey

Waiyego S. (2004). "Engendering Political Space: Women's Political Participation in Kangema, Murang'a District, 1963 – 2002" MA Thesis, Kenyatta University.

Wanyama, F. (2010). "Voting Without Institutional Political Parties." In Kanyinga, *et. al.* (Eds.). *Tensions and Reversals in Democratic Transitions: The Kenya 2007 General Elections.* Nairobi: Society for International Development (SID) and Institute for Development Studies (IDS).

Wanyande, P. (2006). "Electoral Politics and Election Outcomes in Kenya." *African Development* Vol. XXX1, No. 3, 2006 pp. 62-80.

WAR/c. 468 (29th January, 1955). War Council Minutes: Report by Emergency Joint Staff.

WAR/c. 670 (6th July, 1955). War Council Minutes: Report by Emergency Joint Staff.

Wasserman, G. (1976). *Politics of decolonization*. Cambridge University Press.

Weber, E. (1976). *Peasants and Frenchmen: The Modernization of the Rural France* 1870-1914. Stanford: California – Stanford University Press.

Wekesa P. (2007). The History of Community Relations across the Kenya-Uganda border: The case of the Babukusu and the Bagisu, c. 1884-1997. Nairobi: PhD Thesis, Kenyatta University.

Wekesa P. (2010). "Old Issues and New Challenges: The Migingo Island Controversy and the Kenya-Uganda Borderland" in *JEAS Vol.4 No.2* July London: Routledge Taylor and Francis Group.

Weru G. (1995). "Special Report" Daily Nation, Nairobi Kenya, August 23, 1995 Pg. Viii –ix.

White, R. F. (2007). "A Prolegomenon to a General Theory of Assassination." *Assassination Research*, 5(1).

Widner, J. A. (1993). *The rise of a party-state in Kenya: From" Harambee!" to" Nyayo!"*. Univ. of California Press.

Wiebe, M. (2003). Assassination in Domestic and International Law: The Central Intelligence Agency, State-Sponsored Terrorism, and the Right of Self-Defence. *Tulsa J. Comp. & Int'l L.*, *11*, 363.

Wilcox, L. M. (1980). *Bibliography on terrorism and assassination*. Laird Wilcox.

Wilkinson, D. Y. (Ed.). (1976). *Social Structure and Assassination Behaviour: The Sociology of Political Murder*. Schenkman Publishing Company.

Wilson, C. (2015). *Order of assassins: The psychology of murder*. Diversion Books.

Zeleza, T. (1989): "The Establishment of Colonial Rule, 1905-1920", in Ochieng' W.R. (Ed.), *A Modern History of Kenya, 1895-1980*, Nairobi, Evans Brothers LTD.

Zolberg, A. (1966).*Creating Political Order: The One-Party States of West Africa*. Chicago: Rand McNally, p. 45.

Index

Manilal Ambalal Desai, 133
Manilal Desai, 133, 136
Marjorie Oludhe Macgoye, 188
Martin Shikuku, ii, 7, 13, 163,
164, 165, 167, 170, 173, 204
Mashujaa Day, 198
Masinde Muliro, 4, 7, 167
Mau Mau, ii, 1, 3, 5, 6, 11, 12, 42,
44, 49, 50, 51, 52, 53, 55, 56, 57,
59, 60, 61, 62, 64, 65, 66, 67, 69,
75, 77, 78, 80, 81, 82, 84, 88, 91,
103, 108, 128, 130, 134, 137,
165, 175, 178, 200, 205, 206,
207, 2018, 209, 210, 2011, 2013,
2014
Mau Mau heritage, 11, 49, 50, 51,
59, 61, 64, 65, 67
Mazrui, 72, 99, 184, 185, 208
Mbembe, 18, 20, 130, 208
Meja Mwangi, 187
Memorandum of
Understanding, 108, 196
memorialization, 13, 50, 59, 127,
128, 136
Michael Blundell, 4, 57
Mlolongo, 158
Mohammed Ahmed Bamahriz,
167
Moi, iii, 4, 7, 11, 34, 46, 47, 50,
78, 82, 88, 104, 105, 106, 107,
108, 110, 114, 137, 156, 159,
161, 165, 167, 169, 170, 175,
194, 195, 198, 200, 213
Mombasa African Democratic
Union, 3
Mount Kenya Mafia, 109, 110
Muchoki, ii, 11, 93, 106, 111,
208
Muindi Mbingu, 134
multipartyism, 107
Muriuki, iii, 81, 199
Murunga, 7, 102, 107, 165, 171,
208
Mwai Kibaki, 47, 82, 88, 107,
108, 110, 121, 122, 144, 167, 196

N

NARC, 107, 108, 109, 149, 196,
210
Nasong'o, 107, 141, 208, 209
Nation-building, ii, 9, 11, 12, 13,
16, 22, 40, 69, 77, 93, 94, 95, 96,
99, 100, 103, 104, 105, 107, 110,
112, 113, 114, 115, 118, 119,
120, 121, 122, 123, 125, 127,
132, 163, 193, 197, 198, 207
National Accord, 171, 196, 197
National Alliance Party of
Kenya, 196
National Christian Council of
Kenya, 132
National Commission on the
Status of Women, 146
National Council of Women of
Kenya, 145
National Democratic Party of
Kenya, 147
National Museums and Heritage
Act, 61, 209
National Museums of Kenya,
127, 136, 200
National Rainbow Coalition
(NARC), 107, 196
nationalism, iii, iv, 1, 2, 3, 5, 6, 7,
8, 9, 10, 11, 23, 24, 33, 34, 35,
37, 38, 39, 40, 41, 42, 46, 72, 78,
79, 80, 81, 83, 84, 85, 86, 92, 93,
94, 95, 96, 98, 99, 100, 102, 103,
113, 129, 140, 164, 198, 204,
205, 207, 210
nation-state, 13, 15, 16, 20, 29,
31, 33, 34, 35, 36, 37, 38, 39, 40,
45, 94
Ndeda, ii, 12, 139, 140, 143, 209
Ndiiri, ii, 13, 163
Ngugi wa Thiong'o, 187
Njenga Karume, 45
North Frontier District, 135
North Kavirondo Central
Association, 98

TJRC, 13, 175, 176, 178, 179, 180, 184
Tom Mboya, 4, 45, 100, 104, 108, 136, 152, 163, 175, 181, 183, 186, 187, 188, 193, 203, 212
Trade Union Movement. Mombasa, 134

U
United Nations Committee on the Rights of the Child, 145

W
Wahome, ii, 11, 49, 86
Waki Commission Report, 120
Walter Rodney, 96
Wangari Maathai, 7, 147
Wanyande, 106, 214
war-heritage, 50

Wekesa, ii, 10, 15, 16, 23, 24, 215
White Highlands, 97
William Samoei Ruto, 121
Wole Soyinka, 177

Y
Young Kavirondo Association, 98
Young Kikuyu Association, 2, 3, 98
Young Women Christian Association, 144

Z
Zarina Patel, ii, 12, 127, 132, 134, 203
Zeleza, 97, 140, 215